PUNISHMENT

"In this unique textbook, which is scholarly yet accessible to students, Miethe and Lu approach punishment from a perspective that is both historical and comparative, addressing the global dimensions of punishment as few authors do."

Gray Cavender, Arizona State University

Informed by current scholarship, yet tailored to the needs of undergraduate students, this textbook presents a broad perspective on one of the most fundamental social practices. Punishment is the common response to crime and deviance in all societies. However, its particular form and purpose are also linked to specific structural features of these societies in a particular time and place. Through a comparative historical analysis, the authors identify and examine the sources of similarity and difference in types of economic punishments, incapacitation devices and structures, and lethal and nonlethal forms of corporal punishment over time and place. They look closely at punishment responses to crime and deviance across different regions of the world and in specific countries like the United States, China, and Saudi Arabia. In this way readers gain an appreciation for both the universal and context-specific nature of punishment and its use for purposes of social control, social change, and the elimination of threat to the prevailing authorities.

Terance D. Miethe is Professor of Criminal Justice at the University of Nevada, Las Vegas. He has authored six books in the areas of criminology and legal studies, including *Crime and Its Social Context* (1994); *Whistleblowing at Work: Tough Choices in Exposing Fraud, Waste, and Abuse on the Job* (1999); *Crime Profiles: The Anatomy of Dangerous Persons, Places, and Situations*, 2nd ed. (2001); *Panic: The Social Construction of the Youth Gang Problem* (2002); *The Mismeasure of Crime* (2002); and *Rethinking Homicide: Exploring the Structure and Process Underlying Deadly Situations* (2004, Cambridge). His research articles have been published in all the major journals in criminology and sociology, including *Criminology, British Journal of Criminology, Law and Society Review, American Sociological Review*, and *Social Forces*.

Hong Lu is Associate Professor of Criminal Justice at the University of Nevada, Las Vegas. She has authored numerous articles in the areas of criminology and comparative legal studies appearing in journals such as *Law and Society Review, British Journal of Criminology, Crime and Delinquency*, and *Justice Quarterly*.

PUNISHMENT

A Comparative Historical Perspective

Terance D. Miethe
University of Nevada, Las Vegas

WITHDRAWN

Hong Lu
University of Nevada, Las Vegas

CAMBRIDGE
UNIVERSITY PRESS

PUBLISHED BY THE PRESS SYNDICATE OF THE UNIVERSITY OF CAMBRIDGE
The Pitt Building, Trumpington Street, Cambridge, United Kingdom

CAMBRIDGE UNIVERSITY PRESS
The Edinburgh Building, Cambridge CB2 2RU, UK
40 West 20th Street, New York, NY 10011-4211, USA
477 Williamstown Road, Port Melbourne, VIC 3207, Australia
Ruiz de Alarcón 13, 28014 Madrid, Spain
Dock House, The Waterfront, Cape Town 8001, South Africa

http://www.cambridge.org

First published 2005

Printed in the United States of America

Typefaces Poppl-Pontifex 9.5/14.5 pt. and Poppl-Laudatio   *System* LaTeX 2_ε [TB]

A catalog record for this book is available from the British Library.

Library of Congress Cataloging in Publication Data
Miethe, Terance D.
    Punishment : a comparative historical perspective / Terance D. Miethe, Hong Lu.
     p. cm.
    Includes bibliographical references and index.
    ISBN 0-521-84407-X – ISBN 0-521-60516-4 (pbk.)
    1. Punishment.   2. Punishment – Cross-cultural studies.   3. Punishment – History.
I. Lu, Hong, 1966– II. Title.
    HV8693.M54   2005
    364.6 – dc22   2004049271

ISBN 0 521 84407 X hardback
ISBN 0 521 60516 4 paperback

Physical Processing

Order Type: NTAS

Cust/Add: 170280000/02

Cust PO No.

BBS Order No: C705210   LSSC

0521844407X-18685986

(9780521844079)

Ln:23   Del:1

SIERRA COLLEGE LIBRARY

Cust Ord Date: 27-Mar-2007

BBS Ord Date: 27-Mar-2007

Sales Qty: 1   **#Vols:** 001

Punishment

Subtitle: a comparative historical perspective

HARDBACK   **Pub Year:** 2005   **Vol No.:**   Stmt of Resp: Terence D. Miethe, Hong Lu.

Miethe, Terance D.

Cambridge University Press   **Ser. Title:**   Edition:

Acc Mat:

Tech Services Charges:

   PromptCat Barcode US   Mylar Dust Jacket (Cloth)

   Barcode Label Application   Spine Label Protector US

   Barcode Label Protector   Spine Label PromptCat U

   Base Charge Processing U

Cust Fund Code: **Cust Location:**

Stock Category: **Cust Dept:**

Order Line Notes

Notes to Vendor

Blackwell's Book Services

Sel ID/Seq No:

106437

/407

281303

CONTENTS

FIGURES AND TABLES

PREFACE AND ACKNOWLEDGMENTS

Punishment is a basic fact of human life. We impose punishment in formal and informal settings for a variety of purposes of social control, social change, and order maintenance. Previous studies of punishment also indicate that its nature and prevalence vary over time and place.

Using a comparative historical approach, the goal in this book is to illustrate the similarities and differences in punishment responses over time and place. We review current punishment practices across world regions and use case studies of the United States, China, and Saudi Arabia for detailed investigation of the comparative and historical contexts of punishment. Through this comparative historical perspective, the reader should gain an appreciation of the universal and context-specific nature of punishment practices.

There is an enormous academic and popular literature on punishment. Sociologists and other social scientists have long been interested in the topic of punishment, social control, and the structure of society. Various human rights organizations like Amnesty International and Human Rights Watch also provide current reports and commentary about punishment practices throughout most countries of the world. By providing detailed references to this previous research and a list of suggested readings in each chapter, we hope this book will serve as a research guide and inspire others to further examine the nature and effectiveness of punishment responses to crime and deviance across a wide range of social, political, and economic contexts.

Our views about punishment expressed in this book are a reflection of our personal experiences and academic training. We are especially appreciative of the insights of colleagues and mentors that have shaped our perspective and challenged us to go beyond the conventional wisdom. While we are responsible for any errors of omission and commission in this book, our colleagues have contributed to the potential insights about punishment that derive from this comparative historical study.

The authors would also like to acknowledge the assistance provided by Ed Parsons at Cambridge University Press. He has kept this project on pace and has treated us with dignity, respect, and good humor throughout the publication process.

CHAPTER ONE

Introduction: The Punishment Response

Punishment is the universal response to crime and deviance in all societies. As such, it takes various forms. Criminal sanctions like imprisonment and death sentences are allocated and dispensed by state authorities. Other formal punishments involve civil lawsuits and administrative decrees to either reconcile or restore relations among the parties, compensate for personal injuries, and/or prevent further wrongful conduct through restrictions of ongoing practices. Punishment may also involve various types of informal sanctions by family, peers, and extralegal groups like vigilante committees and paramilitary organizations to promote their own interests.

Different types of punishments are used for different purposes. Criminal sanctions serve to reinforce cherished values and beliefs, incapacitate and deter those who may be considering criminal misconduct, and often function to maintain power relations in a society and to eliminate threats to the prevailing social order. The regulation and maintenance of social order is also an important function of civil and administrative sanctions. Both formal and informal punishments may further serve to dramatize the evil of particular conduct in a society, enhance communal solidarity against external threats, and provide the means for social engineering efforts directed at improving the quality of life.

Even a cursory look at punishments, however, reveals that they vary widely over time and place. Formal sanctions by the state or other "official" bodies were largely unknown in earlier agrarian societies, whereas social order in modern industrial societies is possible in many cases only by an elaborate system of formal sanctions. Variation also occurs in the use of particular sanctions within countries over time. A comparative historical approach offers a valuable way to more fully understand this variation in punishment over time and place.

An investigation of punishments from a comparative historical perspective becomes even more important within the current context of global economies, world systems, and multinational penetration. Within this increasingly smaller and interconnected world system, a comparative historical approach challenges our ethnocentric beliefs of "good" and "bad" practices based on our particular cultural and national experiences. The potential discovery of punishment responses and principles that transcend boundaries of time and space provides an empirical basis for improving our understanding of criminal sanctions and punishments in Western and non-Western societies alike.

The purpose of this book is to explore punishments from a comparative historical perspective. We describe the purposes and types of punishments over time and place. By exploring the use of lethal and nonlethal punishments across different historical periods in particular countries, we illustrate the similarities and differences in punishment responses across contexts. We anticipate doing so will demonstrate the value of a comparative historical perspective for studying crime, deviance, and punishment.

PUNISHMENT AND TYPES OF SANCTIONS

All societies and social groups develop ways to control behavior that violates norms. Socialization is a basic type of social control that seeks conformity through learning processes and the subsequent internalization of group norms as personal preferences. Social control is also achieved directly through external sources that compel individuals to conform through the threat of societal reaction. Regardless of whether conformity results from personal desires or external compulsion, conformity is ultimately achieved through the use and threat of sanctions.

As an instrument of social control, sanctions vary in their nature and source. Positive sanctions are rewards meant to encourage conformity to norms, whereas negative sanctions are punishments to discourage norm violations.[1] Based on their source, sanctions are considered "formal" when they are imposed by the state or by other organizations that have the legitimate authority to do so (e.g., churches, educational institutions, business

TABLE 1.1: Types of Sanctions (examples)

	Positive (rewards)	Negative (punishments)
Formal	Promotions	Fines/forfeitures
	Bonuses	Probation/revocations
	Awards/medals	Incarceration
	Honorary titles	Torture/death penalty
Informal	Kiss/hugs	Gossip
	Praise	Ridicule
	Respect	Ostracism
	Trust	"Street justice"

Source: Adapted from Clinard and Meier (1985)

organizations). In contrast, informal sanctions are unofficial actions by groups and individuals. These include sanctions imposed by family, friends, and quasi-legal bodies such as vigilante groups, paramilitary forces, and local "regulators."

Sanctions also vary according to their magnitude and form (see Table 1.1). As punishments designed to inflict pain, negative sanctions can vary in intensity from minor inconveniences (e.g., small fines) to death (i.e., capital punishment). The form of these sanctions may also differ, involving economic costs, physical restraints, and/or corporal punishment. For example, parents may choose to discipline their children through the denial of their allowance (an economic sanction), "grounding" them to their home (an incapacitative sanction), or by spanking them (corporal punishment). Governments may assign criminal penalties that also include monetary fines, imprisonment, and death sentences.

Positive sanctions also vary in their magnitude. The continuum for positive sanctions may range from a pat on the back and word of praise, to large monetary raises and promotions for high work performance, to the awarding of multimillion-dollar mergers and acquisitions. It is more difficult to view forms of incapacitation and corporal punishment as positive sanctions, unless one considers criminal penalties like suspended jail sentences, the earning of "good time" credits while in prison, pardons of death sentences, and/or the reduction in the number of lashes with a whip as a "reward."

Although both positive and negative sanctions are important for understanding social control in societies, our focus on punishments necessitates an emphasis on negative sanctions. Within the area of negative sanctions, we also focus primarily on state-sponsored sanctions (e.g., criminal penalties, civil litigation judgments) and the actions of various quasi-governmental groups that impose extralegal sanctions. By focusing on these punishment responses in different times and places, we hope to learn about convergent and divergent aspects of societal reaction to deviance in various comparative historical contexts.

THE FUNCTIONS OF PUNISHMENT

The functions of criminal and civil punishments in any society depend largely on the prevailing social, economic, and political conditions in that society. In small, undifferentiated societies characterized by value consensus, sanctions are used to preserve social order by maintaining the status quo and regulating and controlling social relations. In contrast, criminal and civil sanctions in more diversified societies are often viewed as both sources of order maintenance and instruments for the protection of special interests.

Across different times and places, criminal sanctions have been designed to serve multiple purposes. These purposes include the reinforcement of collective values, the protection of the community through the physical incapacitation of convicted offenders, the rehabilitation of the offender, the deterrence of individuals from repeat offending (known as specific deterrence), and serving as an example to deter others from committing crime (known as general deterrence). Some criminal and civil sanctions (e.g., monetary fines, victim compensation) are designed for restorative purposes. In addition, sanctions administered in public places often provide important symbolic functions by either dramatizing the evil of particular conduct or illustrating the fairness of legal proceedings.

> Criminal punishments are used to reinforce collective values, physically incapacitate and rehabilitate offenders, deter misconduct, provide restoration or compensation, and eliminate threats to the prevailing social order.

According to the conflict perspective on law and society, the primary function of legal sanctions is to preserve and protect the interests of those in power. This is done in various ways through the development and application of civil and criminal laws. For example, it has long been argued that the criminal law is designed to criminalize the greedy actions of the powerless and to legitimate the same activities by the powerful.[2] Machiavelli's comment in the seventeenth century that "who steals a handkerchief goes to jail; who steals a country becomes a duke" conveys the same idea.[3] More generally, social control is a major purpose of the law for conflict theorists, both as a mechanism of gaining control over goods or services and as a means of controlling dissent.

The use of legal sanctions to maintain one's cumulative advantage is reflected in a wide range of civil, administrative, regulatory, and criminal laws. For example, the American Medical Association (AMA) in the United States has long been opposed to alternative medical providers (e.g., chiropractors, herbalists) to maintain their financial interests from the monopolistic control of medical treatment and practice. Primary opponents of legalizing marijuana are often groups like the tobacco and distillers industries that desire to preserve their control over the legal drug market. Oil companies are usually the major opposition to mass transit for similar economic reasons. The widespread use of licensing, external auditors and inspectors, building codes and ordinances, and other regulatory activities serves a manifest function of providing some protection to the public, but these same activities are often proposed and developed to preserve a particular group's cumulative advantage.

The primary ways in which legal sanctions serve to control dissent are through various selection processes, civil actions, and the application of criminal sanctions. Access to political power in most countries is limited by money and contacts, and individuals or groups who pose a threat to the prevailing regime may be controlled through adverse publicity, denial of material benefits (e.g., student dissent is controlled by cutting back of student aid programs), civil commitments to mental institutions and rehabilitation centers, and imprisonment for criminal offenses. Federal agencies like the Central Intelligence Agency (CIA), the Federal Bureau of Investigation (FBI), and the Internal Revenue Service (IRS) provide a largely covert but equally effective method of controlling dissent in the United States. The use of secret police organizations and death squads are coercive social control responses to dissent in other countries.

Criminal and civil sanctions also function as a tool for social engineering, or "purposive, planned, and directed social change initiated, guided, and supported by the law."[4] However, the ultimate goal of social engineering varies across theoretical perspectives. Achieving maximum harmony for the greatest good and social integration are the goals of social engineering within a functionalist perspective that emphasizes stability, collective solidarity, and interdependency among the units and institutions within social systems. Social integration is important in conflict theories of social order only when efforts at social engineering result in maintaining one's position. To conflict theorists, the control of dissent and those who pose a serious threat to prevailing interest groups is the role of the social engineering function of both criminal and civil sanctions.

THE NATURE OF PUNISHMENT AND SOCIETAL COMPLEXITY

It is a widely held belief among sociolegal scholars that criminal and civil sanctions are developed and shaped by the prevailing social conditions in a society. This link between punishments and the structure of society is reflected in Emile Durkheim's views about punishment and types of solidarity in societies; Philippe Nonet and Philip Selnick's analysis of transitional legal systems and the movement from repressive to responsive law; Donald Black's work on the behavior of law; Michel Foucault's treatise on changes over time in the state's power to control the body, mind, and "souls" of its subjects; and Norbert Elias's argument about the growth of "civilized sensibilities" in modern society that shape how punishment is dispensed.[5] Although these authors vary in their focus on particular elements, there is a general agreement that the nature of punishment changes through the historical transition from primitive or early tribal law to the development of modern legal systems.

Early tribal law or what is also called "primitive" legal systems is linked to small, homogeneous, and undifferentiated societies. Social order is maintained through informal sanctions that are connected to shared customs, norms, and traditions. Laws reflect and protect these most cherished values and beliefs. Although punishment is often viewed as a simple, automatic response to deviance, Durkheim contends that punishments under certain conditions also serve as social rituals to bring together community members and provide a forum for reaffirming and intensifying their commitment to these shared values and a common identity.[6] Repressive justice is often administered in these homogeneous societies characterized by what Durkheim calls mechanical solidarity, with diffuse forms of ritual punishments being used to reaffirm collective values and denounce "evil."[7]

The demise of early tribal societies is often associated with the social forces of increased population, increased heterogeneity, urbanization, industrialization, and modernization. During the transitional stage of societal evolution, new forms of social organization develop to regulate and coordinate activities and to maintain order. This transitional period is often associated with the development of the state as the primary institution in society, the enforcement of laws according to geography or jurisdiction rather than kinship, and the definition of crime or deviance as a public rather than private harm (e.g., the state is the "victim" of crime in modern societies). Both law and social order are precarious in this temporary, transitional stage of societal development.

The basic problem of integration in highly diverse societies is often considered the major catalyst for the emergence of a formally codified legal system. Modern societies are typically so complex and diverse that it is problematic to assume that informal sanctions (like interpersonal agreements, social customs, or moral precepts) alone are capable of regulating and maintaining social order. Instead, societal integration in this context necessitates a legal system that is comprehensive, responsive to changing political and economic conditions, and is generally accepted as the legitimate authority. Whether formal codified legal systems are successful in achieving their multiple functions is the key question that underlies much of the current theory and research in the sociological study of law.

It is widely assumed that the transition from simple to complex legal systems is also reflective of changes in the nature of social control and types of sanctions. Greater reliance on formal mechanisms of social control (like criminal sanctions, civil commitments, administrative and regulatory laws) is assumed to occur in modern societies because informal controls (like customs, traditions, ridicule, gossip, praise, or verbal criticism) are considered insufficient to maintain conformity in industrialized societies. Changes in sanctions often associated with increasing societal complexity involve the shift from repressive sanctions (e.g., punishments that serve to denounce, stigmatize, and degrade the offender) to restitutive sanctions (e.g., punishments that serve to restore or compensate for the disruptive relationship rather than stigmatizing the offender per se). John Braithwaite defines these types of restitutive sanctions as efforts at "reintegrative shaming."[8]

An examination of punishment from a comparative historical perspective provides an opportunity to directly assess the accuracy of these ideas about the social structure of societies and punishment. For example, have punishments become more restitutive and less punitive over time? Have formal sanctions replaced informal sanctions as the primary glue that maintains social order in modern societies? Do these patterns differ across specific countries in the modern world? Answers to these fundamental sociological questions about punishment and society require a comparative historical approach.

EFFECTIVENESS OF CRIMINAL AND CIVIL SANCTIONS

The effectiveness of state-sponsored sanctions in maintaining social integration and fostering constructive social change has been widely addressed in a number of different areas. Civil litigation in the United States and most Western democracies has skyrocketed over the last two decades, characterized as an "explosion" by some legal scholars.[9] An increasing number of citizens have turned to civil litigation to resolve interpersonal disputes (e.g., divorce, child custody, landlord–tenant disputes, prohibited employment practices). Most states and all federal agencies in the United States now provide civil remedies and other legal protections against retaliatory punishment of employees who file reports to external agencies about fraud, waste, and abuse in their workplace.[10] Criminal sanctions such as monetary fines, suspended jail sentences and probation, and imprisonment are widely imposed on convicted criminals across countries.

In general, civil and criminal sanctions are considered an effective instrument of social integration and change when they accomplish two goals.[11] First, sanctions should be based on clearly articulated standards of expected behavior that include established norms and provisions for the violation. Second, these patterns of expected behavior must be internalized by citizens and followed as personal preferences (i.e., things that people want to do) rather than just because they are legally required. Of course, it is possible to have effective sanctions without either of these conditions (e.g., by using the coercive power of the state to control criminal dissent or regulate contractual arrangements). However, exclusively coercive methods of social control are often thought to have only a limited lifespan. The rapid rise and fall of prevailing political regimes that rely exclusively on force to maintain conformity are a general testament to the long-term ineffectiveness of this method of social control.

The effectiveness of criminal sanctions is often judged within the context of deterrence. Numerous studies have examined whether specific criminal sanctions deter convicted offenders from repeating criminal behavior or serve to deter others from committing criminal acts. Although the specific and general deterrent value of specific punishments is subject to much debate, criminal sanctions are usually considered to be most effective for instrumental crimes (i.e., planned crimes done for some future goals) by persons with low commitment to crime as a way of life.[12]

The study of the death penalty and other criminal sanctions affords the opportunity to examine several aspects about the effectiveness of law as an instrument of social change. First, we will explore how the death penalty has been used throughout history as a method for controlling dissent and threats to prevailing interests (e.g., the increased use in capital punishment in China in the past decade as a response to rising economic crimes). Second, as a general deterrent, capital punishment and extrajudicial executions in particular countries at particular times (e.g., post-Mao China; lynchings during the postbellum South) should be especially effective because the means in which death sentences were administered in these contexts (i.e., swift, certain, severe punishments in a public setting) should maximize their deterrent value. Through the historical and comparative analysis of lethal and nonlethal punishments, the current investigation will also provide evidence of the effectiveness of criminal sanctions in various historical and cultural contexts.

DISPARITIES IN CRIMINAL AND CIVIL SANCTIONS

An extensive literature exists on the issue of disparities or differential treatment in the access and application of criminal and civil law. This literature includes studies of differential access to civil remedies by disadvantaged groups (e.g., the poor, ethnic and racial minorities); the differential success of individual plaintiffs and corporations in civil disputes; and the nature and magnitude of gender, race, and class disparities in the imposition of criminal sanctions.[13]

Within the area of the criminal justice system, the question of differential treatment focuses on whether group differences exist in charging and sentencing decisions after adjustments are made for a wide variety of legal factors (e.g., seriousness of the charge, defendant's prior record) that should influence these decisions. Both gender and race differences are often found in research on court practices in the United States, with males and African Americans the groups most disadvantaged by differential treatment. These social differences are found in studies that focus on the death penalty as well as research on other types of criminal sanctions.[14]

Donald Black's theory of the behavior of law offers an interesting basis for examining differential treatment in the imposition of criminal sanctions. According to Black, the quantity of law (e.g., the frequency of its application) and its style (e.g., penal, compensatory, therapeutic, or conciliatory) vary by particular aspects of social life.[15] For example, law has a penal style when it is directed toward people of low rank stratification, but it is compensatory when applied upward (e.g, a higher ranking person kills a person from a lower social position). Among people of equal rank, law has a conciliatory style. The comparative analysis of criminal sanctions provides a clear forum for evaluating Black's theory of differential legal treatment across different social and political contexts.

THE VALUE OF A COMPARATIVE HISTORICAL APPROACH

Although crime and punishment are universal features of contemporary societies, it would be a serious mistake to view punishment as an automatic or uniform response to particular types of misconduct. In fact, how acts are defined and their legal treatment reflect the prevailing social, political, economic, and historical conditions of a society at any given point in time. In some contexts particular criminal acts (e.g., adultery, rape, drug use, political corruption) may be considered normatively acceptable in some cultures and in other contexts vile acts deserving of the most severe punishment. Even within the same country over time, the legal acceptance of particular punishments for particular criminal offenses is context-specific. Drug offenses, for example, are capital crimes in some historical periods in the United States, England, and China, but not in other time periods.

The strength of a comparative historical analysis lies in its ability to identify patterns that are robust across time and space, transcending both the comparative and historical context. The discovery of such patterns is essential for both theoretical and practical reasons because it allows us to more clearly specify the nature of the link between crime and punishment. Exceptions to these patterns are no less important because they help restrict our claims of universalism and necessitate the further investigation of the basis for these exceptions. The dramatic globalization of the modern world and the emergence of a world system perspective in various arenas of social life provide the current background for a fuller understanding of crime and punishment from a comparative historical framework.

> A comparative historical analysis provides the unique ability to identify patterns of punishment over space and time.

The major limitation of a comparative historical perspective involves the adequacy of available data and the selection of the particular comparative cases. Problems with the absence of available data on criminal or civil case processing and historical records of these practices are compounded as the number of comparative cases increases. The selection of the particular comparative cases raise questions about the generality of the conclusions. By selecting countries with varied legal and cultural traditions for detailed analysis, the current study is designed to offer sufficient diversity in the selection of comparative cases to permit an extensive comparative analysis of crime and punishment.

THE CURRENT APPROACH

The current study involves a comparative historical analysis of lethal and nonlethal punishments. Our comparative analysis will focus on punishment in three countries (the United States, China, and Saudi Arabia) that represent variation in both culture and legal tradition. As a former British colony, the United States's law and culture are reflective of a Western European tradition. The United States is also a highly industrialized society. The People's Republic of China represents a socialist legal system and an Eastern culture that has experienced major political and economic upheaval within the last century. Saudi Arabia is physically located within the Middle East and its legal system and culture are firmly rooted in the Islamic faith.

When compared with other countries with similar legal and cultural traditions, our selection of the United States, China, and Saudi Arabia as case

studies provides enough diversity for a comprehensive comparative historical analysis of punishment across world regions. For each of these countries,
we will examine the nature and prevalence of economic, incapacitative, and
corporal punishments over time. By exploring the relationship between deviance and punishment across these contexts, we hope to illustrate the value
of a comparative historical approach for understanding basic issues in the
study of crime, deviance, and its control.

The remaining chapters of this book are organized as follows: Chapter 2
examines different types of sanctions for deviance, including informal sanctions, civil sanctions, and criminal punishments. Chapter 3 reviews the
current world practices regarding economic, incapacitative, and corporal
sanctions. As the most severe and notorious criminal sanction, particular attention is given to the use of capital punishment across different geographic
regions of the world.

Detailed case studies are conducted in the next three chapters to examine
the historical context of punishments. Chapter 4 describes punishment in
Colonial America and the United States. Chapter 5 examines punishment
throughout the history of China. Chapter 6 explores punishments under
Islamic law and uses Saudi Arabia's practices as a particular example. Within
each of these case studies, however, comparative practices are also examined
with other countries that have similar cultures or legal traditions.

The final chapter focuses on issues in the sociological study of punishments. Based on our comparative historical analyses in previous chapters,
we address here fundamental issues about the effectiveness of sanctions in
maintaining social integration and implementing social change, the deterrent effect of punishments, the nature and magnitude of differential treatment, the relationship between legal and extrajudicial punishments, and the
accuracy of current theories about crime, punishment, and the structure of
society. As a result of these comparisons, we provide empirical evidence of the
strengths and limitations of a comparative historical perspective for studying
punishments.

Notes

1. Robert F. Meier. 1989. *Crime and Society*. Boston: Allyn and Bacon. Pages 33–4. For
    other discussions of types of sanctions, see Marshall B. Clinard and Robert F. Meier.
    1985. *Sociology of Deviant Behavior*. 6th ed. New York: Holt, Rinehart and Winston.
    Page 14.

2. For applications of a conflict perspective and discussions of its basic principles, see Willem Bonger. 1916. *Criminality and Economic Conditions.* Boston: Little, Brown; Richard Quinney. 1973. *Critique of Legal Order.* Boston: Litttle, Brown; Richard Quinney. 1977. *Class, State, and Crime.* New York: McKay; William Chambliss and Robert Seidman. 1982. *Law, Order, and Power.* 2nd ed. Reading, MA: Addison-Wesley.

3. Quoted in James Inverarity, Pat Lauderdale, and Barry Feld. 1983. *Law and Society: Sociological Perspectives on Criminal Law.* Boston: Little, Brown. Page 9.

4. Steven Vago. 1994. *Law and Society.* 4th ed. Upper Saddle River, NJ: Prentice-Hall. Page 15.

5. Emile Durkheim. 1933 [1893]. *The Division of Labor in Society.* Translated by George Simpson. New York: Free Press. First published in 1893; Phillipe Nonet and Philip Selznick. 1978. *Law and Society in Transition: Toward Responsive Law.* New York: Octagon Books; Donald Black. 1978. *The Behavior of Law.* New York: Academic Press; Michel Foucault. 1977. *Discipline and Punish: The Birth of the Prison.* New York: Pantheon; Norbert Elias. 1978 [1939]. *The Civilizing Process I: The History of Manners.* New York: Urizen Books; Norbert Elias. 1982. *The Civilizing Process II: Power and Civility.* New York: Pantheon.

6. Emile Durkheim. 1938. *The Rules of Sociological Method.* New York: Free Press.

7. Emile Durkheim. 1933 [1893]. *The Division of Labor in Society.* Translated by George Simpson. New York: Free Press. First published in 1893.

8. John Braithwaite. 1989. *Crime, Shame, and Reintegration.* New York: Cambridge University Press.

9. See Jethro Lieberman. 1983. *The Litigious Society.* New York: Basic Books; Marc Galanter. 1983. "Reading the Landscape of Disputes: What We Know and Don't Know (and Think We Know) About Our Allegedly Contentious and Litigious Society." *UCLA Law Review* 31 (October): 4–71; Terance D. Miethe. 1995. "Predicting Future Litigiousness." *Justice Quarterly* 12(3): 407–28.

10. See Terance D. Miethe. 1999. *Whistleblowing At Work: Tough Choices in Exposing Fraud, Waste, and Abuse on the Job.* Boulder, CO: Westview.

11. Steven Vago. 1981. *Law and Society.* Upper Saddle River, NJ: Prentice-Hall. Pages 231–2.

12. William J. Chambliss. 1967. "Types of Deviance and the Effectiveness of Legal Sanctions." *Wisconsin Law Review* Summer: 703–19. For a review of the current literature on deterrence, see Daniel S. Nagin. 1998. "Criminal Deterrence Research at the Outset of the Twenty-First Century." In Michael Tonry (ed.), *Crime and Justice: A Review of Research.* Volume 23. Chicago: University of Chicago Press. Pages 1–42.

13. For reviews of the literature of disparities in the access and application of law, see Barbara Curran. 1977. *The Legal Needs of the Public: The Final Report of a National Survey.* Chicago: American Bar Foundation; William Chambliss and Robert Seidman. 1982. *Law, Order, and Power.* 2nd ed. Reading, MA: Addison-Wesley; Anne Strick. 1977. *Injustice for All.* New York: Penguin; Samuel Walker, Cassia Spohn, and Miriam DeLone. 2003. *The Color of Justice: Race, Ethnicity, and Crime in America.* 3rd ed. Belmont, CA: Wadsworth.

14. For a review of studies of disparities in criminal processing, see Samuel Walker, Cassia Spohn, and Miriam DeLone. 2003. *The Color of Justice: Race, Ethnicity, and Crime in America.* 3rd ed. Belmont, CA: Wadsworth; Cassia C. Spohn. 2000. "Thirty Years of Sentencing Reform: The Quest for a Racially Neutral Sentencing Process." In Julie

Horney (ed.), *Policies, Processes, and Decisions of the Criminal Justice System: Criminal Justice 2000.* Volume 3. Washington, D.C.: U.S. Department of Justice. National Institute of Justice. Pages 427–502; Marjorie S. Zatz. 2000. "The Convergence of Race, Ethnicity, Gender, and Class on Court Decisionmaking: Looking Toward the 21st Century." In Julie Horney (ed.), *Policies, Processes, and Decisions of the Criminal Justice System: Criminal Justice 2000.* Volume 3. Washington, D.C.: U.S. Department of Justice. National Institute of Justice. Pages 503–52.

15. Donald Black. 1978. *The Behavior of Law.* New York: Academic Press.

Suggested Readings

Donald Black. 1978. *The Behavior of Law.* New York: Academic Press.

John Braithwaite. 1989. *Crime, Shame, and Reintegration.* New York: Cambridge University Press.

William Chambliss and Robert Seidman. 1982. *Law, Order, and Power.* 2nd ed. Reading, MA: Addison-Wesley.

Emile Durkheim. 1933 [1893]. *The Division of Labor in Society.* Translated by George Simpson. New York: Free Press.

David Garland. 1990. *Punishment and Modern Society: A Study of Social Theory.* Chicago: University of Chicago Press.

Phillipe Nonet and Philip Selznick. 1978. *Law and Society in Transition: Toward Responsive Law.* New York: Octagon Books.

Steven Vago. 1994. *Law and Society.* 4th ed. Upper Saddle River, NJ: Prentice-Hall.

CHAPTER TWO

Punishment Philosophies and Types of Sanctions

Punishments vary in their underlying philosophy and form. Major punishment philosophies include retribution, deterrence, rehabilitation, incapacitation, and restoration. The form of punishment may be classified as either formal or informal in terms of the organization and legitimate authority of the sanctioning body. Sanctions also vary in their valence or direction. Positive sanctions for "good behavior" include various types of praise, awards, and rewards, whereas negative sanctions are associated with various types of punishments. Our focus on punishment dictates an emphasis on negative sanctions.

This chapter reviews these punishment philosophies and the types of punishment within a comparative historical context. Detailed comparisons of current practices across world regions and case studies in particular countries will be conducted in later chapters. Here, our focus is on the general philosophical orientations and justifications for punishment and their various forms.

PHILOSOPHIES OF PUNISHMENT

Punishment serves numerous social-control functions, but it is usually justified on the principles of retribution, incapacitation, deterrence, rehabilitation, and/or restoration. The specific principles that underlie these dominant philosophies for punishment are summarized below.

RETRIBUTION

One of the oldest and most basic justifications for punishment involves the principles of revenge and retribution. This equation of punishment with the gravity of the offense is embedded in the Judeo–Christian tradition in the Mosaic laws of the Old Testament that emphasize the idea of "an eye for an eye." Neither constrained by questions of offender culpability nor directed at preventing future wrongdoing, offenders under a retributive philosophy simply get what they deserve. Punishment is justified on its own grounds, a general principle that has remained popular throughout Western history in both law and widespread public beliefs about how justice should be dispensed in democratic societies.

The classical retributive principle of "let the punishment fit the crime" was the primary basis for criminal sentencing practices in much of Western Europe in the nineteenth century. This principle of punishment was subsequently modified in neoclassical thought to recognize that some offenders who commit similar offenses may be less blameworthy or culpable due to factors outside of their control (e.g., diminished capacity, mental disease or defect, immaturity). Under this revised retributive theory of just deserts, punishment should fit primarily the moral gravity of the crime and, to a lesser extent, the characteristics of the offender.

A current example of retributive principles being used as the basis for punishment involves mandatory sentencing policies and sentencing guidelines systems in the United States. Mandatory sentences dictate uniform sanctions for persons who commit particular types of offenses (e.g., enhanced penalties for crimes committed with firearms), whereas determinate sentencing guidelines prescribe specific punishments based on the severity of the criminal offense and the extensiveness of the offender's prior criminal record. Consistent with a retributive philosophy, punishment under these sentencing systems focuses primarily on the seriousness and characteristics of the criminal act rather than the offender.

Although retribution is often linked to criminal sanctions, it is equally applicable to other types of legal sanctions and informal sanctions. For example, civil litigation that is based on the principle of strict liability is similar to retributive philosophy in that compensatory and punitive damages focus on the gravity of the prohibited act rather than characteristics of the offender. Lethal and nonlethal sanctions that derive from blood feuds between rival families, range wars in agrarian communities, terrorist attacks on civilian and government targets, and acts of "street justice" by vigilante groups and other extrajudicial bodies are often fueled by the twin motives of revenge and retribution. Various economic punishments and sanctions that restrict business practices (e.g., asset forfeitures, injunctions, product boycotts, worker strikes and slowdowns, revocation of licenses, decertification of programs, cease-and-desist orders, denial of benefits) may be justified on various utilitarian grounds like protecting society or deterring wrongdoing, but they may ultimately reflect the widespread belief in letting the punishment fit the crime.

Retribution as a penal philosophy has been criticized on several fronts when it is actually applied in practice. First, strict retributive sanctions based solely on the nature of the offense (e.g., mandatory sentences for drug trafficking, the use of firearms in the commission of crimes) are often criticized as being overly rigid, especially in societies that recognize degrees of individual culpability and blameworthiness. Second, the principle of *lex talionis* (i.e., the "eye for an eye" dictum that punishment should correspond in degree and kind to the offense) has limited applicability. For example, how do you sanction in kind acts of drunkenness, drug abuse, adultery, prostitution, and/or traffic violations like speeding? Third, the assumption of proportionality of punishments (i.e., that punishment should be commensurate or proportional to the moral gravity of the offense) is untenable in most pluralistic societies because there is often widespread public disagreement on the severity of particular offenses.[1] Under these conditions, a retributive sentencing system that espouses proportional sanctions would be based on the erroneous assumption that there is public consensus in the rankings of the moral gravity of particular types of crime.

Even with these criticisms, however, the retributive principle of *lex talionis* and proportionality of sanctions remains a dominant justification of punishment in most Western cultures. Retribution under a Judeo–Christian religious tradition offers a divine justification for strict sanctions and it clearly fits popular notions of justice (e.g., "he got what was coming to him"). The dictum of "let the punishment fit the crime" also has some appeal as a principled, proportional, and commensurate form of societal revenge for various types of misconduct.

INCAPACITATION

A primary utilitarian purpose for punishment involves various actions designed to decrease the physical capacity of a person to commit criminal or deviant acts. This principle of incapacitation focuses on the elimination of individuals' opportunity for crime and deviance through different types of physical restraints on their actions. The conditions of confinement may be so deplorable that they reduce the offender's subsequent desire to engage in misconduct, but such a deterrent effect is not a necessary component of incapacitation in its pure and earliest form. In other words, a night in the "drunk tank," confinement in the military stockade, or the "grounding" of a wayward adolescent are often considered useful incapacitative strategies even when these practices do not lead to subsequent reform in one's behavior.

A plethora of devices, techniques, and structures have been used throughout history as means for incapacitation. The early tribal practices of banishment to the wilderness, the English system of "transportation" of convicts to other colonies in the seventeenth and eighteenth centuries, the exile of citizens in ancient Greek society, and political exile in more modern times are examples of incapacitative sanctions because they involve the physical removal of persons from their former communities, thereby restricting their physical opportunity for misconduct in the original setting. The stocks and pillory in English history and Colonial America were devices used for both public ridicule and incapacitation. Other types of incapacitating hardware are as diverse as electronic shackles for monitoring offenders in open spaces, Breathalysers that prevent drunk drivers from starting their cars, "kiddie harnesses" to restrict the movement of young children in public places, and chastity belts for limiting sexual promiscuity.

The function of incapacitation may also be served by other types of legal and extralegal restrictions on one's behavior. Other legal forms of incapacitation involving civil or administrative decrees include court-ordered injunctions, federal boycotts and restraint-of-trade agreements, restraining orders in domestic violence cases, cease-and-desist orders, revocations of licenses, foreclosures, and the passage of certification requirements to perform particular tasks (e.g., college degree requirements for teaching, passing medical board and bar exams for practicing medicine or law). Many of these actions are economic sanctions in that they carry financial consequences for those involved, but these civil and administrative rules can also be seen as incapacitative in that they place physical restrictions on one's possible actions. Ostracism, the spreading of adverse publicity, "lumping" (i.e., doing nothing and not responding to one's inquiries), and censorship are some of the extralegal and informal means of physically restricting one's behavioral opportunities.

The most widely known type of incapacitation involves some form of in-carceration, or what others have termed "penal bondage."[2] Aside from their incapacitative effect on restricting immediate criminal opportunities, penal bondage of criminals, vagrants, debtors, social misfits, and other disadvan-taged groups across time periods and geographical contexts has often in-cluded a component of forced labor (e.g., public works projects, forced servi-tude in military campaigns) as a condition of confinement.

Physical structures for incapacitation may have different purposes or functions besides the physical restraint of the body. These places of con-finement are described across time and space in context-specific terms like dungeons, towers, workhouses, gulags, jails, prisons, labor camps, "readjust-ment" centers, correctional or treatment facilities, cottages, sanitariums, and mental institutions. The specific language used for descriptive purposes also signifies their functions beyond physical incapacitation.

During the last half century, several new forms of incapacitation have emerged. For example, shock incarceration programs involve short-term in-carceration of juvenile offenders to show them the pains of imprisonment and scare them into a future life of conformity. Work release programs and place-ment in halfway houses are temporary incapacitation programs designed to maintain community ties and ease the adjustment from prison to conven-tional life. Another variant of incapacitation, intensive-supervision probation (ISP), leaves adjudicated criminals in their community but under the watchful eye of probation officers or other legal authorities.

The recent model of selective incapacitation in the United States is de-signed to target criminal offenders thought to have the greatest probability of repeat offending and place greater restraints on the nature and conditions of confinement for these "high-risk" offenders. Although research suggests that a small pool of people commits the predominant share of violent and property crime, efforts to successfully predict these high-risk offenders suf-fer from numerous ethical and practical problems, including high rates of both "false positives" (i.e., falsely labeling someone as a high-risk offender) and "false negatives" (i.e., releasing high-risk offenders because they were erroneously characterized as low-risk).[3]

Contrary to early historical patterns of incapacitation that emphasized the reduction of the physical opportunity for crime and deviance, modern versions of this philosophy are more "forward-looking" in terms of focusing on the utility of punishments for changing offenders' criminal motivations once they are no longer physically restrained from committing deviance. In this way, incapacitation is united with other utilitarian philosophies for punishment. Different types of incapacitative sanctions may serve as the initial framework for establishing successful programs of deterrence and rehabilitation.

DETERRENCE

The doctrine of deterrence asks a fundamental question about the relationship between sanctions and human behavior: Are legal and extralegal sanctions effective in reducing deviance and achieving conformity? Punishment is said to have a deterrent effect when the fear or actual imposition of punishment leads to conformity.[4] The deterrent value of punishments is directly linked to the characteristics of those punishments. Specifically, punishments have the greatest potential for deterring misconduct when they are severe, certain, and swift in their application. Punishments are also widely assumed to be most effective for instrumental conduct (i.e., deliberate actions directed at the achievement of some explicit goal) and for potential offenders who have low commitment to deviance as a livelihood (e.g., the person is not a professional criminal).[5]

Deterrence is based on a rational conception of human behavior in which individuals freely choose between alternative courses of action to maximize pleasure and minimize pain. From this classical perspective on crime and punishment, criminal solutions to problems become an unattractive option when the costs of this conduct exceed its expected benefit. Swift, certain, and severe sanctions are costs that are assumed to impede the likelihood of engaging in deviant behavior. From a deterrence standpoint, any type of punishment (e.g., monetary, informal, incapacitative, corporal) has a potential deterrent effect as long as it is perceived as a severe, certain, and swift sanction.

The research literature on the effectiveness of criminal punishments outlines the four major types of deterrence, which include the following:

- *Specific deterrence* involves the effectiveness of punishment on that particular individual's future behavior. Recidivism rates (e.g., rates of repeat offending among prior offenders) are often used to measure the specific deterrent value of punishments.

- *General deterrence* asks whether the punishment of particular offenders deters other people from committing deviance. A comparison of crime rates over time or across jurisdictions is typically used to ascertain the general deterrent value of punishment.

- *Marginal deterrence* focuses on the relative effectiveness of different types of punishments as either general or specific deterrents. For example, if recidivism rates for drunk drivers are higher for those who receive monetary fines than those who received jail time, jail time would be rated higher in its marginal deterrent value as a specific deterrent for drunk driving. Similarly, debates about capital punishment often focus on the marginal deterrent value of life imprisonment compared to the death penalty as a general deterrent for murder.

- *Partial deterrence* refers to situations in which the threat of sanction has some deterrent value even when the sanction threats do not lead to law-abiding behavior. For example, if a thief picked or "lifted" someone's wallet rather than robbing them at gunpoint (because the thief was fearful of the more serious penalty for committing an armed robbery), the thief would be treated as a "successful" case of partial deterrence. Similarly, tougher fines for speeding passed in a jurisdiction would serve as a partial deterrent under these two conditions: (1) the average motorist under the new law exceeded the speed limit by 5 miles an hour and (2) the average motorist under the old law exceeded the speed limit by 10 miles an hour. The average motorist is still exceeding the speed limit but he or she nonetheless is driving slower.

When the philosophy of deterrence is used in the context of penal reform, it is often as a justification for increasing the severity of sanctions, particularly in Western developed countries.[6] Legislative responses to terrorist attacks, drug trafficking, child abductions, and violent crimes on school property have been directed primarily at increasing the severity and/or duration of punishments (e.g., being a drug "kingpin" and participation in lethal terrorist attacks are now capital crimes under U.S. federal law). Although these greater punitive measures may serve to pacify widespread public demands to "get tough" on crime, the specific and general deterrent effect of such efforts is probably limited without attention to the other necessary conditions for effective deterrence (i.e., high certainty and high celerity of punishments).[7]

Empirical efforts to assess the effectiveness of deterrence are limited by several basic factors. First, persons may abide by laws or desist in deviant behavior for a variety of reasons other than the looming threat or fear of legal sanctions. Some of these nondeterrence constraints on behavior include one's moral/ethical principles, religious beliefs, physical inability to commit the deviant act, and lack of opportunity. Second, neither swift nor certain punishment exists in most legal systems in the contemporary world. The majority of criminal offenses are typically unknown to the legal authorities and, even among the known offenses, only a small proportion result in an arrest and conviction. The typical criminal penalty and civil suits are often imposed or resolved months, if not years, after the initial violation. Third, the severity of punishment actually received by offenders is often far less than mandated by law, due to the operation of such factors as plea bargaining, charge reductions, jury nullifications, executive clemency and pardons, and "good time" provisions. Under these conditions, it is unsurprising that the deterrent effect of criminal and civil sanctions has not been clearly demonstrated across a variety of contexts.

REHABILITATION

Although it may seem contradictory or at least somewhat odd to assert that we punish for the treatment and reform of offenders, this basic principle underlies the rehabilitation purpose of punishment. The ultimate goal of rehabilitation is to restore a convicted offender to a constructive place in society through some combination of treatment, education, and training.[8] The salience of rehabilitation as a punishment philosophy is indicated by the contemporary jargon of "correctional facilities," "reformatories," and "therapeutic community" now used to describe jails, prisons, and other institutions of incapacitation.

The link between places of incapacitation and reform is established throughout much of written history. The earliest forms of penal confinement in dungeons, towers, caves, and other dark and dreary places were largely incapacitative in their primary function, but some degree of moral and spiritual enlightenment was expected of those condemned to long periods of solitary confinement. This idea of restraint to reform is evident within the context of religious penance in Judeo–Christian practices in Western Europe and the British colonies in North America and elsewhere. It is also manifested in U.S. history in the early development of reformatories and penitentiaries. These large-scale incarceration structures punished misguided youth and criminals by isolating them so they could reflect on their deviant actions, repent, and subsequently reform their behavior. Confinement and reflection for spiritual reform are also of central importance in the religious principles found in Hinduism and Buddhism.

In contrast to retribution that emphasizes uniform punishments based on the gravity of the misconduct, rehabilitation focuses on the particular characteristics of individual offenders that require treatment and intervention. This individualized treatment approach is logically consistent with indeterminate sentencing structures that give judges enormous discretion to tailor punishments for the greatest good to the individual offender and provide parole boards with equally high discretion to release or retain offenders for future treatment. Through the application of current theories of human behavior and the latest therapeutic techniques for behavioral modification, rehabilitation experienced growing acceptance in many countries throughout much of the twentieth century.[9]

Even though "correctional" institutions continue to espouse the benefits of rehabilitation and specific treatment programs (e.g., drug treatment, anger management, job training), support for rehabilitation in the United States was dealt a major blow in the mid-1970s with publication of a report that concluded that rehabilitation efforts had no appreciable effect on recidivism.[10] National fiscal restraints, declines in correctional budgets for program development, high public outcry for more severe and longer prison sentences, and a growing crime-control political ideology that focuses on suppression of criminal behavior rather than its early prevention are current conditions in Western societies that are largely antithetical to the ideas of treatment and rehabilitation.[11]

RESTORATION

One of the most recent goals of punishment derives from the principles of restoration. As an alternative to other punishment philosophies (e.g., retribution, incapacitation, rehabilitation), restorative justice fundamentally challenges our way of thinking about crime and justice. The global victims' rights movement is a relatively new phenomenon, but, the general roots of restorative justice can be traced back to the early legal systems of Western Europe, ancient Hebrew justice, and precolonial African societies.[12]

Restorative justice literally involves the process of returning to their previous condition all parties involved in or affected by the original misconduct, including victims, offenders, the community, and even possibly the government.[13] Under this punishment philosophy, the offender takes full responsibility for the wrongdoing and initiates restitution to the victim. The victim and offender are brought together to develop a mutually beneficial program that helps the victim in the recovery process and provides the offender a means of reducing their risks of re-offending.

The theory of reintegrative shaming developed by John Braithwaite is based on the principles of restorative justice.[14] Offenders take personal responsibility for their actions and condemnation is focused on the deviant act, rather than the offender, and its impact on the victim and the community. Both the offender and the community need to be reintegrated as a result of the harm caused by the criminal behavior. Community mediation groups, neighborhood councils, local support groups, and victim–offender conferences are the primary means of achieving these restorative efforts.

The principles of restorative justice have been applied to the study of both criminal and civil sanctions. For example, the institutionalized practice of "written apology" and "letter of forgiveness" in the Japanese criminal justice system is designed to express remorse and make restitution. By accepting the apology, the victim forgives the offender.[15] In all cases of restorative justice, the goal is to restore both the individual parties and their community's sense of wholeness.

TYPES OF FORMAL AND INFORMAL SANCTIONS

The various philosophies of punishment are manifested in practice by the allocation of various types of formal and informal sanctions. Formal legal punishments involve pain or other consequences normally considered unpleasant that are intentionally administered by officials with the legitimate authority to do so.[16] Legal officials in this context are judges, government agencies, administrative bodies, executive boards, councils, tribunals, and other individuals and groups that are formally authorized to impose these sanctions. In contrast, informal sanctions are those imposed by individuals or groups that lack this legitimate authority. Friends, family members, vigilante committees and civilian "regulators," paramilitary organizations, and law enforcement personnel operating outside their official capacity are examples of informal sanctioning bodies. Regardless of their formal or informal status, punishment is a ubiquitous feature of social control in the modern world.

There are various ways to classify the enormous variety of formal and informal punishments.[17] We group these sanctions into three major categories: (1) *economic punishments* that involve direct financial consequences to offenders, (2) *incapacitative sanctions* that physically restrain behavioral patterns, and (3) *corporal punishments* that involve death or physical suffering through the direct application of physical force on the human body. Sanctions that cover multiple types of punishment are classified here according to their primary consequences to the offender (e.g., economic boycotts are classified as economic sanctions even though they may physically incapacitate and harm residents of the affected area).[18] The nature of specific punishments within these general categories is highlighted below.

ECONOMIC SANCTIONS

Economic sanctions are financial penalties imposed for wrongdoing. As such, these sanctions are used around the world for purposes of retribution, deterrence, and restoration.[19] Large fines levied against persons who commit economic crimes such as embezzlement, stock fraud, and insider trading may be viewed as an appropriate retributive response for these offenses. Given that their crimes involve economic activities, severe financial penalties for misconduct seem especially salient for many white-collar offenders, and there is some evidence that such offenders are most likely to be deterred by economic punishments.[20] Financial restitution by offenders to their victims is an obvious example of economic punishments based on restorative principles. The most common types of economic sanctions are described below.

Monetary Fines

In many countries, monetary fines are commonly used to sanction traffic violations and less serious criminal offenses (e.g., public drunkenness, disorderly conduct, petty theft). A particular monetary amount can also be paid in lieu of jail or prison sentences for particular offenses. Fines are often imposed in addition to other sentences as well. For example, Michael Fay, an American teenager, received a sentence of $1,400 fine, four months in jail, and six lashes for vandalizing several cars in Singapore in 1994.

Given social class disparities in the ability to pay financial penalties, a number of European countries (e.g., Finland, Sweden, Germany) have developed a structured system of economic sanctions called "day fines," based on the amount of money an offender earns in a day's work. Day fine programs have been praised for reducing discrimination in sentencing (because the fine is relative to one's income) and for being fair and just (because offenders literally "pay for their crimes," but not beyond what is financially feasible).[21]

Sanctions involving monetary fines are also commonly found within the context of white-collar crime. Upon successful criminal prosecution, corporations and their agents are often levied with large financial penalties that are deemed commensurate with the gravity of the misconduct. However, for most types of corporate crime (e.g., unlawful regulatory practices, environmental crimes, prohibitive personnel practices, crimes against investors/competitors), it is often the threat of criminal prosecutions and adverse publicity that leads to out-of-court settlements that involve fines and other monetary sanctions. A federal regulatory agency (like the U.S. Internal Revenue Service, Environmental Protection Agency, or Securities and Exchange Commission) commonly serves as the enforcement and sanctioning body for these corporate offenses.

ECONOMIC SANCTIONS:

- monetary fines/bail
- civil suits
- asset forfeiture/foreclosure
- denial of financial benefits
- injunctions/boycotts/strikes
- license revocation

Financial Sanctions in Civil Litigation

Financial sanctions within the context of civil litigation involve economic settlements and the awarding of compensatory and punitive damages in civil suits. Both alimony payments and child support are types of financial sanctions that evolve from civil litigation among former family members. Civil suits involving many types of personal injury (e.g., product liability, medical malpractice, prohibited personnel practices such as discriminatory hiring/firing) are economic sanctions with both restorative and deterrence components. Specifically, compensatory damages in civil litigation is designed for restorative purposes (i.e, to return and "make whole" the situation before the wrongful conduct was done), whereas punitive damages are directed at deterring similar misconduct in the future by the offending party.

Although assessing compensatory damages is a common goal in civil courts throughout the world, economic sanctions involving punitive damages are usually found only in developed countries. However, even within developed countries, great variation is found in the use of these practices as well as the size of awards. For example, the German civil courts do not award punitive damages by law, and compensatory awards for "pain and suffering" are relatively small compared to American practices.[22]

The civil litigation "explosion" in the United States in the last quarter century has been blamed for a variety of societal ills. These include: (1) the rising cost of health care, (2) decreased availability of particular types of medical doctors (e.g., obstetricians) because of the onerous cost of medical malpractice insurance, (3) the increased price of consumer goods due to companies offsetting their losses in product liability suits, and (4) an erosion of trust in fellow citizens due to fears of being sued. Both federal and state legislation has been proposed to limit the size of jury awards in personal injury cases.

The effectiveness of civil litigation in controlling organizational misconduct depends on both the nature of the economic sanction and the organizational response. For many companies, severe economic sanctions should send a clear message about the unacceptability of particular practices. If, however, financial sanctions are viewed as just "one of the costs of doing business," they will largely be ineffective. For example, the multibillion-dollar settlement levied against the tobacco industry in the United States for misleading both Congress and the American public about the dangers of tobacco use has increased the price of cigarettes and other tobacco products. However, this litigation has had negligible effects on the tobacco industry's desire to restrict production and distribution of their product.

Other Economic Sanctions

Several other types of economic sanctions are used for purposes of social control. They include asset forfeiture and foreclosure, denials of financial benefits, and economic restraints on practices such as injunctions, boycotts, protests, and strikes. This class of economic sanctions is imposed within different formal settings (e.g., they may be criminal penalties, civil judgments, or decrees by administrative or regulatory agencies) and within informal contexts of daily life (e.g., individuals may choose to boycott a particular store because they were poorly treated).

Asset forfeiture as an economic sanction has received recent attention in the United States in the context of prosecution of drug offenders and organized crime syndicates. Under both federal and state laws, offenders' property can be seized and their assets forfeited to the government if they were involved in a criminal enterprise and that property was purchased or received from their material participation in this criminal enterprise. For example, financial institutions that "launder" money received from illegal activities (e.g., drug trafficking, off-track betting) may have some of their profits and the specific building in which these illegal transactions took place seized and forfeited to the U.S. government. Foreclosures by financial institutions are similar types of asset forfeiture. A person's car, home, and/or business becomes the property of the financial institution that provided the economic backing or loan for this property. Asset forfeiture has been increasingly used in China as a supplementary criminal penalty for persons convicted of bribery and corruption.

The denial of financial benefits is another form of economic sanctions. These sanctions may involve government benefits (e.g., welfare payments, unemployment compensation, living in government-subsidized housing, food vouchers, education grants and scholarships) and benefits provided by one's employer (e.g., pension funds, sick leave, paid vacations, lower insurance premiums). The withholding or denial of these material benefits may dramatically impact the quality of one's life. Hence, the mere threat of denial of these benefits is an insidious but often effective method of social control.

Finally, various physical restraints on practices may serve as both incapacitative and economic sanctions. These include the following legal and extralegal actions: injunctions, embargoes and boycotts, cease-and-desist orders, revocation of licenses, the invocation of licensing and certification requirements, suspensions, and expulsions. These sanctions have been applied to individuals, various groups, and even to entire nations (see Table 2.1). Their economic basis derives from the fact that such physical restraints will ultimately have direct consequences on the economic well-being of those so affected. Accordingly, they can be treated as somewhat special forms of economic sanctions.

TABLE 2.1: International economic sanctions (examples)

Country and decade	Actions
18th and 19th Centuries:	
1765: American colonists vs. Britain	Boycott of English goods because of the Stamp Act.
1883–85: France vs. China	France declared rice contraband.
1930s and 1940s:	
1935 League of Nations vs. Italy	Trade embargo/restrictions for Invasion of Abyssinia.
1939–41: USA, UK, and others vs. Japan	Trade boycott/financial restriction to prevent Japan's movement toward southern Indo-China.
1946–48: The Arab League vs. Zionist movement in Palestine/Israel	Trade embargo in opposition to creation of an Israeli state.
1950s and 1960s:	
1951: UK vs. Iran	Oil import embargo for nationalizing Anglo-Iranian Oil Co.
1954: USSR vs. Australia	Import boycott of wool for not extraditing Soviet defector.
1960: USA vs. Cuba	Trade embargo and cessation of economic aid for Cuba's drawing closer to Soviet Union.
1962: West Germany vs. USSR	Trade embargo and cessation of economic aid for construction of Berlin Wall by East Germany.
1966: United Nations (UN) vs. Rhodesia	Trade embargo to end racial discrimination policies and the unilateral declaration of independence.
1970s and 1980s:	
1971: France vs. Algeria	Oil import boycott for nationalizing a French oil company.
1977: United Nations vs. South Africa	Arms embargo against apartheid.
1980: USA vs. USSR	Grain export embargo for invasion of Afghanistan.
1990s and 2000s:	
1990: United Nations vs. Iraq	Trade embargo and financial restrictions for Iraq's invasion and occupation of Kuwait.
2000: USA vs. North Korea	Continuation of trade embargo.

Source: Simons (1999); Miyagawa (1992)

INCAPACITATIVE SANCTIONS

Sanctions that confine individuals or limit their physical opportunities for unacceptable behavior are ubiquitous over time and geographical context. These incapacitative sanctions may be justified solely on their preventive value, but they can also serve multiple functions when the conditions of confinement are so deplorable that they deter the individual from future deviant behavior. As illustrated below, numerous devices, techniques, and physical structures have been employed throughout history for purposes of incapacitation.

Banishment and Exile

One of the most basic means of social control is the physical removal of deviants and dissidents through banishment and exile. Exile is the physical banishment of dissidents and persons of higher social status in a society (e.g., political rivals, religious leaders, social reformers).

Banishment and exile have several obvious advantages compared to other methods of physical restraint. For example, they are both cheap and efficient methods of social control, involving in most cases little more cost than the proverbial "one-way ticket out of town." Acts of banishment and exile also have strong symbolic value as punishments and may uniquely enhance community solidarity. The public degradation ceremonies in which these sanctions are pronounced may serve to dramatize the evil of the offender and the offense, ultimately leading to greater community solidarity and reinforcing the prevailing power relations in the community. Ironically, these punishments are often considered more humane and less likely to create martyrs than alternative sanctions (e.g., death, penal servitude) even though banishment and exile to hostile lands often result in the same outcomes.

Banishment in various forms has been practiced in a variety of different cultures and societies. Anthropological accounts of life in early tribal societies reveal that banishment was used for serious breaches of customs and folkways. Both the Greek and Roman civilizations practiced banishment, as did

INCAPACITATIVE SANCTIONS:

- banishment/exile/transportation
- chains/stocks/pillory/handcuffs
- electronic anklets/bracelets
- dungeons/hulks/jails/prisons/reformatories/labor camps
- supervised probation
- "grounding"/school detention

later European communities. During the eighteenth century, an estimated 97 percent of the noncapital sentences in Amsterdam included banishment.[23]

The practice of banishment reached an unprecedented level in England through the system called "transportation." For over 200 years starting at the end of the sixteenth century, England used transportation to its colonies as a means to rid the homeland of criminal felons and various "rogues, vagabonds, and beggars."[24] An estimated 50,000 English prisoners were sent to the American colonies prior to the Revolutionary War.[25] The annual number of convicts shipped to Australia and other British colonies peaked at 5,000 per year in the early 1830s, representing about one-third of convicted offenders in English courts.[26]

Banishment to other countries has shifted in the modern world from the removal of a criminal underclass to the expulsion of political exiles and other dissidents. Foreign nationals and ethnic minorities have often been the targets of organized "relocation" campaigns and lethal violence in nearly all regions of the world, including Southeast Europe (e.g., the ethnic conflict in Bosnia, Croatia, Serbia), the Middle East (e.g., the Kurds in Iraq, the Palestinians on the Gaza Strip), the Caribbean and Central American (e.g., the persecution of Dominican nationals of Haitian origin, attacks on the indigenous community of Acteal in Mexico), and Asia (e.g., the Uighurs and Falun Gong in China). Rather than transportation to distant countries, many of the new types of banishment involve segregation in geographical regions within the same country. These segregation areas are similar to the reservations used to control the indigenous native populations in North America during the nineteenth and twentieth centuries.

Incapacitative Devices

The earliest physical restraints on offenders reflected elements of both incapacitative and corporal punishment. Confinement in chains, stocks (i.e. a wooden frame that binds the person's hands and feet in a locked position), or yokes around the person's neck were physically uncomfortable and caused pain to the body. The pillory (i.e., a device that forced the wearer to stand with head and hands locked in place) was even more notorious for extracting physical pain, as it often involved nailing the person's ears to the wooden blocks. Technological advances in the modern world have led to the emergence of incapacitative devices that do not impose corporal punishment. Electronic monitoring ankle bracelets, handcuffs, and fingercuffs are examples of these less invasive restraint devices.

Stocks and the pillory were commonly displayed in cities and towns throughout medieval Europe and in Colonial America. These incapacitation devices were located in open public places to ridicule or humiliate the offender and to serve as a visible deterrent for other potential offenders. Public scorn for some offenders was met with verbal and physical abuse of the prisoner, frequently involving a barrage of attacks with rotten eggs and fruit. The potential specific and general deterrent effect of public shaming was probably a more important purpose underlying these punishments than their incapacitative effects per se.

Modern incapacitative devices provide less stigmatizing and more reintegrative punishments. Persons under electronic monitoring remain in the community and are encouraged to maintain and enhance family relations and employment opportunities. As punishments that promote social integration rather than isolation of the offender, the theory of reintegrative shaming would predict that these sanctioning devices should be more effective than their historical counterparts in reducing future criminal behavior.[27]

Incapacitative Structures

Popular images of incapacitation focus on the physical facilities or structures for penal confinement. From this perspective, incapacitation is equated primarily with the notion of institutional confinement. Physical structures for incapacitation for particular offenses at various times and in different countries are described by the following terms: dungeons, gaols (i.e., jails), towers, hulks (i.e., abandoned ships), workhouses, penitentiaries, prisons, reformatories, labor camps, centers and cottages, halfway houses, sanitariums, mental institutions/hospitals, correctional facilities, and therapeutic communities/environments.

The particular language used to describe these penal structures is instructive because it reflects through time a movement toward rehabilitation and treatment as a major goal within these incapacitative structures. Ironically, the term "warehousing" is now being used to describe the overall correctional philosophy in the United States, a word that is more synonymous with an incapacitative function and far removed from the language of rehabilitation and treatment.

Current incapacitative facilities for criminal offenders in most countries involve temporary holding institutions (e.g., jails) and long-term facilities (e.g., prisons). Jails in the United States are restricted to misdemeanors and felony sentences of less than one year. Prisons are reserved for commitments of longer than one year. Some correctional institutions like drug treatment centers and mental hospitals involve both voluntary commitments and court-ordered commitments. Both jails and prisons involve court-ordered incapacitation. The length of such confinement in these latter facilities depends in most jurisdictions on the seriousness of the offense and the offender's prior criminal record.

Other Types of Incapacitation

The final type of incapacitation involves short-term incapacitation and confinement that monitors offenders within the community. Shock incarceration is a temporary incapacitation program in which the convicted offender is given a brief period of confinement in an institution (e.g., one day to one week) and then released back to the community. Types of supervised probation involve monitoring within the community by legal officials (e.g., police, correctional officers, probation officers). Supervised probation is considered an incapacitative sanction because there are conditions of confinement placed on those given probationary sentences (e.g., restrictions on contact with particular people, restrictions on travel, mandatory curfews, prohibitions against alcohol use). Other types of short-term incapacitative sanctions include after-school detention and the confinement of troubled youth at home through "grounding."

CORPORAL PUNISHMENT

Corporal punishment involves the infliction of pain on the offender's body. Pain and suffering are the primary and immediate goal of corporal punishment. This type of punishment is used for various purposes, including retribution (e.g., removing the tongue of a liar or hands of a thief), specific and general deterrence, the rehabilitation of the offender, and the extraction of confessions. In other words, most corporal sanctions are also "future-directed," designed to change the behavior of those punished and to send a strong message to other potential offenders of the price of wrongdoing.

The particular means of inflicting corporal punishment are virtually limitless, restricted only by the imagination and standards of human decency. However, the methods of choice for torture and inflicting pain are also linked to customs, rituals, and the availability of technology within particular countries at particular times. The outcome of corporal punishment ranges from short-term pain, to permanent disfiguration and injury, to death. Death has been both an intentional and unintentional outcome of corporal punishment throughout history. Mistakes caused by the inexperience or overzealousness of the sanctioner and poor medical treatment are common reasons why nonlethal corporal sanctions sometimes have deadly consequences.

> **CORPORAL PUNISHMENT:**
>
> - flogging/whipping
> - branding
> - stretching (racking)
> - keel-hauling
> - dunking stools
> - electric shock
> - raping/sodomizing
> - amputations
> - other disfigurements/mutilations
> - capital punishment

Corporal punishments are popular in the modern world in particular contexts (e.g., the spanking of children by parents, coerced confessions for wrongdoing, the use of physical punishments under Islamic law and in developing countries). However, corporal punishment gained its greatest notoriety in earlier historical periods. The most infamous periods of corporal punishment occurred during the Spanish Inquisition (1478–1834), the reign of Henry VIII (1509–1547) and the Elizabethan period (1558–1603) in England, the "reign of terror" (1793–4) during the French Revolution, the Puritan settlements of the seventeenth century, and the mass genocides and democides of the twentieth century (e.g., the Holocaust in Nazi Germany, Khmer Rouge in Cambodia, the Turk–Armenian genocides, the slaughter and torture of different groups in Africa [Sudan, Burundi, Uganda, Nigeria]).[28]

Flogging

Flogging involves the whipping of the body with some object (e.g., stick, leather straps, branches, cords). Flogging is a common form of corporal punishment used by parents on their children and state authorities to inflict injury on offenders and dissidents.

Early legal codes (e.g., Mosaic codes, Roman laws, the Tang Code in Imperial China) and military decrees specified the types of offenses punishable by whipping (e.g., petty theft, vagrancy, blasphemy) and the particular number of lashes to be inflicted. Under Henry VIII, England passed the Whipping Act of 1530. This law was directed at vagrants whose idleness was considered an economic threat and "revenue problem" for the Crown.[29] Public floggings in the early American colonies were used to enforce discipline, vilify evil and enhance community solidarity, and to deter others. Whipping was especially common in Virginia and other southern colonies to punish slaves and to prevent slave revolts. As a mechanism for gaining compliance to institutional rules, flogging has a long history within the context of prisons and labor camps.

> An especially cruel form of flogging involved the Russian knout. It was made of leather strips fitted with fishhooks. During the whipping, the hooks would dig into the body and rip away pieces of flesh. Death sometimes occurred because of the gravity of blood loss.
>
> *Source:* Schmallenger & Ortiz (2001:67)

> One of the most publicized floggings in recent times involved the caning of Michael Fay. Fay was an American teenager given six lashes for vandalizing cars in Singapore in 1994. The incident created a major international uproar, regarding the subjugation of a foreign teenager to such a severe corporal punishment.

Branding

Another type of corporal punishment is the practice of branding. Criminals and dissidents in various historical contexts have been physically branded with a mark or letter on the body that signifies their offense (e.g., "T" for thieves, "B" for blasphemers, "R" for rogues, "A" for adultery). Branding served primarily as a means of public stigmatization or shaming of the accused. The branding on the forehead or other parts of the face was an especially vivid warning to others of the offender's previous behavior.

Depending on the particular historical context, branding varied both in its form and location on the body. The French branded criminals with the royal emblem on the shoulder. This practice was later changed to the burning of a letter on the shoulder to represent the convicted offense.[30] Facial branding in England was replaced with hand branding around the early 1700s. The early American colonists also burned particular letters on offenders' hands and forehead. Facial branding was more often imposed on more serious offenses at this time (e.g., blasphemy) and for repeat offenders. Rather than being physically branded, female offenders were forced to wear letters symbolizing their crimes on their clothing. This practice of sewing letters on garments of criminals was called the "scarlet letter."[31]

The practice of physical branding by state authorities has been largely abolished in modern industrial societies. However, these practices continue in many developing countries and in the extrajudicial sanctions by vigilante groups and paramilitary forces against other civilians. Various "hazing" incidents of particular people and groups also sometimes result in temporary types of branding (e.g., spray painting letters directly on individuals and their clothing, graffiti on personal property). These latter forms of branding may be less intrusive than actual physical branding, but they are similar in terms of their goals of stigmatization and social control.

Mutilations

As a type of corporal punishment, physical branding falls under the more general category of mutilations. Some societies justified mutilations on the grounds of retribution and the law of retaliation (*lex talionis*). For example, the removal of particular body parts may be deemed to "fit the crime" (e.g., the hands of thieves, tongues of liars, genitals of sex offenders, eyes of spies, feet of deserters, or ears of eavesdroppers). However, some cultures justify bodily mutilations in terms of their incapacitative and deterrent function.

Regardless of their philosophical rationale, mutilations carry enormous symbolic weight in a society. State-sponsored mutilations are "theatrical" punishments that dramatize to citizens the evils of the original misconduct.[32] They also demonstrate the supreme power of the prevailing authority to exact incredible pain and physical suffering on its subjects. The gravity of public humiliation and shaming of the offender associated with mutilation is best represented by the practice of hand amputations for particular misconduct in different cultures. Aside from the physical incapacitation caused by amputation, this type of mutilation has symbolic importance for public degradation because it leaves the offender permanently tainted with only one hand for both eating and cleaning body parts after bodily secretions.

Many of the most gruesome and appalling types of bodily mutilation emerged during the Middle Ages. The Holy Inquisition era in medieval Europe was instrumental in the development of numerous devices and techniques

to extract confessions and punish heretics and nonbelievers. Stretching machines like the rack, presses and
other crushing devices, bludgeoning tools, cages with
spikes to impale the occupant, and specially designed
cutting tools to slowly bleed and disembowel (i.e., removing internal organs) were some of the common
tools of inquisitors of this era.

> Disemboweling involves the tearing out of internal organs. Hearts and kidneys were common targets of these mutilations because they were seen as the roots of the criminal's wicked disposition.
>
> *Source:* Newman (1978:47)

Earlier civilizations (e.g., ancient Greece, the Roman
Empire, and the Song Dynasty in China) also used mutilation as forms of
corporal punishment. These involved such practices as slicing, whipping, and
beating. As with other methods of mutilation (e.g., boiling in oil or water,
burning, cutting off the ears of offenders in the pillory), death often resulted
from the most serious types of bodily mutilations. Bodily desecrations and
mutilations were often conducted posthumously for particularly notorious
offenders (e.g., rival leaders, political dissidents). These post-death mutilations
included the bludgeoning, burning, dismemberment, and subsequent display
of body parts in public places.

Bodily mutilations in various forms have continued in many countries
in the modern world. Islamic countries like Saudi Arabia, Iran, and Iraq continue to perform amputations on particular offenders. Genital mutilation (e.g.,
removal of the female clitoris) is practiced in many countries of Africa and
the Middle East to control sexual pleasure and promiscuity.[33] During civil
wars and other types of civil strife across the last half of the twentieth century, both migrants and the indigenous populations have been physically
mutilated through acts of torture, rape, and bludgeoning. Even with greater
international scrutiny of these practices, physical mutilations in many countries continue to take place in the process of police interrogations of criminal
suspects and in the context of maintaining discipline and control of prison
inmates.

Capital Punishment

Because it results in the death of the accused, capital punishment is the ultimate corporal sanction. The wide variety of methods of execution used
over time and place can be distinguished according to whether they involve instant or slow death. Beheadings, hangings, and strangulations have

been identified as the most common means for merciful or instant death.[34] The use of firing squads, gas chambers, and lethal injections are modern forms of instant death. In contrast, lethal methods associated with a slow or lingering death included the acts of burning, boiling, stoning, crucifixion, draw and quartering, and being "broken on the wheel." These methods of capital punishments and the context in which they have been used are described below.[35]

MERCIFUL AND INSTANT EXECUTION METHODS:

- beheading
- hanging
- strangulation/garroting
- burying alive
- drowning/"walking the plank"
- dropping from high places
- shootings/firing squads
- gas chambers
- electrocutions
- lethal injections

SLOW AND LINGERING EXECUTION METHODS:

- burning
- boiling
- slicing
- crucifixion
- draw and quartering
- "broken on the wheel"

BEHEADING. Beheading is a quick death that occurs when the head is separated from the body using an ax, sword, or machine. It was considered an honorable form of punishment for nobles and conquered enemies in ancient China and early Egypt. However, it has been applied in most countries to nobles and commoners alike. An ax and chopping block were the basic tools for decapitation in medieval Europe. A sword was the tool for samurai warriors and "field" executions in civil wars in early historical periods.

The guillotine, invented at the beginning of the French Revolution, was the method of beheading used almost exclusively in Europe. Comparable beheading machines in England and Scotland in the 1500s were nicknamed the "Halifax Gibbet" and the "Scottish Maiden." These machines were developed to provide a reliable, efficient, and cheap method for mass numbers of executions. Thousands of French citizens lost their heads in the guillotine during the "reign of terror" of 1793–4. The guillotine represented a major technological advancement over other beheading machines in that it stabilized the head and used a tilted blade for a cleaner decapitation.

HANGING AND STRANGULATION. These methods of instant death include various types of executions by ropes and cords around the neck. Condemned persons across history have been hung from trees, walls, horses, lampposts, bridges, and physical structures erected for these executions. A lynching is often considered an extrajudicial hanging, meaning that it is committed by vigilante groups and other parties that do not have the formal legal authority to do so. The practice of garroting is strangulation by a double cord passed through a hole in an upright post. Strangulations in Imperial China were committed in the following way: The executioner threw the victim down upon his face, then straddled the victim and began twisting a cord around his neck until the victim died. Compared to other methods such as beheading, hanging has always been considered a more lowly and less dignified form of capital punishment in Western societies.

Public hangings have been major public spectacles throughout history.[36] "Hanging days" often created a carnival-like atmosphere that drew huge crowds. These executions were ritualistic events, involving processionals from the jail to the gallows, fiery orations that whipped up the frenzy of the crowd, and fairly elaborate protocol for the preparation of the condemned for hanging (e.g., the recording of their "last words," constraints on the body) and postexecution practices (e.g., the nature of bodily desecration, whether autopsies were performed).

> It has been said that some 72,000 people were hanged during the reign of Henry VIII (1509–47) and that vagabonds were strung up in rows of 300–400 at a time in the Elizabethan period (1558–1603) in English history.
>
> Source: Rusche and Kirchheimer (1939:19)

The public hanging was designed for both retributive and deterrence purposes. However, many countries abolished public executions in their early history due to the unpredictability of the public reaction (i.e., applause or condemnation). As a result of social class differences, many witnesses of public executions had more in common with the condemned than the ruling authority and violent riots would break out during the execution in response to perceived injustices. By weakening the potential general deterrent value of punishment and the legitimacy of the ruling authority, public executions became a liability. England abolished public executions in 1868.[37] With some exceptions in particular states, public executions in the United States have been largely discontinued since the end of the 1800s.[38]

Lynchings by extrajudicial bodies have been widely-used methods of informal social control in various societies. Thousands of blacks in the post-Civil War period in the United States were victims of these hangings by members of vigilante groups such as the Ku Klux Klan and other self-appointed regulators. During this same period, lynchings of suspected horse thieves, cattle rustlers, and other deviants were also commonly performed by quasi-government officials and citizens on the lawless western frontier. Various "death squads" in other countries have also used lynchings for "ethnic cleansing," distributing "street justice," and other purposes. Based on reports from human rights groups like Amnesty International, these types of extrajudicial executions still occur in all major continents and regions of the world.

SHOOTINGS AND FIRING SQUADS. Another type of instant death involves executions by shootings and firing squads. In China, these executions are conducted by the firing of a single bullet at point-blank range to the back of the head. Firing squads of different numbers of shooters are used in other countries. The condemned is shot from a distance and a target (e.g., a white patch over the heart) is often used for directing the executioners' aim. When practiced in the United States, some members of the firing squad receive "blanks" so that the specific person who fires the fatal shot is unknown.

Firing squads are common in military summary judgments throughout history. However, numerous citizens have been executed by this method in both legal and extrajudicial punishments. The wider availability of guns in contemporary society has led to the greater choice of shootings as a means of dispensing "street justice." Ironically, one of the reasons why Dr. Joseph Ignace Guillotine was commissioned by the French government to develop his machine for mass executions was to "preserve precious materials such as bullets which were wasted with a firing squad."[39]

Shooting as a method of execution received notoriety in the United States with the death of Gary Gilmore in Utah by firing squad in 1977. This was the first execution in the United States since a temporary moratorium was placed on the death penalty as a result of the *Furman v. Georgia* ruling of 1972. Gilmore was an exceptional case because he actually fought efforts to appeal his death sentence. Firing squads are now used in only three states — Idaho, Oklahoma, and Utah.

GAS CHAMBER. The use of lethal gas as a state-sponsored sanction achieved its greatest notoriety within the context of the mass extermination of Jews in the Holocaust of Nazi Germany. Several million citizens were killed by gas in concentration camps and by other methods during this period. Lethal gas attacks have been used as corporal punishment more recently in the ethnic genocide of the Kurds in Iraq.

As a form of punishment for criminal misconduct, lethal gas has been restricted to practices within the United States. The gas chamber was developed in this country in the mid-1920s, primarily as a response to adverse public reactions to the brutality of electrocutions and hangings. The first person to die in the gas chamber was a Chinese–American murderer named Gee Jon in 1924. Cyanide gas pellets are dropped into a pan of distilled water and sulfuric acid. Upon breathing these fumes, the person dies within minutes.

Over the past three decades, lethal gas has been used for executions in several U.S. states (Arizona, California, Maryland, Missouri, Wyoming). During the 1950s and early 1960s, about a third of all U.S. executions were conducted in gas chambers.[40]

ELECTROCUTION. Instant death for convicted criminals by electrocution has been used exclusively in the United States. It began in the late 1800s and was the dominant method of state-sponsored execution in this country for most of the twentieth century. Although recently replaced by lethal injection as the dominant method, electrocution remains a possible method of execution in twelve states.[41] During the execution, the accused is strapped to the chair (often wooden, but some are metal) and the executioner throws a switch that sends cycles of about 2,000 volts of electricity through the body.

Aside from its use in legal executions, electricity has been widely applied as both a method of treatment and torture. "Shock" therapy is a behavioral modification approach that seeks to change one's behavior through the pairing of a stimulus (e.g., cigarettes, alcohol, sexual lust) with an immediate painful response (i.e., electric shock). As nonlethal corporal punishment, electric nodes are attached to sensitive body parts (e.g., genitals) and volts of electricity are passed through the body. Torture through electric shock is most commonly used by military and quasi-military organizations, law enforcement personnel, and prison authorities for extracting confessions, maintaining discipline, and dispensing "justice."

LETHAL INJECTION. A relatively new means of instant death involves lethal injections. This type of capital punishment began in the United States in 1982 and has been used in only a few other countries (e.g., Guatemala, China). Over 90 percent of the legal executions in the United States are now conducted by lethal injection.[42] The process of lethal injection typically involves strapping down condemned persons on a stretcher or hospital gurney, moving them to the death chamber, and then giving them three lethal chemicals through an intravenous injection.

Compared to other lethal methods that disfigure and desecrate the body, lethal injection is often seen as a more humane and "therapeutic" punishment. It is often described by its advocates as similar to "falling asleep." Ironically, this approach is often viewed as too painless by those who believe that "doing justice" and general deterrence require more lingering and excruciating pain before death.

CRUCIFIXION. Used mainly in the Roman republic, crucifixion involved a slow death through the hanging of the accused on a cross. The person was first whipped to bring about a loss of blood and weakness, and then attached to a cross with leather cords or nails to the hands and feet. A crucified person sometimes survived for several days before finally dying of thirst, exposure, or blood poisoning from the nails. The crosses were placed on hills and along well-traveled roads to send a message to others.

BOILING TO DEATH. Boiling in oil or water was a multipurpose form of corporal punishment. It was used as an execution method, torture technique, and as a way to stun the person before hanging. Boiling was instituted as a legal punishment in England by King Henry VIII in the 1500s. Boiling to death in oil or water were specifically inflicted upon those passing false coin (i.e., counterfeiters and forgers) in France until the late 1700s. The pouring of boiling metal down the throat of persons during hanging is a variation on this basic method.

BREAKING ON THE WHEEL. An especially torturous and agonizing method of capital punishment in early historical periods involved the "wheel." The victim of this method was stretched on a wooden wheel and his or her overhanging limbs broken by the executioner with a metal rod or pole. After pulverizing the bones so they fit around the outside of the wheel, the executioner would often roll the victim around town. Death came from a blow to the rib cage with the metal rod.

The first reported case of being "broken at the wheel" was in fourth century Egypt. The original device was named "the Catherine Wheel" and involved strapping the accused to a wheel that was then lowered on another wheel with metal spikes, disemboweling the victim. Modifications of the device were popularized across Europe during the Middle Ages.

BURNING AT THE STAKE. Fire as a method of execution has been used throughout history. It was included in the "eye for eye" doctrine of the Hammurabi Code of 2000 B.C. as the punishment for anyone who destroyed a neighbor's possessions through arson. The Assyrians, the French and Spanish Inquisitors, and the Puritans of early New England colonies used burning as an instrument of terror and the punishment for various offenders including witches and heretics. The burning of the body had great symbolic value within some religious contexts. For example, burning carried a special horror for medieval Christians because it destroyed the body, scattered the ashes, and thereby made it impossible to have a proper burial. Even among the worst criminals of this era, it was believed that hopes of forgiveness for their sins and the prospects of eternity in paradise were unattainable without a proper Christian burial.[43]

DRAWING AND QUARTERING. The act of drawing and quartering is often viewed as one of the most brutal methods of execution. Offenders sentenced to this death were first hanged until near death, taken down from the gallows, their limbs tied to horses, and then pulled apart as the horses ran in different directions. Disembowelment (i.e., the ripping out of internal organs) and the removal of genitals often occurred while the accused was still alive prior to the drawing and quartering. The body parts were usually shown to the offender and then burned in a fire.

Sir William Wallace, the Scottish patriot, was executed by this method in 1305. His body parts were strewn over all corners of Great Britain as a warning to others of the consequences of dissension. Robert-Francois Damien was killed by drawing and quartering for his attempt to assassinate King Louis XV of France in 1757. The following sentence pronounced in the courthouse in which Damien was convicted graphically illustrates the brutality of this method in combination with other torture:

> the flesh will be torn from his breasts, arms, thighs, and calves with red-hot pinchers, his right hand, holding the knife with which he committed the said parricide, burnt with sulphur, and, on those places where the flesh will be torn away, poured with molten lead, boiling oil, burning resin, wax and sulphur melted together and then his body drawn and quartered by four horses and his limbs and body consumed by fire, reduced to ashes and his ashes thrown to the winds.[44]

Given the various desecrations inflicted on Damien's body prior to drawing and quartering, it is remarkable to note that newspaper accounts indicate that the physical strength of Damien prevented the horses from separating his limbs. The executioner was forced to hack off Damien's arms and legs. This quartering occurred while he was still alive. Possibly because of this gruesome public spectacle, Damien was the last person in France executed by the method of drawing and quartering.

STONING. The method of lapidation (i.e., stoning) involved the tossing of heavy rocks and stones at the victim until death. Stoning was recognized in the Mosaic code and is still used in a few countries (e.g., Afghanistan and Iran). "Pressing" is another type of stoning that involves placing large stones on the chests of victims until the weight crushes them. Historically, stoning was a common method of execution for women who committed adultery.

SUMMARY

Punishment for misconduct is ubiquitous over time and place. It is justified on the philosophical basis of retribution, incapacitation, deterrence, rehabilitation, and restoration. It takes various forms. These general forms of punishment include economic sanctions (e.g., monetary fines), incapacitative sanctions (e.g., imprisonment), and corporal sanctions (e.g., capital punishment).

Although sanctions are primary instruments of social control, they vary in their form, duration, and intensity over different contexts. The similarities and differences in sanctioning practices across world regions in contemporary society are described in the next chapter.

Notes

1. For example, public surveys in the United States on the seriousness of particular offenses reveal enormous variation across individuals and social groups in their ratings of the perceived seriousness of many white-collar offenses (e.g., employee theft, stock fraud), ordinary property offenses (e.g., breaking/entering, shoplifting), and victimless crimes (e.g., prostitution, gambling, drug use). See, for studies of public ratings of the seriousness of crime, Peter Rossi, Emily Waite, Christine Bose, and Richard Berk. 1974. "The Seriousness of Crime: Normative Structure and Individual Differences." *American Sociological Review* 39: 224–37; Terance D. Miethe. 1984. "Types of Consensus in Public Evaluations of Crime: An Illustration of Strategies for Measuring 'Consensus.'" *Journal of Criminal Law and Criminology* 75(2): 459–73; Francis Cullen, Bruce Link, and Craig

Polanzi. 1982. "The Seriousness of Crime Revisited: Have Attitudes toward White-Collar Crime Changed?" *Criminology* 20: 83–102.

2. Pieter Spierenburg. 1995. "The Body and the State: Early Modern Europe." In Norval Morris and David J. Rothman (eds.), *The Oxford History of the Prison*. New York: Oxford University Press. Pages 49–77.

3. See Joan Petersilia, Peter W. Greenwood, and Marvin Lavin. 1978. *Criminal Careers of Habitual Felons*. Santa Monica, CA: Rand Corp. Page 5; Peter Greenwood. 1982. *Selective Incapacitation*. Santa Monica, CA: Rand Corp.; Stephen D. Gottfredson and Don M. Gottfredson. 1992. *Incapacitation Strategies and the Criminal Career*. Sacramento, CA: Information Center, California Division of Law Enforcement.

4. It is important to note that conformity after the imposition of punishment may be due to deterrence or a wide variety of other factors (e.g., decreased opportunity to commit offenses, maturation, the development of alternative interests). Accordingly, a reduction in criminal behavior after the threat or application of punishment should be treated as a necessary but not a sufficient condition for the demonstration of a deterrent effect. For a comprehensive treatment of deterrence and the difficulties with testing this idea, see Jack Gibbs. 1975. *Crime, Punishment, and Deterrence*. New York: Elsevier.

5. See William J. Chambliss. 1967. "Types of Deviance and the Effectiveness of Legal Sanctions." *Wisconsin Law Review* Summer: 703–19. For a review of the more recent literature on deterrence, see Daniel S. Nagin. 1998. "Criminal Deterrence Research at the Outset of the Twenty-First Century." In Michael Tonry (ed.), *Crime and Justice: A Review of Research* Volume 23, pages 1–42; Raymond Paternoster. 1987. "The Deterrent Effect of the Perceived Certainty and Severity of Punishment: A Review of the Evidence and Issues." *Justice Quarterly* 4(2): 173–217.

6. Developing countries, in contrast, often have less emphasis on procedural justice considerations, allowing for a swifter, more certain, and more punitive response to particular types of civil unrest or disorder. For example, in a series of "strike-hard" campaigns to crack down on crime, the Chinese courts were granted authority to forgo many legal requirements by quickly processing criminal cases and executing the sentence.

7. In fact, the available empirical evidence strongly supports the contention that all three elements are important for deterrence, but that the certainty of punishment is even more important than severity in leading to law-abiding behavior. See Jack P. Gibbs. 1975. *Crime, Punishment, and Deterrence*. New York: Elsevier; Raymond Paternoster. 1987. "The Deterrent Effect of the Perceived Certainty and Severity of Punishment: A Review of the Evidence and Issues." *Justice Quarterly* 4(2): 173–217; Daniel S. Nagin. 1998. "Criminal Deterrence Research at the Outset of the Twenty-First Century." In Michael Tonry (ed.), *Crime and Justice: A Review of Research* Volume 23, pages 1–42.

8. See Todd R. Clear and George F. Cole. 2000. *American Corrections*. 5th ed. Belmont, CA: West/Wadsworth. Page 513.

9. The "He Ara Hou" program in New Zealand is a recent penal initiative designed specifically to rehabilitate members of its Maori minority who are in the prison population. To help rehabilitate these offenders, the "He Ara Hou" program emphasizes case management, individualized help, and academic skills. Prison activities are flexibly scheduled, and officers are given wide discretion to help encourage offenders to achieve their goals. See Greg Newbold and Chris W. Eskridge. 1996. "History and Development of Modern

Correctional Practices in New Zealand." In Charles B. Fields and Richter H. Moore, Jr. (eds.), *Comparative Criminal Justice – Traditional and Nontraditional Systems of Law and Control*. Prospect Heights, IL: Waveland. Pages 453–78.

10. See Robert Martinson. 1974. "What Works? Questions and Answers About Prison Reform." *The Public Interest* 35 (Spring): 22. Martinson acknowledged the limitations of making generalizations from his work (given that only a few programs were actually evaluated and their research designs were flawed) and that other programs worked, but it was not clear why they worked. However, as pointed out by a reviewer of our book, the continual restatement of the overgeneralization from Martinson's original report has reified it.

Aside from the Martinson report, there were also political and ideological factors associated with the decline in rehabilitation. These factors are represented by the "get tough on crime" mentality that led to such policies as mandatory sentencing and "three strikes and you're out" legistation.

11. This does not necessarily imply that rehabilitation is ineffective. In fact, some rehabilitation programs have recently shown positive results. For example, there was a threefold increase in the number of inmates completing educational coursework in the inaugural year of "He Ara Hou" program in New Zealand in 1990. Significantly more inmates are enrolling in education programs, and there has been a huge reduction in misconduct, suicides, and assaults among inmates in this program. See Greg Newbold and Chris Eskridge. 1996. "History and Development of Modern Correctional Practices in New Zealand." In Charles B. Fields and Richter H. Moore, Jr. (eds.), *Comparative Criminal Justice – Traditional and Nontraditional Systems of Law and Control*. Prospect Heights, IL: Waveland. Page 472. For a general discussion of "what works" in corrections, see D. A. Andrews, I. Zinger, J. Bonta, R. D. Hoge, P. Gendreau, and F. T. Cullen. 1990. "Does Correctional Treatment Work? A Psychologically Informed Meta-Analysis." *Criminology* 28: 369–404; R. Izzo and R. R. Ross. 1990. "Meta-Analysis of Rehabilitation Programs for Juveniles: A Brief Report." *Criminal Justice and Behavior* 17: 134–42.

12. See Evelyn Zellere and Joanna B. Cannon. 2000. "Restorative Justice, Reparation, and the Southside Project." In David R. Karp and Todd R. Clear, *What is Community Justice*. Thousand Oaks, CA: Sage. Pages 89–107.

13. Frank Schmalleger and John Ortiz Smyka. 2001. *Corrections in the 21st Century*. New York: Glencoe McGraw Hill. Page 486.

14. John Braithwaite. 1989. *Crime, Shame, and Reintegration*. Cambridge, UK: Cambridge University Press.

15. Philip L. Reichel. 1999. *Comparative Criminal Justice Systems*. 2nd ed. Upper Saddle River, NJ: Prentice-Hall.

16. Graeme Newman. 1978. *The Punishment Response*. Philadelphia: J. P. Lippincott. Page 7.

17. For example, Jeremy Bentham in the late 1700s identified eleven different types of punishment. These included capital punishment, afflictive punishments (e.g., whipping, starvation), indelible punishments (e.g., branding, amputation, mutilation), ignominious punishments (e.g., stocks, pillories, and other public sanctions), penitential punishments (e.g., censured by one's community), chronic punishments (e.g., banishment, exile, imprisonment), restrictive punishments (e.g., license revocation, administrative sanctions), compulsive punishments (e.g., restitution, requiring periodic meetings with

court officials), pecuniary punishments (e.g., fines), quasi-pecuniary punishments (e.g., denial of service), and characteristic punishments (e.g., mandating the wearing of prison uniforms by incarcerated offenders). Jeremy Bentham. 1789. *An Introduction to the Principles of Morals and Legislation.* London: T. Payne.

18. It is recognized that these three types of sanctions are not exhaustive of all possible types of sanctions (e.g., community service and "symbolic" sanctions that ridicule or humiliate the offender are not included) and that the categories are not mutually exclusive (e.g., injunctions are economic sanctions that may be physically incapacitating; amputation is corporal punishment that is incapacitative both physically and economically). However, within our classification scheme, we have attempted to classify and describe sanctions that cover multiple dimensions of punishment based on their primary consequences (i.e., is it financial, restrictive of movement, or corporal punishment of the body). The idea of "symbolic" sanctions can be discussed within the context of any of these three major forms of punishment because they all have symbolic value to the state and the individual.

19. It is also possible to argue that monetary sanctions also serve an incapacitative function when the sanctions are so severe that they place extraordinary physical restrictions on the offender's subsequent behavior. The proverbial "fall from grace" of corporate executives who become bankrupt from financial injunctions and penalties for misconduct would be an example of the possible incapacitative effects of monetary sanctions.

20. White-collar crimes are typically defined as crimes committed by people of high respectability or high social status in the course of their occupations. The term "corporate crime" is used to describe criminal misconduct that is done for the benefit of the corporation, whereas the term "occupational" crime is used to describe white-collar crimes that are committed for personal goals of the individual offender. For a discussion of the deterrent effect on economic sanctions on corporate crime, see Charles A. Moore. 1987. "Taming the Giant Corporation: Some Cautionary Remarks on the Deterrability of Corporate Crime." *Crime and Delinquency* 33: 379–402.

21. Erika Fairchild and Harry R. Dammer. 2001. *Comparative Criminal Justice Systems.* 2nd ed. Belmont, CA: Wadsworth/Thomson Learning. Page 224.

22. See Anthony J. Sebok. 2001. "How Germany views U.S. Tort Law: Duties, Damages, Dumb Luck and the Differences in the Two Countries' Systems." tsebok@findlaw.com. Monday, July 23, 2001.

23. See Pieter Spierenburg. 1995. "The Body and the State: Early Modern Europe." In Norval Morris and David J. Rothman (eds.), *The Oxford History of the Prison.* New York: Oxford University Press. Page 53.

24. For a description of these classes of people in England, see Lionel Rose. 1988. *Rogues and Vagabonds: Vagrant Underworld in Britain 1815–1985.* London: Routledge Press.

25. Abbott Emerson Smith. 1947. *Colonists in Bondage.* Chapel Hill: University of North Carolina Press.

26. Clive Emsley. 1987. *Crime and Society in England, 1750–1900.* London: Longman. Page 223.

27. John Braithwaite. 1989. *Crime, Shame, and Reintegration.* Cambridge, UK: Cambridge University Press.

28. Genocide is often defined as "a form of one-side mass killing in which a state or other authority intends to destroy a group, as that group and membership in it are defined by the perpetrator." See Frank Chalk and Kurt Jonassohn. 1990. *A History and Sociology of Genocide.* New Haven, CT: Yale University Press. Democide is the killing of members of the general population by the state that do not target a particular ethnic, racial, or religious group. See Gerald Scully. 1997. *Murder by the State.* Washington, D.C.: National Center for Policy Analysis.

29. Vagrancy was considered a revenue problem for most British monarchs because their expenditures for war, personal protection, and pleasure were subsidized primarily from taxes and labor of ordinary people. The threat of public whipping under this law was designed to help Henry VIII generate revenue and preserve his power.

30. Frank Schmalleger and John Ortiz Smyka. 2001. *Corrections in the 21st Century.* New York: Glencoe McGraw Hill. Page 68.

31. See Graeme Newman. 1978. *The Punishment Response.* Philadelphia: J. P. Lippincott. Page 119.

32. See Pieter Spierenburg. 1995. "The Body and the State: Early Modern Europe." In Norval Morris and David J. Rothman (eds.), *The Oxford History of the Prison.* New York: Oxford University Press. Pages 52–3.

33. Amnesty International reports that an estimated 135 million of the world's girls and women have undergone genital mutilation, and 2 million girls a year are at risk of mutilation — approximately 6,000 per day. It is practiced extensively in twenty eight countries in Africa and is common in some countries in the Middle East (e.g., Egypt, Oman, Yemen, the United Arab Emirates). Female genital mutilation also occurs, mainly among immigrant communities, in parts of Asia and the Pacific, North and Latin America, and Europe. Amnesty International. 1997. *Female Genital Mutilation: A Human Rights Information Pack* [AI Index: ACT 77/05/97].

34. Pieter Spierenburg. 1995. "The Body and the State: Early Modern Europe." In Norval Morris and David J. Rothman (eds.), *The Oxford History of the Prison.* New York: Oxford University Press. Page 53.

35. For a good source of information on the different methods of capital punishment, see Mark Grossman. 1998. *Encyclopedia of Capital Punishment.* Santa Barbara, CA: ABC-CLIO Publishers. Our general descriptions of particular methods of capital punishment are derived from this book and other sources.

36. The same arguments apply to beheadings and other types of executions that have taken place in public settings. Crowds in the thousands witnessed the beheading of dissidents and citizens via the guillotine in the French Revolution. Similar size crowds are common in public executions in contemporary China.

37. Graeme Newman. 1978. *The Punishment Response.* Philadelphia: J. P. Lippincott. Page 144.

38. See Raymond Paternoster. 1991. *Capital Punishment in America.* New York: Lexington Books. Page 7.

39. Mark Grossman. 1998. *Encyclopedia of Capital Punishment.* Santa Barbara, CA: ABC-CLIO Publishers. Page 106.

40. See M. Watt Espy and John Ortiz Smykla. 1991. *Executions in the United States, 1608–1991: The Espy File.* [Data File]. Inter-University Consortium for Social and Political Research. Ann Arbor: University of Michigan.

41. See Bureau of Justice Statistics. 2002. *Capital Punishment 2001*. Washington, D.C. December 2002. NCJ 197020.

42. Ibid.

43. Michael Kronenwetter. 2001. *Capital Punishment: A Reference Handbook*. 2nd ed. Santa Barbara, CA: ABC-CLIO.

44. Michel Foucault. 1977. *Discipline and Punish*. New York: Pantheon. Page 4.

Suggested Readings

Frank Chalk and Kurt Jonassohn. 1990. *A History and Sociology of Genocide*. New Haven, CT: Yale University Press.

Michel Foucault. 1977. *Discipline and Punish*. New York: Pantheon.

David Garland. 1990. *Punishment and Modern Society: A Study in Social Theory*. Chicago: University of Chicago Press.

Jack P. Gibbs. 1975. *Crime, Punishment, and Deterrence*. New York: Elsevier.

Norval Morris and David J. Rothman. 1995. *The Oxford History of the Prison*. New York: Oxford University Press.

Graeme Newman. 1978. *The Punishment Response*. Philadelphia: J. P. Lippincott.

Geoff Simons. 1999. *Imposing Economic Sanctions: Legal Remedy or Genocidal Tool?* London: Pluto Press.

CHAPTER THREE

Contemporary Punishments in Comparative Perspective

All societies in the modern world use punishment for various purposes of social control. Through the threat and application of economic, incapacitative and corporal sanctions, both industrial and developing societies have been able to maintain social order, regulate interpersonal and international relations, and minimize threats to the existing authority. From a comparative perspective, the interesting question is the generalizability of these practices over countries and geographical regions. In other words, are punishment responses uniform across context, and, if not, what is the nature of these context-specific differences?

Using available data from various sources, the current chapter explores the relative prevalence of different types of sanctions across world regions. We compare different continents and geographical regions in their current use of different types of economic, incapacitative, and corporal sanctions. However, aside from comparisons based on geographical location, differences across levels of economic development are also examined in this chapter. More detailed comparative and historical analyses of particular countries (e.g., United States, China, Saudi Arabia) are addressed in subsequent chapters.

BASIC PROBLEMS IN COMPARATIVE STUDIES

As is true of all comparative studies, there are three fundamental problems in the systematic examination of punishment across different countries and world regions. These basic problems involve the unit of analysis, definitional issues, and data limitations.

An initial concern in comparative studies involves the selection of units of analysis. Within the current study of punishments, the issue focuses on variation within our comparative units. For example, does the comparison of punishments across world regions (e.g., Europe vs. Asia) mask serious variation within these regions? Similar problems face comparative analyses on the basis of groupings of countries by economic development (e.g., developed vs. developing countries). This basic problem exists even in simple comparisons between countries because of differences in local jurisdictions, provinces, or states therein. Unfortunately, there is no easy solution to this problem because there is variation within comparative units no matter how restrictive the units of analysis (e.g., judges within the same court may differ in their sanctioning practices).

The compromise reached here and elsewhere about within-group variation involves common sense and an appropriate balance between the specificity and generality. For example, it makes little sense to classify North America as a world region that does or does not have capital punishment because one country in this region allows for legal executions (i.e., United States) and the other countries in the region do not (i.e., Canada, Mexico). However, it is reasonable to consider in comparative analysis the United States as pro-capital punishment because it is permitted under federal law and most state codes within this country. For purposes of generality, this classification would be justified even though some specific states in this country prohibit the death penalty. We will employ a similar logic throughout our comparative analyses in a concerted effort to make general statements about punishment over time and place without grossly distorting and minimizing differences within context.

The definitional issue involves how we classify and count different types of punishments in different countries. Take, for instance, structures of penal confinement (e.g., jails, prisons, workhouses, labor camps, etc.). Lacking a clear and uniform definition of this concept, different countries may classify these practices differently. Are temporary "holding tanks" uniformly counted one way or another? How about being "grounded" to your room – is this uniformly dismissed as a type of penal confinement? The same definitional problems apply to types of economic sanctions (e.g., Is the giving up of personal property such as chickens or a horse counted the same as monetary fines?).

Even in serious corporal punishment like executions, there is enormous definitional ambiguity about what "counts." For example, how are extra-judicial executions counted (e.g., summary executions of ordinary citizens or perceived dissidents by paramilitary forces or vigilante groups)? What about "purges" and "disappearances" sponsored by the prevailing legitimate authorities, and deaths in custody due to deplorable conditions of confinement? Also, how about nonlethal corporal punishments (e.g., amputations, whippings, and beatings) that inadvertently result in death? Depending on how these practices are defined, the classification of particular countries as "abolitionist" or "retentionist" of capital punishment is extremely dubious.

The solution to this definitional problem is greater clarity and specificity in terms of what behaviors fall within these general categories. Unfortunately, even with more refined definitions, there will always be some subjective differences in the interpretations that underlie these classification and counting practices.[1] Such problems are compounded in comparative analysis because of differences in culture and language. Despite these limitations, however, a comparative approach still has the best potential for understanding general similarities and differences across context.

Another basic problem with comparative studies involves the availability of data. Countries vary dramatically in the quantity and quality of data on types of sanctions. Some countries have archives and repositories that collect, disseminate, and store national data. Other countries collect little or no systematic information on national practices or collect this information but do not disseminate it. The quality and representativeness of the data are also uneven across countries. Monthly and annual data can be gleaned from archival records and government reports in some countries but not in others. Furthermore, some types of sanctions (e.g., numbers of executions, counts of inmates in prison) are more readily available and routinely disseminated than other sanctions (e.g., number/amount of monetary fines).

This problem with missing data, however, is inherent in any type of social research. The usual solution to this problem is (1) to focus on those units with the most comprehensive data and that contain multiple measures of the key analytic variables (so that reliability and consistency of findings can be compared across measures) and (2) to provide some assessment of the potential bias in findings that results from focusing solely on the units with more complete information. We employ a similar strategy in our comparative analyses of punishments.

It is important to emphasize that these three basic problems of the unit of analysis, definitions, and data availability are endemic to all comparative and noncomparative research. There are both practical and structural obstacles to the resolution of these problems, but their effects on our substantive conclusions can be minimized somewhat by common sense, logical reasoning, and the exercise of appropriate caution when making inferences about general practices. With these caveats in mind, we now turn our attention to the comparative analysis of the current use of economic, incapacitative, and corporal sanctions across geographical regions.

ECONOMIC SANCTIONS

As described in chapter 2, economic sanctions are financial penalties that are imposed for wrongdoing. Common economic sanctions include monetary fines, financial damages imposed in civil suits, asset forfeitures and foreclosures, injunctions and other restraints on economic activities (e.g., embargoes, boycotts, production strikes), and revocation of licenses. Economic sanctions are used across the world for purposes of retribution, deterrence, and restoration.

Comparative data on different types of economic sanctions are limited in many countries. Of the different types of economic sanctions, the most comprehensive data exist on national and international embargoes (e.g., U.S. and UN sanctions against Iraq, oil embargoes, restrictions on financial aid and productions between countries [North vs. South Korea]). For economic sanctions against individual offenders (rather than corporations or countries), the most complete information is available on monetary fines. Unfortunately, comprehensive national data on fines are available in only a few industrial countries. Accordingly, our observations about the prevalence of economic sanctions on individual offenders are somewhat speculative.

Our preliminary analysis of regional differences, however, indicates enormous variation within each world region. This variation is of sufficient magnitude to make between-region comparisons almost meaningless. Instead,

TABLE 3.1: Recent embargoes and boycotts (examples)		
Boycott nation/group	**Targeted nation/product**	**Type of boycott/embargo**
Great Britain and EEC (1982)	Argentina for invading Falkland Islands	Trade/financial embargo
United Nations (1990–2003)	Iraq for invading Kuwait	Trade/financial restrictions
USSR (1990)	Lithuania's unilateral declaration of independence	Trade embargo
U.S. (2001–2)	Afghanistan under Taliban rule	Trade embargo on defense aid
U.S. (1993)	Burma's military regime	Trade embargo on defense aid
U.S. (1960–2003)	Cuba's political alliances	Trade/financial embargo

National and international boycotts have been initiated by consumer groups for various alleged reasons to restrict the profits and practices of the following organizations/companies: Nestle's (for dumping infant formula on developing countries), Microsoft (for monopoly control efforts), Nike (for exploitive labor practices), ExonMobil (for endangering the environment), Petco (for animal cruelty), Taco Bell (for unfair labor practices), *LA Times* Newspaper (for its anti-Israel tone), University of California-Berkeley (for being unpatriotic to U.S. policies).

country variation in economic sanctions is better represented by level of economic development in countries rather than their regional location per se. Countries with high economic development, by definition, have the financial means of using a variety of economic sanctions to control behavior. Given their relative economic position, it should not be surprising to find that such economic sanctions as injunctions, embargoes, boycotts, restraint of trade agreements, and damages from civil litigation are most commonly used within economically advanced societies. In fact, when these types of economic sanctions are employed in less-developed countries, it is almost always a more economically advanced country imposing the sanction upon them to gain compliance (see Table 3.1).

Anthropological and cross-cultural studies of developing countries reveal that economic sanctions are used for punishment and restitution in cases of minor crimes. Thefts and interpersonal disputes may be compensated through exchanges of goods or services for greater value than the original offense. However, economic sanctions have also been used within the context of reparation and compensation for more serious crimes. Under Islamic law, for example, murderers may be spared a death sentence if the victim's family agrees to the payment of financial compensation.

Economic sanctions also appear to be increasingly used to punish corporate offenders in developing countries. For example, India has an estimated 60 million to 115 million child laborers, the largest number of working children in the world. To address this problem, the Indian government passed the Bonded Labor System Abolishing Act in 1976 making employers that hire child labor subject to a jail sentence (three months to one year) and/or fines (from 10,000 to 20,000 rupees).[2] Similarly, media outlets in some countries (e.g., Saudi Arabia, Egypt) that violate the ban on free speech law and are viewed as "radical opposition groups" are frequently given monetary fines for their actions either in isolation or in conjunction with other penalties.[3] Foreign broadcasting services may be fined up to $55,000 for engaging in domestic politics in Singapore.[4]

Data on monetary fines in developed countries are sketchy but provide some idea of their frequency of use. For example, about 60 percent of convicted traffic offenses and about one-third of nontraffic offenses in New Zealand resulted in monetary penalty.[5] In contrast, monetary fines for traffic violations are nearly universal sanctions in the United States, either as the sole punishment or in use with other sanctions (e.g., suspension or revocation of the driving license). Day fines are commonly used in criminal cases in various developed countries (e.g., Germany, Sweden, Finland, France), but have diminished in other countries (e.g., England, Austria, Hungary) because of numerous problems in their application.[6]

Although these data suggest variation in the use of monetary fines in developed countries, it is probably true that economic penalties for minor offenses are pervasive across both developing and developed countries. However, collective forms of economic sanctions (e.g., injunctions, embargoes, restraint of trade agreements) are more commonly practiced by the more economically developed countries of the modern world.

INCAPACITATIVE SANCTIONS

Sanctions that confine individuals or limit their physical opportunities for various types of deviance and dissent are found in current practices in all regions

TABLE 3.2: Incarceration rates for select countries			
North America:		**Eastern Europe:**	
United States (1999)	680	Russian Federation (1999)	730
Canada (1998–9)	110	Czech Republic (1999)	225
Central America:		Turkey (1998)	100
Belize (1999)	460	**Central Asia:**	
Mexico (1999)	145	Kazakhstan (1997)	495
Guatemala (1999)	70	Kyrgyzstan (1997)	440
Caribbean:		Turkmenistan (1999)	135
Dominica (1999)	420	**South Central Asia:**	
Trinidad & Tobago (1999)	350	Thailand (1999)	325
Jamaica (1999)	170	Malaysia (1999)	125
South America:		India (1998)	40
Suriname (1999)	435	**Eastern Asia:**	
Chile (1999)	205	Mongolia (1999)	245
Brazil (1999)	115	China (1999)	110
Northern Europe:		Japan (1999)	40
Lithuania (1999)	385	**Western Asia:**	
England & Wales (1999)	125	United Arab Emirates (1998)	250
Sweden (1999)	60	Israel (1999)	150
Iceland (1998)	35	Yemen (1998)	85
Southern Europe:		**North and Central Africa:**	
Portugal (1999)	130	Tunisia (1996)	250
Italy (1999)	90	Sudan (1997)	115
Greece (1999)	70	Chad (1996)	40
Western Europe:		**West Africa:**	
Germany (1999)	95	Cape Verde (1999)	185
France (1999)	90	Cote d'Ivoire (1998)	95
Monaco (1998)	40	Mali (1998)	30
Oceania:		**Eastern and Southern Africa:**	
Fiji (1999)	145	Botswana (1999)	400
Australia (1999)	110	Kenya (1996)	140
Vanuatu (1999)	25	Malawi (1999)	70

Source: Roy Walmsley (2000)

of the world. The most comprehensive data on incapacitative sanctions involve incarceration and state-ordered probation or supervision of convicted offenders. Incapacitation rates based on these measures reveal wide variation both between and within geographical region (see Table 3.2).

When the median incarceration rates are computed for all countries with data within each region, the highest incarceration rates are seen within Caribbean countries (median = 300), followed by countries in Southern Africa (median = 260) and Central Asian countries of the former Soviet Union (median = 260).[7] In contrast, countries in South Central Asia had the lowest incarceration rates (median = 45).

An examination of regional differences in incarceration rates masks variation within countries. Accordingly, the five countries with the highest incarceration rates per 100,00 population include the following: the Russian Federation (730), the United States (680), the Cayman Islands (665), Belarus (575), and Kazakhstan (495). The lowest incarceration rates per 100,000 population are found in Vanuatu (25), Andorra (30), Nepal (30), Mali (30), and the Solomon Islands (30). Countries within each region can be found to be located above and below the median incarceration rate of 125 per 100,000 across all countries. This latter finding further highlights the importance of country-specific analyses rather than regional comparisons.

Data from the United Nations survey indicate that countries also vary widely in their use of probation. For example, the highest probation rates per 100,000 population in 1994 were in North American countries. The rate of probation was 536 per 100,000 in the United States and 269 per 100,000 in Canada. Only England and Wales had a probation rate that approached this level (217 per 100,000). The countries with the lowest rates of probation in the UN survey were spread across geographical regions. For example, Indonesia had a probation rate of less than one person per 100,000, and the following countries had rates of less than twenty per 100,000: Qatar (1.9), Nicaragua (4.2), Chile (8.8), Lithuania (9.6), Republic of Moldova (10.0), Bulgaria (10.1), Malta (13.7), and the Marshall Islands (14.8).[8]

> Two types of probation exist in the current world criminal justice systems: suspended sentences with and without formal supervision. The United States best represents probation with community supervision by criminal justice officials. Japan is an example of probation systems in which supervision is performed informally by members of the community.

When compared to patterns for incarceration rates, these data on probation rates show that both types of incapacitative sanctions are related in practice. Countries like the United States have relatively high rates of both incarceration and probation, whereas countries like the Marshall Islands have relatively low rates for each type of incapacitation. However, there are clear exceptions to this positive relationship between incarceration and probation. For example, Belarus has a high incarceration rate but a relatively low rate of probation.

CORPORAL PUNISHMENT

Corporal punishment involves the infliction of pain on the offender's body. Worldwide human rights organizations (e.g., Amnesty International, Human Rights Watch) and other international organizations (e.g., United Nations) provide periodic reports on the nature and magnitude of different types of corporal punishment. These special reports often include summary descriptions of cases of capital punishment, extrajudicial killings, torture, deaths in custody, the treatment of political dissidents, and "disappearances" of civilians.

The most comprehensive comparative data on corporal sanctions involve capital punishment. Sufficient information is available to classify nearly 200 countries according to whether they have currently retained or abolished capital punishment for ordinary crimes (e.g., murder, rapes). Reports of extrajudicial killings by paramilitary forces and vigilante groups are also relatively comprehensive when compared to other types of corporal punishment.

To examine more fully the nature of current worldwide trends in capital punishment, comparisons of "retentionist" and "abolitionist" countries are made on the basis of several factors. These include differences by world region and level of economic development. These comparisons of legal and extrajudicial executions are then followed by a comparative analysis of corporal punishments in terms of the relationship between state-sponsored violence and the control of civil unrest. The results of these international comparisons are described below.

GEOGRAPHICAL DIFFERENCES IN CAPITAL PUNISHMENT

The social and legal acceptance of the death penalty has changed dramatically across countries in the past century. Patterns of both retention and abolition of capital punishment are found within and across continents and regions, but the most common worldwide trend in the last half century has been toward the abolition of capital punishment in both law and in practice.

According to the most recent report by Amnesty International (as of January 2003), a total of seventy-six countries have abolished capital punishment for all crimes; fifteen other countries have abolished it for

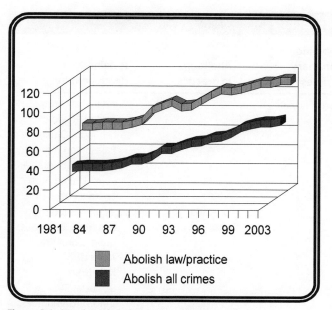

Figure 3.1. Number of abolitionist countries over time
Source: Amnesty International 2001, 2003

ordinary crimes only (but retain it for crimes under military law or for crimes committed under exceptional circumstances); another twenty countries are abolitionist in practice (because they have not executed anyone in the past ten years); and the remaining eighty-four countries in the world have retained the use of the death penalty.[9]

When the three types of abolition are combined, the majority of countries in the world in the twenty-first century have now eliminated the death penalty for ordinary crimes by law or practice. This pattern is in sharp contrast to the mid-1960s, when less than twenty-five countries were identified as having abolished capital punishment for these crimes.[10] As shown in Figure 3.1, the number of countries that have abolished capital punishment has grown considerably in the past three decades.

An examination of current practices indicates the greater prevalence of legal executions in some world regions than others. The nature of geographical differences in the legal status of capital punishment, arranged according to the predominance of retentionist countries within each geographical region, is summarized in Table 3.3 and described below.

TABLE 3.3: Death penalty across world regions*

Region	Abolition for all crimes	Abolition – ordinary crimes	Abolition in practice	Retained death penalty
MIDDLE EAST		Israel [1954]		Bahrain, Iran, Iraq, Jordan, Kuwait, Lebanon, Oman, Palestinian Authority, Qatar, Saudi Arabia, Syria, United Arab Emirates, Yemen
CARIBBEAN	Dominican Rep. [1966] Haiti [1987]		Grenada	Antiqua-Barbuda, Bahamas, Barbados, Cuba, Dominica, Jamaica, St. Kitts-Nevis, St. Lucia, St. Vincent-Grenadines, Trinidad-Tobago
ASIA				
Central	Turkmenistan [1999]			Kazakstan, Kyrgyzstan, Mongolia, Uzbekistan, Tajikistan
East	Nepal [1997]			China, Japan, Korea (North), Korea (South), Taiwan
Southern	Cambodia [1989] East Timor [1999]		Bhutan, Maldives, Sri Lanka	Afghanistan, Bangladesh, India, Myanmar, Pakistan
Southeast	Azerbaijan [1998] Georgia [1997]		Papua, New Guinea, Brunei-Daussalam	Indonesia, Laos, Malaysia, Philippines, Singapore, Thailand, Vietnam
Southwest		Turkey [na]		Armenia
AFRICA				
Central			Cent. Africa Repub.	Burundi, Chad, Congo (Dem. Repub.), Rwanda
East	Djibouti [1995] Seychelles [1993]			Eritrea, Ethiopia, Kenya, Somalia, Tanzania, Uganda

Region	Abolition for all crimes	Abolition – ordinary crimes	Abolition in practice	Retained death penalty
Northern				Algeria, Egypt, Libya, Mauritania, Morocco, Sudan, Tunisia
Southern	Angola [1992] Mauritius [1995] Mozambique [1990] Namibia [1990] South Africa [1997]		Madagascar	Botswana, Lesotho, Malawi, Swaziland, Zambia, Zimbabwe
Western	Cape Verde [1981] Cote D'Ivoire [2000] Guinea-Bissau [1993] Sao Tome-Princ. [1990]		Burkina Faso, Congo (Repub.) Gambia, Mali, Niger, Senegal, Togo	Benin, Cameroon, Comoros, Equatorial Guinea, Gabon, Ghana, Guinea, Liberia, Nigeria, Sierra Leone
NORTH AMERICA	Canada [1998]	Mexico [na]		United States
CENTRAL AMERICA	Costa Rica [1877] Honduras [1956] Nicaragua [1979] Panama [na]	El Salvador [1983]		Belize, Guatemala
SOUTH AMERICA	Colombia [1910] Ecuador [1906] Paraguay [1992] Uruguay [1907] Venezuela [1863]	Argentina [1984] Bolivia [1997] Brazil [1979] Chile [2001] Peru [1979]	Suriname	Guyana
EUROPE Central	Austria [1968] Czech Republic [1990] Germany [1987] Hungary [1990] Poland [1997] Slovak Republic [1990] Liechtenstein [1987] Switzerland [1992]			
Eastern	Estonia [1998] Lithuania [1998] Moldova [1995] Ukraine [1999]	Latvia [1999]	Russian Federation	Belarus

(*continued*)

TABLE 3.3 (continued)

Region	Abolition for all crimes	Abolition – ordinary crimes	Abolition in practice	Retained death penalty
Northern	Denmark [1978] Finland [1972] Iceland [1928] Norway [1979] Sweden [1972]			
Southern	Italy [1994] Malta [2000] San Marino [1865] Vatican City [1969]	Greece [1993]		
Southeast-ern	Bulgaria [1998] Croatia [1990] Cyprus [2002] Macedonia [1991] Romania [1989] Slovenia [1989] Yugoslavia (FR) [2002]	Albania [2000] Bosnia-Herz. [1997]		
Southwest-ern	Andorra [1990] Portugal [1976] Spain [1995]			
Western	Belgium [1996] France [1981] Repub. of Ireland [1990] Luxembourg [1979] Monaco [1962] Netherlands [1982] United Kingdom [1998]			
OCEANIA	Australia [1985] Kiribati [ne] Marshall Islands [ne] Micronesia (Fed.St.) [ne] New Zealand [1989] Palau [na] Solomon Islands [ne] Tuvalu [ne] Vanuatu [ne]	Cook Islands [na] Fiji [1979]	Nauru, Samoa, Tonga	

*Country classification based on CIA World Factbook (2002).

[ne] = no executions since independence. [na] = not available or unknown date.

Source: Amnesty international Reports (ACT 50/0400, April 2000; Jan 2003)

The Middle East

The highest concentration of countries that have retained the death penalty in the twenty-first century is in the Middle East. None of these countries have abolished capital punishment completely. Israel restricts the death penalty to "exceptional crimes" such as crimes committed under military law or crimes committed in wartime.[11] The other countries in the Middle East have retained and used capital punishment for ordinary crimes during this century. Capital punishment has long been practiced in this region of one of the earliest-known civilizations.

According to information compiled in annual reports by Amnesty International,[12] death sentences have been given in the twenty-first century in the vast majority of Middle Eastern countries (12/14) and executions have been carried out in most of these countries.[13] Iran, Saudi Arabia, and Iraq have the largest number of known executions, averaging around 100 death sentences per year in each country. Given the secrecy surrounding many criminal trials and summary judgments by state officials, the actual number of death sentences imposed in these countries is believed to be far higher than reported.

Capital offenses in this region continue to encompass a wide range of crimes. During the past decade, people have been executed for violent crimes, sex offenses, drug-related crimes, apostasy (i.e., the rejection of Islam by one who professes Islamic faith), "collaboration with the enemy," and various other antigovernment activities. Iraqi authorities in 2001 decreed as capital offenses the acts of homosexuality, incest, rape, prostitution, and providing accommodations for prostitution.[14] Saudi Arabia has executed people for a variety of offenses, including the practice of witchcraft, magic, charlatanism, and sorcery.[15]

An assortment of lethal methods are used in the Middle East for executions in public and private settings. Capital methods in Iran over the past decades, included stoning (most often for adultery), hanging, and beheading by sword (commonly for prostitution). Hangings have also occurred in Lebanon and Kuwait, whereas firing squads have been used in United Arab Emirates, Iraq, and by the Palestinian Authority. Crucifixion has followed executions in both Saudi Arabia and Yemen.

Although many executions in the Middle East are carried out secretly and in private settings (like inside prisons), public executions have occurred recently in various countries. For example, Amnesty International reported a surge in public executions in Iran during a three-month period in 2001.[16] A public hanging in Lebanon in 1998 was broadcast on television stations, and several Syrian nationals have also been executed recently in public places. An estimated 50,000 people witnessed an execution involving a "high-attention" crime in Yemen in 2000.[17]

Capital trials and the subsequent imposition of the death penalty in most Middle Eastern countries are largely secretive, quick, and inquisitorial proceedings with few legal safeguards for the accused. Confessions are often extracted through extreme torture and a system of inquisitorial justice is reflected in low levels of legal representation of the accused, a focus on fact-finding, and the dual role of the judge as both investigator and adjudicator. Although some adversarial elements may exist in the areas of the right to confront one's accusers, remaining silent, and a slight presumption of innocence,[18] these basic rights of defendants facing capital punishment in Saudi Arabia and other Islamic countries are largely disregarded throughout the entire criminal court process. Similar to other world regions, extrajudicial executions and summary or "field" judgments against political opposition parties in the Middle East are clear instances of executions that lack any legal safeguards for the accused.

Caribbean Countries

The next-most-concentrated area for the retention of capital punishment involves countries in the Carribean. Over three-quarters of these countries (ten of thirteen) have retained capital punishment. Legal executions, however, have been relatively rare in this region since the beginning of the twenty-first century. Death sentences continue to be imposed in most of these countries, but only the Bahamas and Cuba had reports of executions during this period.[19] Hanging and shooting by firing squads are the primary lethal methods used in the Caribbean. Various international organizations (e.g., Amnesty International, Human Rights Watch, United Nations) have reported numerous cases of torture, brutality, deaths in custody, and inhumane conditions of confinement for death-row inmates and other prisoners in many of these countries.

Aside from legal executions, several countries within the Caribbean have a long and tumultuous history of extrajudicial executions by security forces and opposition groups. For example, the Haitian National Police have been linked to numerous cases of summary executions and have avoided criminal prosecution through a well-entrenched system of judicial impunity.[20] These security forces have also remained inactive when mobs of people have carried out "popular justice" in public areas. Even though the death penalty has been abolished since 1987, assassinations and other violent acts against public figures, journalists, and political opponents are other forms of death sentences given out in Haiti over the past decade.

The use of extrajudicial executions by law enforcement agents and security forces is also common in the Dominican Republic, another "abolitionist" country in this region. International agencies report hundreds of cases of killings in the Dominican Republic by security forces "under disputed circumstances" (e.g., the authorities allege that the victims were killed in gunfire exchanges with criminal suspects although this account is disputed by eyewitness testimony or other evidence).[21] Similar patterns are found in Jamaica, where numerous complaints of police brutality and extrajudicial executions have been levied against specialized police units that were developed in response to high crime rates in this country.[22] Unlawful shootings of unarmed civilians by law enforcement officials have also been reported in Cuba. Unfortunately, the actual number of civilian killings by death squads, military and security forces, or other extrajudicial bodies throughout the Caribbean and other world regions is largely unknown.

Asian Countries

Countries within the Asian continent are diverse in terms of their sociopolitical composition and their use of the death penalty. Currently, nearly two-thirds of the countries in this region have retained capital punishment (see Table 3.3). Most of these countries that retain the death penalty have conducted at least one execution since the start of the new century. At least half of the countries in each region of Asia still retain the death penalty.

Variation does exist, however, across the Asian continent. The highest concentration of countries with capital punishment involves Eastern and Central Asia, where over 80 percent of the included countries retain it. Country-level support for capital punishment is lower in the entire Southern region of Asia (including the countries in the south, southeast, and southwest regions), but even here a majority of countries retain the death penalty.

EAST ASIA. The world leader in the use of the death penalty is China. Although no official count of executions and death sentences is available, media accounts and human rights organizations report that at least 2,468 people were executed and more than 4,000 were given a death sentence in China in 2001.[23] These same sources estimated that over 1,000 executions and at least 1,500 death sentences were imposed in 2000.

As will be discussed more fully in chapter 5, the widespread use of the death penalty as a response to social, economic, and political conditions in China has a long history. The dramatic rise in death sentences in China at different times in the past two decades is a direct result of national "strike-hard" campaigns designed to crack down on various types of crime, including violent crimes, drug offenses, and other nonviolent offenses such as corruption, pimping, tax fraud, producing and selling harmful food, and theft.[24] Mass sentencing rallies are not uncommon, and these rallies are often broadcast live on state television. Actual executions are done out of public sight, especially after the passage of the 1996 Criminal Procedural Law (CRL).[25] The primary method of execution involves a shooting at point-blank range, but lethal injection has also been formalized as an option for execution under current Chinese criminal procedural law.[26]

In addition to the extensive use of the death penalty, other acts of state-sponsored violence have also taken place in China in the past decade. Primary among these offenses include the issue of human rights protection for groups and individuals who may threaten the stability and unity of the prevailing Chinese government (e.g., Falun Gong, Tibetan Buddhists, Muslim ethnic groups like the Uighurs). Human rights organizations report numerous instances of deaths in custody because of torture or deplorable conditions and essentially extrajudicial executions through secret trials and summary judgments against persons labeled "separatists" or "terrorists."[27]

Other countries within East Asia have also conducted executions in the new century (e.g., Japan, North Korea, Taiwan), but with a far lower frequency than China. North Korea has substantially reduced its number of capital offenses, restricting the death penalty to intentional murder and crimes that threaten the state (e.g., conspiracy against state power, high treason, terrorism, antinational treachery).[28] Death sentences have continued to be pronounced in courts in South Korea, but no executions have occurred since 1998.[29] Mandatory death sentences for a wide variety of crimes are the current practice in Taiwan, with at least twenty-seven executions having taken place in 2000 and 2001.[30] Japan has executed by hanging five people during this same time period.[31] Nepal has abolished the death penalty since 1997, but its political instability has been associated with over 200 deaths from unlawful or extrajudicial executions, torture by police, and numerous "disappearances" of citizens.[32]

CENTRAL ASIA. Death sentences were imposed and executed in most countries in Central Asia during this period. Unofficial sources (e.g., television reports) indicate that Kazakstan has averaged about forty to sixty executions per year compared to about five to ten executions per year in other countries in this region (e.g. Uzbekistan, Tajikistan). Central Asia has been plagued by many forms of social and political unrest in the past decade, including high levels of political violence (e.g., assassinations and attempts to kill political officials in Uzbekistan and Tajikistan) and civil unrest, torture, and forcible deportation involving ethnic and religious minorities (e.g. ethnic Uighurs in Kazakstan and Kyrgyzstan, unregistered religious denominations in Turkmenistan).[33]

SOUTHEAST ASIA. Southeast Asia is the next-most-concentrated area for retaining capital punishment within the continent. Most countries within this region have executed people in either 2000 or 2001. Singapore, Vietnam, and Thailand led the region in terms of the largest number of recorded executions. Amnesty International reported that 340 people were hanged in Singapore between 1991 and 2000, giving it one of the world's highest execution rates per population size.[34] Death sentences have been imposed on at least 1,800 people in the Philippines since capital punishment was restored in 1984, but only seven executions have taken place in this time period.[35]

Although the death penalty can be imposed for a variety of criminal offenses in this region,[36] capital punishment has been most widely used for drug trafficking in Southeast Asian countries. Over 80 percent (17/21) of the executions in Singapore in 2000 were for drug trafficking, and a similar proportion was found in Thailand and Vietnam.[37] The death penalty for drug offenses is either prohibited or less commonly given in other world regions. A diversity of methods are used for the execution of drug traffickers and other offenders in the region, including firing squads (Indonesia, Thailand,

Vietnam), hanging (Malaysia, Singapore), and lethal injection (the Philippines, Thailand).[38]

Particular countries within Southeast Asia have also been involved in numerous allegations and documented cases of extrajudicial killings by security forces and opposition groups. The Special Rapporteur for the United Nations in 1996 sent reports to the following countries in this region regarding alleged cases of extrajudicial, summary, or arbitrary executions: Indonesia, Malaysia, Papua-New Guinea, the Philippines, and Thailand.[39] Human rights organizations in the last several years have also reported thousands of civilian killings and extrajudicial executions within Indonesia (e.g., killings in the context of the pro-independence movement in Aceh and Papua), the Philippines (e.g., summary executions of suspected drug dealers, the killing of indigenous people in land disputes, deaths from military counterinsurgency operations), and Thailand (e.g., killings by police "death squads" of over 300 suspected drug traffickers, the widespread disappearance of civilians under dubious circumstances).[40]

SOUTHERN AND SOUTHWEST ASIA. Both the Southern and Southwest regions of Asia retain capital punishment in about half of the countries. However, executions have been reported in only three of these countries (Afghanistan, Bangladesh, Pakistan) during the 2000–1 time period.[41] Extrajudicial executions by police and opposition forces as well as deaths from torture and other human rights abuses have continued to be a serious problem within these regions.

Over fifty people in Afghanistan in 2001 were executed after trials, and scores of religious and ethnic minorities were victims of extrajudicial killings by Taleban forces in military operations.[42] Summary executions of captured fighters were reported on both sides of the Afghanistan conflict (i.e., both Taleban and United Front forces were involved in these practices). The majority given a death sentence in Pakistan were for murder. Nearly 4,000 people are currently on death row in Pakistan.[43] Deaths from torture, extrajudicial executions by police forces, and "honor" killings (e.g., killing of wives for adultery) were also relatively common. Nearly 1,000 criminal suspects were killed in "encounters" with police in the Punjab province in Pakistan during a three-year period in the late 1990s.[44] Although the number of executions in India is unknown, death sentences continue to be imposed and thousands of deaths have occurred in this country over the past decade from extrajudicial executions and torture by security forces and other armed groups.[45] Several countries in these regions (e.g. Cambodia, Sri Lanka, Turkey) also have long histories of extrajudicial violence, but they have abolished capital punishment in law or in practice.

The methods of execution in these southern regions of Asia have included hanging (e.g., Bangladesh, India, Myanmar, Sri Lanka), firing squads (e.g., Afghanistan), and stoning (e.g., Pakistan). One Pakistani murderer was sentenced to be "publicly strangled, cut into pieces, and thrown into acid."[46] Most legal executions are conducted in public places, but usually in the absence of the large crowds and sentencing rallies found in other settings like China.

Africa

The death penalty in law and practice continues to be used in the majority of African countries in the early twenty-first century.[47] However, there are large regional differences on this continent. Central and North Africa have the highest concentration of countries that still impose death sentences and have conducted legal executions in the last several years. The vast majority of countries in East Africa also have recently imposed death sentences upon criminal convictions, but no record of legal executions has been reported by government officials or human rights groups within this region. In contrast, available evidence suggests that capital sentences have not been given or executed in the vast majority of countries in both the regions of West and Southern Africa.[48]

As is true of other regions, the legal status and practice of capital punishment in Africa cannot be fully understood without examining the wider context of social and political unrest that has long plagued this region. Over the past three decades, most countries in this region have experienced massive social and political turmoil resulting from natural disasters (e.g., drought and mass starvation), democide, genocide, numerous coups to overthrow existing governments, pro-independence movements, and extensive poverty and despair. As reported in several recent books, the estimated number of deaths in this region from democide and genocide is simply staggering:

■ Up to 300,000 Ugandans were killed under the Ida Amin regime in the mid-to late 1970s.[49]

■ The prolonged conflict in Burundi between the Hutus and Tutsis resulted in the deaths of an estimated 100,000 Hutus by the Tutsis-dominated government in Burundi in 1972, the killing by the army of another 20,000 Hutus in a village struggle in 1988, and the subsequent retaliation in the early 1990s by Hutus "hit squads" that massacred an estimated 500,000 Tutsis people.[50]

■ Acts of democide and genocide over the last half century are responsible for the deaths of an estimated 1.1 million people in Sudan, 600,000 in Uganda, 400,000 in Nigeria, 200,000 in Mozambique, 125,000 in Angola, 50,000 in Algeria and Equatorial Guinea, 30,000 in Rwanda, and 20,000 in Chad.[51]

Reports of extrajudicial executions, deaths in custody through torture, and disappearances of civilians and political officials have gone unabated in many parts of Africa at the turn and beginning of the twenty-first century. For example, the Special Rapporteur for the United Nations in 1996 sent reports of alleged cases of extrajudicial, summary, or arbitrary executions to the governments of the following thirty-four countries in Africa: Algeria, Angola, Botswana, Burkina Faso, Burundi, Cameroon, Central Africa Republic, Chad, Comoros, Cote d'Ivoire, Djibouti, Egypt, Equatorial Guinea, Ethiopia, Ghana, Guinea, Kenya, Lesotho, Liberia, Malawi, Mali, Mauritania, Morocco, Niger, Nigeria, Rwanda, Senegal, Sierra Leone, South Africa, Sudan, Togo, Tunisia, Zaire, and Zimbabwe.[52] Africa represented over a third of the countries that received this notification by the United Nations. Human rights groups have also reported cases of extrajudicial executions and killings under suspicious circumstances in the vast majority of countries in this region.[53]

Many countries in Africa that have legally abolished capital punishment are still practicing executions through extrajudicial means. In fact, across the entire African continent, the level of legal executions is relatively low compared to other world regions. However, when the amount of extrajudicial executions through democide and genocide in the past three decades are considered, Africa would be rated as one of the top regions of the world in terms of state-sponsored violence.

North America

Countries in North America vary widely in their use of the death penalty in law and in practice. The United States averaged about fifty-four executions per year over the past decade (from 1991–2000), and more than 3,500 inmates remained on death row at the end of 2001.[54] A total of 820 inmates have been executed in the United States since the late 1970s. Mexico has abolished capital punishment for ordinary crimes (like murder and armed robbery), but military forces and armed civilian groups have been implicated in extrajudicial executions, the disappearance of citizens, and the massacre of indigenous populations (e.g, the 1997 massacre of forty-five people in the community of Acteal).[55] Canada abolished the death penalty for all crimes in 1998, and its Supreme Court has recently placed limits on the government's extradition of Canadian citizens who are charged with capital crimes in other countries.[56]

Capital punishment in the United States is allowed in thirty-seven states for murders done under special circumstances (e.g., excessive brutality, wider public threat, child victims). Federal law also permits death sentences for acts of treason, terrorism, murder, and major drug trafficking. Lethal injection is the primary method of execution in most states with the death penalty, but hanging, firing squads, and electrocutions are also possible methods in other states. The history and practice of capital punishment in the United States will be discussed more fully in chapter 4.

Central America

Most countries in Central America have legally abolished capital punishment for either ordinary crimes or all crimes. The exceptions are Belize and Guatemala. Belize has not had a legal execution since 1985, but death sentences continue to be given in the early twenty-first century.[57] Guatemala executed two people in 2000 by lethal injection, and these executions were broadcast on television.[58] Firing squads were used in the televised execution of two men in 1996.[59]

Similar to other world regions, civil conflict and rising crime rates have been the basis for reports of extrajudicial killings throughout Central America. For example, United Nations investigators reported that over 300 lynchings took place in Guatemala between 1996 and 2001, most involving citizens alarmed by rising crime who took the law into their own hands.[60] The death of youth gang members in Honduras has been attributed to "social cleansing" by individuals who may be acting with the consent or complicity of local police, whereas the national police in El Salvador have been linked to killings of unarmed citizens.[61]

South America

Guyana and Suriname are the only countries in South America that have retained capital punishment. Suriname has not had an execution in over ten years. Death sentences continue to be imposed in Guyana, but there has not been an execution in this country in the twenty-first century.

Several countries within South America have had long histories of extra-judicial killings by national security forces, paramilitary groups, and armed citizen-opposition groups (e.g., Chile under Augusto Pinochet's "Caravan of Death" in the 1970s, Peru's "death squads" associated with the intelligence services in the 1980s and early 1990s). Death squads and other killings by security forces and opposition groups continue to plague civilians in Brazil, Columbia, Venezuela, and Ecuador. It has been estimated that internal conflict within Columbia has resulted in at least 300 disappearances and over 4,000 killings of civilians outside combat for political motives by armed groups.[62] Extrajudicial executions are widely suspected in the recent killing of 100 people by a so-called extermination group operating inside the police force in the state of Portuguesa in Venezuela.[63]

Europe

Capital punishment has been essentially eliminated in most of Europe. Only Belarus and the Russia Federation in the region of Eastern Europe have not legally abolished the death penalty, and Latvia reserves it to only special circumstances.[64] Countries within other regions of Europe (especially those in Central, Northern, Southwestern, and Western Europe) have abolished the death penalty in both law and practice.

Civil strife and political unrest in Europe at the turn of the twenty-first century has been restricted primarily to the former Eastern bloc countries (e.g., the former Soviet Union) and the Baltic region. The conflict in the former country of Yugoslavia has resulted in thousands of deaths under suspicious circumstances and the displacement of various ethnic groups (e.g., Serbians, Croatians). Numerous extrajudicial executions by military forces and opposition groups have been reported within this context. A similar situation applies to the current conflict in Russia between the Chechen rebels and the Russian Federation. Extrajudicial killings by government security forces, however, have also been noted in areas of Western Europe, including those associated with prolonged attacks between Protestants and Catholics in Northern Ireland, the Basque separatist movement in Spain, and the search for international terrorist groups in various countries.

Oceania

Countries within the area of the South Pacific Ocean have the lowest acceptance of capital punishment in both law and practice. None of these countries have conducted an execution within the last ten years, and most of them have abolished the death penalty for all crimes. Based on reports filed by the United Nations and various human rights groups, countries within this region also have relatively few instances of deaths in custody and extrajudicial, summary, or arbitrary executions by government forces or opposition parties in their recent histories.[65]

LEVEL OF ECONOMIC DEVELOPMENT

It is widely assumed that the death penalty is more prevalent in less economically developed countries than industrialized nations. This presumed inverse relationship between development and death penalty practices is often attributed to the greater need for a variety of state-sponsored mechanisms of social control (including capital punishment) in countries with high levels of poverty and economic despair, enormous inequality in the distribution of wealth across social groups, and volatile political structures that emerge as sources of both relief and further repression within these developing nations. Capital punishment in developing countries often serves as a vivid reminder of the prevailing sources of power and control.

In contrast, industrialized nations often have a wider array of effective mechanisms of social control at their disposal that lessen the need for capital punishment to help preserve social order. These alternatives include the ability to control dissent through civil litigation, denial of material benefits, licensing requirements, inspections, imprisonment, asset forfeiture and foreclosures, and the enforcement of various types of administrative and regulatory laws. Capital punishment in most industrialized nations is currently viewed as largely uncivilized and unnecessary as a mechanism of social control in the modern world.[66]

When death penalty practices are compared across levels of economic development, the conventional wisdom surrounding capital punishment and economic development is generally supported, but there are numerous exceptions. The United States and Japan are the only large industrialized countries of the world that have retained the death penalty.[67] In contrast, nearly two-thirds of the developing countries (i.e., defined by GDP per capita of less than $4,000 [US] in 2000) have retained the death penalty in law.[68] The exceptions involve abolitionist's practices in less-developed countries across geographical regions, including those in Western Africa (e.g., Cape Verde, Cote d'Ivoire, Guinea-Bissau, Sao Tome), Southern Africa (e.g., Angola, Mauritius, Mozambique, Namibia), the Caribbean (e.g., Haiti, Dominican Republic), Central America (e.g., Costa Rica, Honduras), South America (e.g., Ecuador, Venezuela), and Central and Eastern Asia (e.g., Turkmenistan, Nepal). This long list of exceptions across world regions suggests that the level of economic development, in and of itself, is not necessarily a good predictor of the legal status of the death penalty in a particular country.

STATE-SPONSORED VIOLENCE AND CIVIL UNREST

A final approach for examining the death penalty from an international perspective involves its relationship to general levels of civil strife and political unrest. Specifically, is the legal status of the death penalty in a country simply representative of a wider sociopolitical context in which various forms of state-sponsored violence (e.g., deaths in custody, extrajudicial executions, genocides) are relatively commonplace? To address this question, countries listed in a 1996 United Nations report for various types of human rights violations were compared in terms of their death penalty practices during this same period.[69]

Regardless of the particular measure of lethal human rights violations (e.g., extrajudicial executions, deaths in custody, deaths by excessive force by law enforcement officials, deaths from attacks by civil defense forces and paramilitary groups), there is a strong correlation between capital punishment and other types of state-sponsored violence.[70] For example, over three-quarters of the eighty-nine countries that had alleged cases of extrajudicial, summary, or arbitrary executions had legally retained the death penalty. Nearly 90 percent of the countries with reports of deaths in custody involved pro-death penalty countries, and over 70 percent of countries with reports of deaths from excessive force by law enforcement and security officers were countries that retained capital punishment. Stronger relationships between capital punishment and other forms of violence were observed for "communal violence" (i.e., acts of violence by one social group against another in which government forces supported one side or did not intervene to stop the violence).[71] In fact, all eight countries that were involved in these practices between 1992 and 1996 had the death penalty.

Although these analyses reveal a strong association between pro-death penalty countries and their participation in other types of state-sponsored violence, there are several aspects of this relationship that deserve special notice. First, there are numerous exceptions to this pattern, including several countries (e.g., Cambodia, Chile, Colombia, Israel, Haiti) that have abolished capital punishment for at least ordinary crimes, but have continuing histories of civil violence, death squads, and "disappearances" that are linked to acts of either commission or omission by state authorities. Second, several retention-ist countries (e.g., Cameroon, Ethiopia, Indonesia, Myanmar, the Philippines, Uganda) rarely conduct legal executions but they have extensive reports of extrajudicial executions. As illustrated by the killings of drug traffickers by police "death squads" in Thailand,[72] high levels of extrajudicial executions in these countries may be serving as a swift, certain, and severe alternative or substitute for formal legal treatment.

SUMMARY

This chapter has examined current practices in economic, incapacitative, and corporal sanctions in world regions and by level of economic development in societies. Both economic and incapacitative sanctions are more prevalent in Western societies characterized by higher levels of economic development. Corporal punishment (e.g., state-sponsored executions, extrajudicial killings, torture, and deaths in custody) is more prevalent in less-developed countries in Africa, Asia, and Central and South America. These techniques of physical punishment are relatively less common in highly industrialized societies in Europe. Major exceptions to these patterns involve the United States and Japan, highly industrialized societies that retain capital punishment as a legal sanction.

Although these contemporary patterns give us some idea of the preva-lence of different sanctions in a comparative perspective, they do not fully address how these types of punishment reflect changes in social, political, and economic institutions in particular countries over time. Such a comparative historical perspective on punishment in particular countries with different legal traditions is examined in the next three chapters.

Notes

1. For an example of these interpretive and classification problems as they are related to the official counts of crime in the United States and other countries, see Clayton Mosher, Terance Miethe, and Dretha Phillips. 2002. *The Mismeasure of Crime*. Beverly Hills, CA: Sage.
2. See Human Rights Watch. 1996. "The Small Hands of Slavery – Bonded Child Labor in India." New York: Human Rights Watch. [HRW Index No.: ISBN 1-56432-172-x.]. September 1, 1996.
3. See Human Rights Watch. 2001. "Defending Human Rights – The Role of the International Community, Saudi Arabia." New York: Human Rights Watch.
4. Human Rights Watch. 2002. "Singapore: Asia's gilded cage." Human Rights Features. New York: Human Rights Watch. April 17, 2002.
5. New Zealand Ministry of Justice Report. 2000. *Report of Monetary Penalties in New Zealand*. Available through the following Web site: www.justice.govt.nz/pubs/reports/2000.
6. For example, the decline of "unit fines" in England has been attributed to the dramatic increase in fines for offenders of moderate and high income for relatively trivial offenses, to unreliable means of obtaining accurate information on offenders' financial resources, and to over-rigidity and complexity in calculating the appropriate fines. For a review of various types of day fine systems, see New Zealand Ministry of Justice Report. 2000. *Report of Monetary Penalties in New Zealand*. Available through the following Web site: www.justice.govt.nz/pubs/reports/2000. For a general discussion of fines and other intermediate sanctions, see Norval Morris and Michael Tonry. 1990. *Between Prison and Probation: Intermediate Punishments in a Rational Sentencing System*. New York: Oxford University Press.
7. For the source of these international data, see Roy Walmsley. 2000. *World Prison Population List (second edition)*. Home Office Research, Development and Statistics Directorate. Research Findings No. 116. These rates should be interpreted with caution, given the variability in the year of data collection, differences in the definition of incarceration, and the general reliability of the data. Nonetheless, they provide a general basis for looking at differences in incapacitative sanctions across countries.
8. See Graeme Newman. 1999. *Global Report on Crime and Justice: Published for the United Nations*. New York: Oxford University Press.
9. Amnesty International. 2003. *The Death Penalty: Death Penalty Statistics*. See Amnesty International's Web site: www.amnesty.org.
10. Roger Hood. 1996. *The Death Penalty: A World-Wide Perspective*. 2nd ed. Oxford, UK: Clarendon Press.
11. Amnesty International Report. 2002. *The Middle East. Israel*.

12. See Amnesty International. 2002, 2001. *Annual Reports.*
13. Middle Eastern countries that have given death sentences in the twenty-first century include Bahrain, Iran, Iraq, Jordan, Kuwait, Lebanon, Oman, Palestinian Authority, Qatar, Saudi Arabia, United Arab Emirates, and Yemen. According to data provided by Amnesty International (2002, 2001), at least one execution was carried out in each of these countries except Bahrain, Lebanon, and United Arab Emirates. No death sentences were imposed or given in Syria in 2001, and no information was available in AI reports on capital punishment in Syria during the year 2000.
14. See Amnesty International Annual Reports 2002. Iraq. The Iraqi government in 1994 also issued a decree expanding the scope of the death penalty by including offenses "sabotaging the national economy" (e.g., forging official documents, possession of medicines and medical equipment, smuggling cars, and large construction equipment). Amnesty International Report. 1996. "Iraq, State Cruelty: Branding, Amputation, and the Death Penalty." [AI Index: MDE 14/03/96].
15. Human Rights Watch. 2001. *Saudi Arabia.*
16. See Amnesty International. 2002. *Annual Reports.*
17. See Amnesty International. 2001. *Annual Reports.*
18. Sam S. Sourryal. 1987. "Saudi Arabia's Judicial System." *The Middle East Journal* 25: 403–7.
19. See Amnesty International. 2002, 2001. *Annual Reports.*
20. See Human Rights Watch. 1997. "The Human Rights Record of the Haitian National Police." New York: Human Rights Watch. January 1, 1997; Human Rights Watch. 1996. "Thirst for Justice: A Decade of Impunity in Haiti." New York: Human Rights Watch. September 1, 1996.
21. See Amnesty International Report. 2002. "Dominican Republic" [AI Index: POL 10/001/2002]; Amnesty International Report. 2000. "Dominican Republic: Killings by Security Forces" [AI Index: AMR 27/001/2000].
22. See Amnesty International Report. 2002. "Jamaica" [AI Index: POL 10/001/2002]; Amnesty International Report. 2001. "Jamaica: Killings and Violence by police – how many more victims" [AI Index: AMR 38/003/2001].
23. Amnesty International. 2002. *Annual Report: China.*
24. See Michael Palmer. 1996. "The People's Republic of China." In Peter Hodgkinson and Andrew Rutherford (eds.), *Capital Punishment – Global Issues and Prospects.* Winchester, UK: Waterside Press. Pages 105–41; Andrew Scobell. 1990. "The Death Penalty in Post-Mao China." *China Quarterly* 123: 503–20.
25. Specifically, the 1996 CPL, Article 212 stipulates that the carrying out of a death penalty shall be publicly announced but shall not be shown to the public. See Wei Luo. 2000. *The Amended Criminal Procedure Law and the Criminal Court Rules of the PRC.* Buffalo, NY: William S. Hein. Page 116.
26. The 1996 Criminal Procedural Law (CPL), Article 212 maintains that the death penalty may be carried out by shooting, injection, or other means. The first lethal injection was carried out by the Kunming Intermediate People's Court in Yunnan Province, a Southwest region of China, on March 28, 1997. See Wei Luo. 2000. *The Amended Criminal Procedure Law and the Criminal Court Rules of the PRC.* Page 117. In addition, the highest-ranking official in the PRC ever sentenced to death, Cheng Kejie, was executed

by lethal injection on September 14, 2000. Cited in wenxuecity.com. December 4, 2002 under *Law and Life*, "Prosecutor disclosing insider information on Cheng Kejie's trial and lethal injection."

27. See Human Rights Watch. 2002. "China: Repression Against Falun Gong Unabated." Press Release Report. New York: Human Rights Watch. [HRW Index No.: 270x]. February 7, 2002 Human Rights Watch. 2001. "China/APEC Summit: Crackdown in Xinjiang." New York: Human Rights Watch. October 18, 2001 Amnesty International Annual Report. 2002, 2001. *China.*

28. A number of human rights groups have noted in North Korea and elsewhere the vague descriptions of various capital crimes in their respective criminal laws. The vagueness of the wording of these statutes is probably intentional in many countries because it allows the prevailing governments enormous leverage in using the death penalty to control individuals and groups that pose a threat to their legitimacy.

29. Amnesty International. 2002. *Annual Report: South Korea.*

30. Amnesty International. 2002. *Annual Report: Taiwan.*

31. Amnesty International. 2002. *Annual Report: Japan.*

32. Amnesty International. 2002. *Annual Report: Nepal.*

33. Amnesty International. 2002, 2001. *Annual Reports: Kazakstan. Kyrgyzstan. Tajikistan. Turkmenistan. Uzbekistan.*

34. Amnesty International. 2002. *Annual Report: Singapore.*

35. Amnesty International. 2002, 2001. *Annual Report: Philippines.* The 2001 report also notes that a temporary moratorium was placed on executions in 2000 following an execution in a disputed region in the country. No executions were reported in the 2002 report.

36. For example, capital crimes in Vietnam include crimes against national security (e.g., treason, taking action to overthrow the government, espionage, rebellion, banditry, terrorism, sabotage, hijacking, destruction of national security projects, undermining peace, war crimes), crimes against humanity, manufacturing/concealing/trafficking narcotic substances, murder, rape, robbery, embezzlement, fraud, and corruption by officials involving over $21,300 [US dollars]. See Amnesty International Report. 2000. "Socialist Republic of Viet Nam: The death penalty – current developments." [AI-Index: ASA 41/001/2000].

37. See Amnesty International. 2001. *Annual Report: Singapore*; Amnesty International. 2002, 2001. *Annual Report: Thailand*; Amnesty International Report. 2000. "Socialist Republic of Vietnam: The death penalty – current developments." [AI-Index: ASA 41/001/2000].

38. Amnesty International. 2002, 2001. *Annual Reports: Indonesia. Malaysia. Philippines. Singapore. Thailand. Vietnam.*

39. United Nations. 1996. "Human Rights Questions: Human Rights Questions, Including Alternative Approaches for Improving the Effective Enjoyment of Human Rights and Fundamental Freedom. Extrajudicial, Summary, or Arbitrary Executions." Report of the Special Rapporteur of the Commission on Human Rights on Extrajudicial, Summary, and Arbitrary Executions. United Nations General Assembly. Fifty-first Assembly. Agenda Item 110 (b).

40. Amnesty International. 2002. *Annual Reports: Indonesia. Philippines. Thailand.*

41. Amnesty International. 2002, 2001. *Annual Reports: Afghanistan, Bangladesh, Pakistan.*
42. Amnesty International. 2002, 2001. *Annual Reports: Afghanistan.*
43. Amnesty International. 2001. *Annual Report: Pakistan.*
44. Amnesty International. 2002, 2001. *Annual Reports: Pakistan.*
45. Amnesty International. 2002, 2001. *Annual Reports: India.*
46. Amnesty International. 2001. *Annual Reports: Pakistan.*
47. Accurate information on the prevalence and nature of capital punishment is missing in many countries in this region. The high level of political and civil unrest that has long plagued many countries in this region also makes problematic in many cases the distinction between legal and extrajudicial executions. Accordingly, we stress that our rankings of countries here and in other regions on their use of capital punishment should be viewed with caution.
48. See Amnesty International. 2002, 2001. *Annual Reports: Regional Index for Africa.*
49. Irving Horowitz. 2002. *Taking Lives: Genocide and State Power.* 5th ed. New Brunswick, NJ: Transaction Publishers. Page 165.
50. Ibid. Page 41.
51. See Rita Simon and Dagny A. Blaskovich. 2002. *A Comparative Analysis of Capital Punishment: Statutes, Policies, Frequencies, and Public Attitudes the World Over.* New York: Lexington Books. Table 6.1.
52. United Nations. 1996. "Human Rights Questions: Human Rights Questions, Including Alternative Approaches for Improving the Effective Enjoyment of Human Rights and Fundamental Freedom. Extrajudicial, Summary, or Arbitrary Executions." Report of the Special Rapporteur of the Commission on Human Rights on Extrajudicial, Summary, and Arbitrary Executions. United Nations General Assembly. Fifty-first Assembly. Agenda Item 110 (b).
53. See Amnesty International. 2002, 2001. *Annual Reports: Regional Index for Africa.* As a somewhat unique form of extrajudicial executions in recent history, it has been reported in Tanzania that thousands of people have been lynched by witch-hunting mobs in the past decade.
54. Bureau of Justice Statistics. 2002. *Capital Punishment 2001.* Washington, D.C.: U.S. Department of Justice. December 2002. NCJ 197020.
55. Amnesty International. 2002. *Annual Report: Mexico.*
56. Amnesty International. 2002. *Annual Report: Canada.*
57. Amnesty International. 2002. *Annual Report: Belize.*
58. Amnesty International. 2001. *Annual Report: Guatemala.*
59. Amnesty International Report. 2000. "Guatemala: Further Executions Loom." [AI-Index: AMR 34/022/2000].
60. Amnesty International. 2002. *Annual Report: Guatemala.*
61. Amnesty International. 2002. *Annual Report: Honduras*; Amnesty International. 2001. *Annual Report: El Salvador.*
62. Amnesty International. 2002. *Annual Report: Columbia.*
63. Amnesty International. 2002. *Annual Report: Venezuela.*
64. The former Soviet Union, before being dissolved in 1991, had one of the highest numbers of executions in the world, averaging between 1,000 and 2,000 executions each year from the 1960s to the 1980s. In 1996, former President Yeltsin suspended the

death penalty until a jury trial system was established throughout the entire Russian Federation. Since 1996, no death penalty sentence has been granted, although public opinion in Russia appears to be highly supportive of the death penalty. See Sergei Ivashko. 2001. "Duma Discusses Abolishment of Death Penalty." Cited in Johnson's Russia List Web site: Johnson@erols.com.

65. United Nations. 1996. "Human Rights Questions: Human Rights Questions, Including Alternative Approaches for Improving the Effective Enjoyment of Human Rights and Fundamental Freedom. Extrajudicial, Summary, or Arbitrary Executions." Report of the Special Rapporteur of the Commission on Human Rights on Extrajudicial, Summary, and Arbitrary Executions. United Nations General Assembly. Fifty-first Assembly. Agenda Item 110 (b).

66. In addition to its use as a mechanism of social control, capital punishment is also used for several other purposes (e.g., retribution, deterrence, social engineering, the symbolic value of particular punishments). These purposes or functions of the death penalty are discussed in chapter 1 and in the remaining chapters.

67. It is important to note that anti-death penalty attitudes and practices have been growing in each of these industrialized countries. The abolitionist movement in the United States is discussed in chapter 4.

68. Similar findings are observed when measures of average personal income are used. For example, among the twenty-five countries with the highest reported income, only four have the death penalty (Japan, United States, Singapore, Kuwait). However, nearly two-thirds of the sixty-one countries with the lowest reported income have retained capital punishment. Thus, the association between pro-death penalty laws and low economic development holds true regardless of how industrial or economic development is measured.

69. The source for these comparisons is the following United Nations Report. 1996: "Human Rights Questions: Human Rights Questions, Including Alternative Approaches for Improving the Effective Enjoyment of Human Rights and Fundamental Freedom. Extrajudicial, Summary, or Arbitrary Executions." Report of the Special Rapporteur of the Commission on Human Rights on Extrajudicial, Summary, and Arbitrary Executions. United Nations General Assembly. Fifty-first Assembly. Agenda Item 110 (b).

70. We define state-sponsored violence as acts of both commission (i.e., acts done by state security forces, military groups, or government officials) and omission (i.e., the failure of state officials to intervene to stop acts of extrajudicial violence).

71. See United Nations Report. 1996. "Human Rights Questions: Human Rights Questions, Including Alternative Approaches for Improving the Effective Enjoyment of Human Rights and Fundamental Freedom. Extrajudicial, Summary, or Arbitrary Executions." Report of the Special Rapporteur of the Commission on Human Rights on Extrajudicial, Summary, and Arbitrary Executions. United Nations General Assembly. Fifty-first Assembly. Agenda Item 110 (b). Page 16.

72. See Amnesty International. 2002. *Annual Report: Thailand.*

Suggested Readings

Amnesty International. 1996–2003. *Annual Reports. Regional and Country Reports.* Available through Amnesty International's Web site, www.amnesty.org.

Roger Hood. 1996. *The Death Penalty: A World-Wide Perspective.* 2nd ed. Oxford, UK: Clarendon Press.

Irving Horowitz. 2002. *Taking Lives: Genocide and State Power.* 5th ed. New Brunswick, NJ: Transaction Publishers.

Human Rights Watch. 1995–2003. *World and Country Reports.* Available through Human Rights Watch's Web site, www.hrw.org.

Norval Morris and Michael Tonry. 1990. *Between Prison and Probation: Intermediate Punishments in a Rational Sentencing System.* New York: Oxford University Press.

United Nations. 1996. "Human Rights Questions: Human Rights Questions, Including Alternative Approaches for Improving the Effective Enjoyment of Human Rights and Fundamental Freedom. Extrajudicial, Summary, or Arbitrary Executions." Report of the Special Rapporteur of the Commission on Human Rights on Extrajudicial, Summary, and Arbitrary Executions. United Nations General Assembly, 51st assembly, Agenda Item 110 (b).

CHAPTER FOUR

Punishment in American History

An interesting case study for a comparative historical analysis of punishment is the United States. As a former British colony before winning its independence at the end of the eighteenth century, the United States' legal tradition is rooted in the English common law. These common law principles have now been largely codified in a bifurcated system of federal and state statutes. Through its colonial and republic periods, the United States has used various types of punishment to maintain social order, eliminate threats to this order, and to implement major social changes. It is a relatively distinct industrialized society in the modern world, however, due to its high rates of incapacitative sanctions and continued use of the death penalty. These general similarities and differences with other countries make the United States an ideal case study for a comparative historical analysis of punishment.

Our examination of economic, incapacitative, and corporal punishment in the United States begins with a general overview of its demographic and structural features. This general profile is then followed by a more detailed historical account of major societal changes and landmark events that influenced the context-specific nature, prevalence, and justifications for different types of sanctions. This chapter concludes with a brief comparative analysis of historical practices in the United States with England and other Western European countries.

OVERVIEW OF STRUCTURAL FEATURES

The United States of America was formed in the aftermath of the Revolutionary War between England and its American colonists in the late eighteenth century. The original thirteen colonies gained their independence from British rule in 1776. This new republic was expanded across North America in the nineteenth and twentieth centuries to include fifty states.

The country covers a land area of over 9 million square kilometers, making it comparable in physical size to China and about half as large as South America. Its terrain and climate are diverse, covering hills and low mountains on the eastern border, a great plain area in its central regions (i.e., the Midwest), deserts in the Southwest, tropical climates in some areas (e.g., the states of Hawaii and Florida), and arctic conditions in others (e.g., the state of Alaska).

Early European settlements began primarily on the eastern coastline and expanded westward. The western frontier was the sparsely inhabited areas west of the original colonies. Due to both its physical terrain and the rugged characteristics of its nonindigenous settlers, the area to the west of the Mississippi River was also called "the Wild West."

Nearly 300 million people are currently legal residents of the United States. Its population is racially and ethnically mixed. National census data from the year 2000 indicate that whites represent the largest racial/ethnic group (77 percent of the total population), followed by African Americans (13 percent), Asians (4 percent), Native Americans (less than 2 percent), Pacific Islanders (less than 1 percent), and "other" categories of race/ethnicity (4 percent). The fastest-growing minority in the United States are black and white Hispanics (i.e., persons of Latin American descent [Cubans, Mexicans, Puerto Ricans, etc.]). When ethnicity is dichotomized as Hispanic or non-Hispanic, an estimated 13 percent of the current U.S. population is classified as Hispanic.[1] Christianity is the dominant religion of over 80 percent of the population. Racial and ethnic conflict, and to a lesser extent religious persecution, has been a central theme throughout American history.

Economically, the United States is a highly industrialized society based on the principle of capitalism and a market-oriented economy. It has a per capita gross domestic product of $37,600 and is considered the largest and most

U.S. STRUCTURAL PROFILE:

- Former British colony
- Geographically diverse
- Nearly 300 million residents
- Mixed racial/ethnic groups
- Christianity dominant religion
- High economic development
- Capitalism and market economy
- Growing class disparity
- Political democracy
- Two major political parties
- Separate executive, legislative, and judicial branches of government
- Hierarchy of federal/state court systems
- "Common law" legal tradition
- Criminal acts classified as felonies or misdemeanors
- Relatively high crime rates and levels of civil litigation

technologically powerful economy in the world.[2] As measures of the quality of life, the United States is consistently ranked higher than most countries in life expectancy at birth, educational attainment, disposable income, and purchasing power. However, its relative economic position to other countries has decreased somewhat since World War II. The onrush of technology has also increased the level of inequality through a "two-tiered labor market" in which those at the bottom become increasingly disadvantaged because of their lack of education, technical, or professional skills compared to those at the top.[3]

The political structure in the United States is a democracy. Members of the executive and legislative branches of government are elected officials, whereas judges and magistrates within the judicial branch are either appointed (e.g., U.S. Supreme Court Justices, U.S. District Court judges) or elected (e.g., local magistrates in state or municipal courts). The legislative branch involves two chambers of Congress (i.e., the Senate and House of Representatives) with mutual authority to develop and ratify laws. A two-party system composed of Democrats and Republicans is the current form of political organization, loosely representing "left" (i.e., liberal) and "right" (i.e., conservative) ideologies, respectively.

The basic legal structure of courts has changed little over American history. A three-tiered hierarchy of courts exists within both the federal and state systems. The lower courts are courts of limited jurisdiction (e.g., small-claims courts, traffic courts, U.S. Customs court). The purview of these lower courts is usually restricted to minor breaches of order and misdemeanors (i.e., criminal acts punishable by less than a year in jail). Courts of general jurisdiction (e.g., circuit or district courts) are the trial courts for more major violations of federal or state statutes (e.g., federal antitrust violations, felony offenses punishable by over a year of imprisonment). The highest level of courts are appellate courts (i.e., intermediate appellate courts and courts of "last resort" like state supreme courts and the U.S. Supreme Court). Appellate courts are limited in their concern to matters of law such as procedural irregularities, whereas trial courts focus on the facts of the case and rendering a verdict or judgment.

The American legal tradition is characterized by the codification of common law principles into civil and criminal statutes. It is a blended system of judge-made law and statutory law. This departure from the "pure" form of English common law was necessitated in early Colonial America by two primary factors: (1) cultural differences across the colonies (e.g., Quakers in Pennsylvania, Puritans in Massachusetts, Dutch settlers in "New Amsterdam" [New York], slaves and indentured servants in Virginia and other southern colonies) and (2) this social diversity and the vast physical area made it impossible for circuit judges to travel around the region, capture the collective will of the people, meet with other circuit judges to quantify these collective sentiments, and ultimately pass on these uncodified principles as the "living law" of the land. Elements of the common law tradition of judge-made law are clearly reflected in the U.S. system of case law and notion of precedent to inform the interpretative context for legal decisions.

Based on current national data on criminal offenses and victimization, the United States is characterized by high rates of serious crimes (e.g., murders, robberies, rapes). Its level of civil litigation (e.g., lawsuits) is also high compared to other countries. As described in the next section, numerous types of economic, incapacitative, and corporal sanctions have been used throughout American history to control crime and deviance.

HISTORICAL CONTEXT FOR SANCTIONS

There are various ways to identify and classify the different historical contexts of punishment in American society. For example, punishment practices can be classified by time (e.g., comparisons over centuries) or by major events that fundamentally changed the social structure and nature of social relations in society (e.g., the abolition of slavery). We combine these approaches by looking at the nature of punitive responses to crime and threats to social order in the following periods: Colonial America, the nineteenth and early twentieth century (i.e., the period of statehood, slavery, and the expanding western frontier), and the last half of the twentieth century.

COLONIAL AMERICA

The early American settlements were colonized by various groups from the continent of Europe. Spanish colonies were the earliest permanent settlement (e.g., Saint Augustine [Florida] in 1565) and were later extended to territories in present-day Texas, California, and the Southwest. The French outposts and settlements were predominant on the St. Lawrence River (e.g., Quebec and Montreal), the Great Lakes, and along the Mississippi (especially in the colony of Louisiana). Dutch colonists settled along the Hudson River in a territory called New Netherlands, with principal settlements in Fort Orange (now named Albany, New York) and New Amsterdam, a tract of land purchased from the Native Americans in 1626 that later became New York City. Both Swedish and Finnish settlers were dominant in the Delaware Valley in the late 1630s.

Compared to the settlements by other European nations, the English colonies in the New World offered its inhabitants more religious freedom and economic opportunities.[4] The Puritans escaped persecution for their religious beliefs by establishing settlements in the Massachusetts Bay Colony in the 1630s. Roger Williams led a group of followers to Rhode Island to allow greater religious freedom among Baptists and other religious groups. Religious tolerance was also standard practice within other colonies in New Jersey and South Carolina, whereas other geographic areas served as safe havens for Catholics (e.g., Maryland colony) and Quakers (Pennsylvania colony). Hopes of religious freedom and economic prosperity stimulated the emigration of thousands of Europeans to the English colonies. Under a system of indentured servitude, the poor could obtain passage across the Atlantic in return for a specific number of years of labor. The colonial population was also bolstered by the transportation of criminals from England as a method of punishment.

Both religion and economic activity served as major mechanisms of social control in early Colonial America. These social-control mechanisms were clearly observed in the early Massachusetts Bay Colony. To the Puritan colonists a person by nature was sinful and able to achieve goodness only through severe and unremitting discipline.[5] Hard work was viewed as a religious duty, and great importance was placed on self-reflection and self-discipline. Deviance was a collective threat to godly communities to be dealt with through swift, certain, and severe punishment.

For various purposes of social control (e.g., deterrence, incapacitation, threat reduction), the Puritan colonies were notorious for their nature and severity of sanctions. Stocks and yokes were commonly used in these communities for various reasons (e.g., public humiliation of offenders, the public "dramatization of evil").[6] Fines of several shillings or pounds were imposed for numerous minor breaches and were often accompanied by public flogging. The threat to Puritans' views by invading Quakers and alternative religious beliefs were met with the most severe corporal punishment. The hanging of alleged witches and heretics across New England in the seventeenth century epitomized this collective response to threat.[7] These different types of public and ritualistic punishments served in many cases to both enhance community solidarity (e.g., to unite the community against "evil") and as a visible reminder of the lack of communal tolerance for deviance.[8]

The Puritan colonies were most well-known for their small and homogeneous character and their conceptions of godly community. They were largely closed societies in which religious values shaped all aspects of daily life, including their conceptions of deviance and its control. In fact, the Puritans were infamous in their equation of crime with sin and their use of biblical scripture as justification for capital punishment. The influence of the Mosaic code of the Old Testament was clearly evident by the fact that a biblical reference was contained in nearly all of the twelve capital laws in Bay Colony's 1641 Body of Liberties: idolatry (idol worship), witchcraft, blasphemy, murder, manslaughter, poisoning, bestiality, sodomy, adultery, and false witness in capital cases.[9] The only capital crime that did not include a biblical reference was the crime of conspiracy and rebellion.

Life in the Southern colonies was different in several fundamental respects from the Northeast colonies. Many of these differences involved the nature of economic activity in Southern colonies, and the exploitation of servants and slaves to farm the land, grow tobacco, and work semitropical crops like rice and indigo. Various marginalized individuals from England (e.g., rogues, beggars, criminals transported to the colonies) came to these settlements as indentured servants who would receive parcels of land when their terms of servitude ended. Unfortunately, high death rates from overwork, malnutrition, and general ill-treatment among these workers forced landowners to constantly import new laborers, greatly enhancing population diversity and the development of a wide class of young males with few bonds to conventional institutions.[10] Slaves and indentured servants were valuable property for landowners in the Southern colonies, and various laws were passed to protect their control over them and punish those who attempted to take their property.

Only gross estimates of the extent of economic, incapacitative, and corporal punishments in Colonial America are available because of the absence of comprehensive historical records and definitional problems. For example, many of the mutual attacks among and between settlers and Native Americans could be interpreted as extrajudicial executions, as were the early lynching practices against slaves and other disadvantaged groups. Even if detailed court records were available across jurisdictions for much of the seventeenth and eighteenth centuries, however, it is unlikely that the deaths within these disadvantaged or marginalized groups would have been counted in official records as "executions."

Economic Punishment

Several basic features of colonial life affected the use of economic sanctions. First, most of the settlers were poor or indentured servants, property-less and with limited financial resources. Their primary financial assets were their bodies for indentured labor. Except in the Southern colonies where large pools of laborers were required for plantation work, the nature and values of daily life in the other colonies (e.g., subsistence living even with great personal effort) were simply not conducive to the widespread use of indentured servitude as a type of economic sanction for wrongdoing. Second, economic sanctions did not fit with the dominant views toward punishment (i.e., retribution, deterrence). Penal philosophy in many colonies demanded swift and severe punishment that involved the direct inflicting of physical pain on the deviant.

Archival records of economic sanctions indicate that these punishments were most often used for minor offenses. Monetary sanctions were applied as surety (i.e., bond) to ensure the offender's later court appearance. They were also offered as alternatives to corporal punishment (e.g., flogging, the stocks). Historical accounts even include cases of people refusing to pay fines on principled grounds (e.g., Quakers who thought Puritan laws against them were fundamentally wrong) and thus "voluntarily" submitting themselves for corporal punishment.[11] Within the context of a wrongful death of a slave by another owner, the offending party was ordered to pay financial restitution to compensate for the loss of the worker. Such compensatory damages were also applied in cases of civil wrongdoing (e.g., a shipping company that loses one's cargo).

TABLE 4.1: Proportion of superior court sentences in Massachusetts (1750–1796) Involving monetary penalties	
Offenses against the state:	79%
Offenses against the person:	57%
Fraud and property offenses:	36%
Moral offenses:	36%
All offenses combined:	45%

Data Source: Kealey (1991)

Archival records from the Superior Court of Massachusetts in the last half of the eighteenth century reveal that monetary sanctions were the single-most common punishment.[12] Monetary penalties were imposed on nearly half (45 percent) of the convicted offenders, whereas the next most frequent sanctions were corporal punishments (18 percent), work service (15 percent), and public shaming (14 percent). The predominance of monetary sanctions is also true among specific offenses. Financial penalties were given to over three-quarters of persons convicted for crimes against the state (e.g., public order crimes) and to at least a third of offenders in other crime categories (see Table 4.1). Another study in Massachusetts in the same time period found that fines were even more common in lower courts, representing an estimated 82 percent of the punishments for less serious crimes.[13]

Despite the scarcity of currency and liquidable property, these court data suggest that colonial judges frequently imposed monetary fines for various purposes of social control (e.g., direct punishment, restitution for goods stolen or damaged, surety bonds in lieu of incapacitation). Similar findings about the prevalence of fines and their assorted uses are observed in other colonies, providing some support for the generalizability of these conclusions.[14] Rather than being the exclusive punishments, monetary sanctions were often imposed in conjunction with corporal punishment and incapacitation. The use of fines and corporal punishment in combination was especially common in the earlier colonial period.

Financial sanctions in Colonial America and elsewhere have always been associated with an explicit class bias in terms of the ability to pay and escape other punishments. Indentured servants, slaves, and the poor, by definition, lack the financial means to provide economic compensation or

> "the rich can elude justice by giving great bail, and feeing lawyers high, who by that and other methods, protract the affair till the action dies away, by one means or another" ...
>
> A quote from Patrick Lyon, a former inmate of the Philadelphia jail in 1799.
>
> *Source:* Hobbs (1991)

punitive damages for their misconduct. Lacking financial resources, corporal punishments and further incapacitation through penal servitude were often the only viable alternative sanctions for these disadvantaged groups. In contrast, the propertied class of gentleman and professionals had both the economic means and opportunity to "pay" for their crimes through monetary sanctions. This fundamental inequality in the very nature of economic sanctions can be traced throughout American history.

Incapacitative Sanctions

All of the early American colonies had some form of physical restraint system for criminals and other wrongdoers. Jails held people awaiting court action and those unable to pay their debts. Stocks and the pillory were physical devices used for similar purposes of temporary restraint.[15] However, physical structures for long-term confinement were largely absent in the American colonies until the late 1700s. This historical situation in America was in sharp contrast with Mother England and its widespread use of a litany of institutions of confinement (e.g., houses of correction, hulks, jails).

Several factors of colonial life contributed to its comparatively low use of institutional confinement. These factors are both practical and philosophical. For example, America was sparsely populated and primarily rural. Permanent physical structures for confinement were unnecessary in most settlements because (1) less serious offenders could be dealt with most effectively through devices like the stocks and corporal punishments (e.g., whipping, branding, other mutilations) and (2) the small numbers of serious wrongdoers could be easily controlled through permanent forms of incapacitation like banishment and death sentences. Philosophically, punishment in most colonies was equated with inflicting physical injuries and confinement was not considered sufficiently painful. The Quakers were the only settlers who believed that reformation was possible through hard labor and reflection in a house of correction.

Changes in the practice and philosophy of incapacitation in the later stages of the colonial period were the result of changes in population growth, its composition, and contemporary social thought of the Enlightenment. Population growth caused wider social problems (e.g. poverty, idleness, predation) and the need for additional methods of social control. A changing correctional philosophy based on the ideas of Cesare Beccaria, Jeremy Bentham, and John Howard provided a more humane and optimistic view of restoration and human improvability. The growth of institutions of confinement coincided with the emergence of the new American republic.

The first large structure for solitary confinement for purposes of reflection and penance was the Walnut Street Jail in Philadelphia, built in 1776. By 1790, this three-story structure contained twenty four separate cells for solitary confinement. "Hardened and atrocious" offenders were placed in solitary confinement without labor.[16] No matter how intolerable the conditions of incarceration, physical confinement for solitary reflection was viewed by reformers as far more humane than corporal punishment (e.g., severe flogging, death) as a way of controlling the behavior of marginal groups of vagrants, debtors, the insane, dissenters, and criminals.

Over the next several decades, however, an alternative penitentiary system was developed in Auburn, New York. This model used a revised congregate system of prison discipline whereby inmates were held in isolation at night but congregated in workshops outside their cells during the day under a strict reign of obedience, discipline, and silence.[17]

In an increasingly industrial age of factory production, most of the emerging states adopted this New York model of confinement because they saw the economic value of exploiting inmate labor to help defray the expenses of the institution and possibly earn a profit for the state. The Quaker model of solidarity confinement and reflection, although possibly enlightening for some offenders, was increasingly viewed as a waste of precious human labor. In contrast, the New York system allowed the introduction of real work discipline and actual industrial production within the penitentiary.[18]

Corporal Punishment in Colonial Times

Corporal punishment was widely used throughout most of the American colonies. The Puritans in New England were infamous in terms of their severe and harsh physical punishments. Most settlements had a public whipping post and pillory for inflicting serious physical pain and public humiliation. Corporal punishment served multiple purposes or functions in these communities, including specific deterrence, general deterrence, retribution, increasing community solidarity, and permanent incapacitation (i.e., death, branding, and other mutilations reduce the physical opportunity for re-offending).

As a lethal form of corporal punishment, capital punishment was used in all of the original American colonies.[19] Several physical and social aspects of these earlier colonies, however, placed limitations on its use. These limiting factors included the following: (1) settlements were small and relatively homogeneous, conditions in which nonlethal informal control mechanisms are highly effective; (2) physical existence and survival was so precarious that other methods (i.e., starvation, disease) would naturally take their toll and remove "undesirables"; (3) the necessity of preserving able bodies for personal protection against hostile attacks; (4) the need for labor to develop the community; and (5) the absence of social conditions often associated with higher levels of crime (e.g., urbanization, substantial poverty).[20]

Based on the most comprehensive data on executions in American history, a total of 1,553 executions were part of the historical record in the American colonies in the approximately 200-year period from 1608 to 1799.[21] The number of executions vacillated over this period, reaching a high of 289 in the 1780s before dropping again.

It is commonly assumed that executions were relatively rare in Colonial America, and to some extent the data presented in Figure 4.1 support that position. However, when converted to rates per population, this picture changes dramatically. Specifically, an execution rate of seventy-two per million population is estimated for Colonial America in the 1780s compared to a rate of 1.8 per million for the United States in the 1990s.[22] This translates into an execution rate in colonial times that is forty times higher than current trends. When coupled with other forms of corporal punishment, it is apparent that colonial justice was especially severe in its physical response to wrongdoing.

Major differences across jurisdictions existed in the type of capital offenses. Across all settlements prior to 1800, about one-third of the executions were for murder and the remainder involved other offenses. However, there was also enormous regional variability in the proportion of executions for murder (see Figure 4.2). These proportions ranged from a high of 83 percent in New Hampshire to a low of 12 percent in New York.

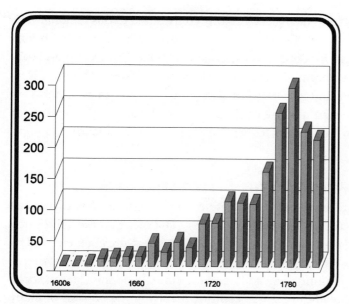

Figure 4.1. Executions in Colonial America (1608–1800)

Data Source: Espy File (1608–1990)

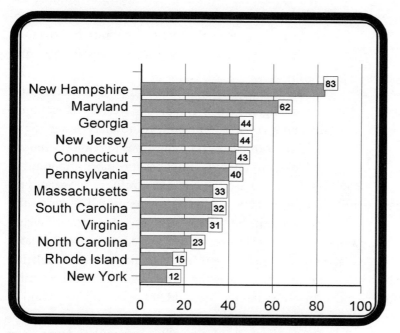

Figure 4.2. Proportion of Executions for Murder in Early Colonies

Data Source: Espy File (1608–1799)

The unique problems facing each colony contributed to this regional variation in the type of capital offenses. For example, two-thirds of the executions in Rhode Island were for piracy, whereas slave revolts (32 percent) and robbery (16 percent) represented the two most prevalent capital crimes in New York. Counterfeiting and forgery were also more common as executable offenses in New York than the other colonies. Massachusetts and Connecticut were the leaders in executions for witchcraft in the seventeenth and eighteenth centuries.

STATEHOOD, SLAVERY, AND THE WESTERN FRONTIER

After the American Revolution, the new republic was faced with various growing pains that affected the nature of society, law, order, and social control. In addition to rapid population growth, the early 1800s were characterized by greater mobility as well as greater socioeconomic differentiation. New territories were settled, continuously adding to the confederation of states. Social change was widespread during this century, involving the erosion of many small and cohesive communities by changing population dynamics, the allure and lore surrounding the expansion of the western frontier, and the development of boomtowns that were temporary havens for a large migratory horde of young men seeking fame and fortune.

The major legal document limiting punishment in the new nation was the ten amendments to the U.S. Constitution known as the "Bill of Rights." Under these rights, the accused is entitled to due process under the law (Fifth Amendment), a speedy and public trial by an impartial jury (Sixth Amendment), and protection against excessive bail, excessive fines, and cruel and unusual punishment (Eighth Amendment).

The use of law as a mechanism of social control also changed in this expanding world. For example, the function of law in prerevolutionary times (especially in northeastern colonies) was to reinforce morals and religious dictates, but it became more important in later years to use the criminal law for purposes of protecting property and physical security. Similar to the worry about the "dangerous classes" in industrializing England, society's well-to-do in the postrevolution period in the United States feared that the economically disadvantaged and malcontents would seek material gain by banding together to deprive the more privileged of their wealth and standing.[23] Under these conditions, it should not be surprising to find in the early 1800s (1) a dramatic increase in prosecutions for offenses against private property (e.g., larceny/theft, burglary), (2) a substantial decrease in offenses against God and religion, and (3) a dramatic increase in the use of hard labor as punishment against the urban poor.[24]

Similar to colonial times, monetary sanctions in the nineteenth and early twentieth century were widely applied for purposes of punishment, compensation, and as a surety bond to help guarantee one's appearance in court. Monetary fines were imposed primarily as punishment for minor criminal offenses, but they were also used in lieu of confinement. The expanding economy also gave rise to the greater accumulations of wealth and property, conditions that increased the opportunity to collect in civil damages. Unfortunately, comprehensive numerical estimates of the prevalence of monetary sanctions in this middle period of American history are unavailable.

Incapacitation of vagabonds, criminals, dissenters, and other "undesirables" changed during this period of western expansion in both its use and purpose. Jails continued to be holding tanks for temporary confinement, and large-scale institutions of confinement were established in each state and many territories. However, by the mid-1800s there was growing disenchantment with early reformative movements that brought about the penitentiary system. Within this period, penitentiaries had become notoriously overcrowded, understaffed, undisciplined, and brutal institutions of confinement that offered little hope of rehabilitation or deterrence.[25]

As a response to the problems with the current incapacitation approach, several changes occurred in the nature and philosophy of confinement. A system of intermediate release was established in which inmates earned enough "marks" to be gradually released back into the community. These types of conditional release programs evolved into modern-day "halfway houses" and the parole system. Another change involved the development of indeterminate sentencing systems and the model of individual treatment. Reformation would be achieved through education and training. Rather than confinement for fixed periods of time, evidence of reform would be rewarded with early release. In the mid-nineteenth century, probation developed as an alternative to confinement and a new type of social incapacitation within one's community.[26]

> John Augustus of Boston is recognized as the originator of probation in the United States. He bailed out offenders at early court hearings, supervised them, and offered guidance until they were sentenced. Over an eighteen-year period (1841–59), Augustus "bailed on probation" 1,152 men and 794 women.
>
> *Source:* Latessa and Allen (1997:110–11)

Comprehensive estimates of the number of jail and prison confinements are not available until the first quarter of the twentieth century. By 1925, state and federal prisons and reformatories contained over 90,000 prisoners, representing an incarceration rate of seventy nine per 100,000 residents.[27] This incarceration rate would skyrocket to nearly 500 per 100,000 population by the end of the twentieth century.

Based on the available evidence, the use of corporal punishments for crimes in the 1800–1950 period was lower than in the previous colonial period. Public whippings were increasingly restricted to particular contexts (e.g., military punishments, disobedience by slaves), and many state statutes removed flogging as an acceptable punishment. The exception to this pattern involved capital punishment by the state authorities and the use of lethal and nonlethal corporal punishment by vigilante groups and "regulators" in the pre- and post-Civil War period.

Capital Punishment

Analysis of the Espy data on executions indicates that this type of corporal punishment generally increased over successive decades throughout the 1800s. Executions ranged from about 200 per decade in the first quarter of the century, and from 350 to nearly 600 per decade at mid-century, to over 1,000 per decade from 1880 to 1899.[28] Murder was the predominant convicted offense for persons executed by local legal authorities in the 1800s, patterns that continued into the twentieth century. The sex, race, and age of those executed in the 1800s also changed little over time (see Figure 4.3). Males, blacks, and adults were far more likely to be executed than their respective counterparts.

During the nineteenth century, capital statutes expanded in several jurisdictions to target particular groups that were considered "problem populations." The most obvious instance of this practice was the "Black Codes" that differentiated capital offenses for blacks and whites. For example, Virginia in the 1830s had only five capital crimes for whites, but for black slaves there were up to seventy offenses punishable by death.[29] Georgia in 1816 had similar types of racial differentiation: The death penalty was mandatory for a black slave or freeman who raped or attempted to rape a white female, an offense that carried only a two-year sentence for a white man.[30]

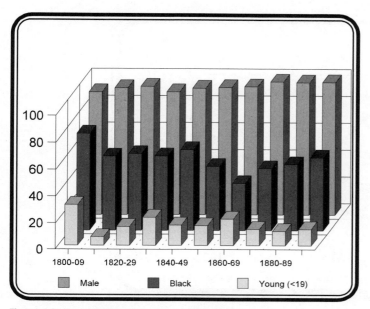

Figure 4.3. Social Profile of the Executed in 1800s
Data Source: Espy and Smykla (1991)

Under the slave-based economies of the South, the problem population was primarily runaway or rebellious slaves and those who provided aid for their insurrection efforts. Both formal legal means (including corporal punishment and capital punishment) and extralegal means (e.g., lynching) were widely used and threatened to maintain control over this social group. These methods of social control against blacks grew as a means of continuing slavery in theory and practice in the postbellum south.

Lynchings in the Nineteenth and Early Twentieth Centuries

Summary executions by groups of individuals acting as a vigilante committee, regulators, or surrogate civil authority within a particular jurisdiction have been a major element of American history. Most of the attention to lynching has focused on the postbellum American South, where vigilante groups used extrajudicial executions for various purposes of social control. However, in the absence of an available and respected legal authority in evolving jurisdictions, lynching was a basic method of social control throughout the entire period of expansion of the American frontier. Its rise and decline in U.S.

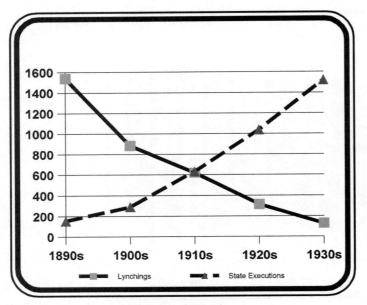

Figure 4.4. Lynchings and State-Based Executions
Data Source: Adapted from Bowers (1984, Tables 2–3)

history coincides with the relative power of local and state authority in handling problem populations and threats to prevailing interests. The perceived legitimacy and effectiveness of these established political institutions are important factors in understanding the prevalence and context of lynching.

Available data on lynching in the latter half of the nineteenth century suggest that it was relatively common, especially compared to legal executions under local and state authority in particular decades. For example, even considering the large number of these extrajudicial executions not recorded or documented, the available count of lynchings in the 1890s (n = 1,540) greatly exceeded the number of executions under both local authority (n = 1,060) and state authority (n = 155).[31] The number of documented lynchings dropped dramatically in subsequent decades as the number of state-sponsored executions increased (see Figure 4.4).

This inverse relationship between the number of lynchings and the number of executions under state authority suggests that acts of collective violence like lynchings are more prevalent when established laws and legal institutions are considered lacking, weak, or openly partisan. Such a set of circumstances are the conditions that appeared to underlie the growth of lynchings in the post-Civil War Reconstruction era and the early twentieth century.[32]

The image and actions of vigilante committees, regulators, and lynch mobs during this general time frame are wide and varied. Vigilante leaders in many cases took pride in their activities, operated in the open, considered their motives to be patriotic and noble, and believed that they were acting in the best interests of their communities.[33] Lynch mobs and other vigilante groups took action in many cases because of the absence or perceived inadequacies of existing laws and legal institutions. The inability of prevailing legal authority to effectively control "problem populations" (e.g., slaves, insurrectionists, rogues, outlaws, abolitionists) was a major factor in the persistence of these sources of extralegal punishments. Although some of these vigilante groups provided at least a semblance of legal procedure and protection to the accused, in most cases it appears that summary judgments were pronounced and carried out quickly with little or no debate or opportunity for legal defense.[34]

The Emancipation Proclamation of 1864 and the subsequent period of Reconstruction had a profound impact on existing laws and the nature of American society. It enforced racial equality under the law and abolished the Black Codes that assigned harsher punishments for blacks and developed separate laws to regulate their behavior. However, this new world order posed a serious social, economic, and political threat to white dominance. Southern whites, in particular, found the law and its administration woefully inadequate for dealing with crime and disorder attributed to blacks. By the end of Reconstruction, several social changes (e.g., Jim Crow laws to establish racial segregation, poll taxes and literacy tests for voting) helped reassert white dominance in the region. More importantly, lynchings in this period became an increasingly prevalent and visible form of social control of free blacks that essentially restored the differential treatment that was the basis for the antebellum Black Codes.[35]

Social Control on the American Frontier

Both law and order were precarious themes on the expanding American frontier in the mid- to late 1800s. Settlers moving west faced all kinds of perils, from climatic disasters (like floods, droughts, and blizzards) to massacres by the indigenous populations, and, in general, a rugged and unpredictable future. At the same time, new settlers and established residents were confronted with hordes of young males with strong ties to nothing except pure self-interest and the dream of quick riches. This period was also characterized as the "era of the outlaw," with the growing availability of banks and businesses to rob in a vast geographical environment with little order and less law. Rapid growth in cow towns (like Dodge City and Abilene) and regional centers (like San Francisco and St. Louis) provided other lucrative opportunities for exploitation, both legitimate and illegitimate.

Although legal officials (e.g., lawmen, territorial judges/magistrates) were available on the expanding frontier, western "justice" was more commonly dispensed in a variety of informal ways. Similar to the lynchings in the South, frontier folk often did not have the patience, resources, or physical opportunities to wait for formal authorities to take action, and they often appeared to have little faith in formal authority's resolution of the issues even if they were readily available. Instead, justice was often meted out via the "quick draw" and vigilante activities of offended parties and concerned citizens who participated in short, informal trials.

TWENTIETH-CENTURY PRACTICES

Major changes in American society in the twentieth century had profound effects on the nature and use of punishment. Sociologically, American society was being transformed to an urban, industrial society with mass migration from both within and outside the country. Many of the early conflicts associated with statehood, civil war, and western expansion had been resolved, but new problems emerged as a result of continuing population concentration and diversity, economic volatility (from the Great Depression to economic prosperity), worldwide wars, and changing political power of various disadvantaged groups (e.g., blacks, women, union workers).

The period beginning in the 1960s was an incredibly tumultuous time in modern American history. Widespread protests about civil rights and the legitimacy of the Vietnam War erupted throughout the country, often resulting in riots and bloody conflicts between police and protestors. Rates of both property and violent crime soared for several decades before dropping in the 1980s, only to rise again in the subsequent decade. This same period saw globalization of the American economy and the establishment of trade agreements and shared production activities throughout the world.

The confluence of different social, political, and economic forces fostered the development and use of various types of sanctions for purposes of social control and social change. Numerous types of legal authority and institutions had now become firmly entrenched in American society to deal with various problems of law and order.

Economic Sanctions

As a sanction for minor criminal offenses, fines have continued to be a major type of economic punishment in the twentieth century. Over the last half century, however, economic fines have been increasingly used to punish various types of corporate deviance. Civil litigation, restraint of trade practices (e.g., product boycotts, embargoes), and asset forfeitures in both civil and criminal cases are the latest forms of economic sanctions in contemporary American society.

Even though no comprehensive measures of the extent of these practices exist, it is an irrefutable fact that economic sanctions are a pervasive method of social control and punishment in modern America. These economic sanctions are justified on multiple grounds, including retribution, incapacitation (i.e., restraint of trade, license revocations), deterrence, and restoration. The magnitude of some of these sanctions is simply staggering[36]:

- The tobacco industry in November of 1998 reached a record $206 billion, twenty five-year settlement with forty six states for various civil damages related to deceiving the public about the health risks of tobacco. Federal litigation also seeks smoking-cessation programs, advertising restrictions, a public education campaign, and the release of industry documents.

- A $2 billion fine was levied against Exxon Corporation in 1985 for overpricing Texas crude oil.

- A $200 million class-action suit was settled in 1985 involving 250,000 Vietnam veterans and seven chemical companies that manufactured the defoliant Agent Orange.

- Union Carbide Corporation was fined $1.37 million in 1986 for numerous health and safety violations.

- Kidder, Peabody, and Company agreed in 1987 to pay a record $25.3 million to settle insider trading charges. In 1992, they agreed to pay an additional $165 million in one of the last remaining insider trading suits from the 1980s.

- A $1.3 billion settlement was reached in 1992 in lawsuits against Michael Milken and associates in illegal stock trading involving "junk bonds."

- The U.S. Department of Justice in 2000 collected $122 million in fines from cases of environmental crime.

The magnitude, diversity, and frequency of economic sanctions in contemporary practice are unparalleled in American history. For example, economic boycotts have been levied by the U.S. government against other countries (e.g., Cuba, Iraq, North Korea), and the threat of the withdrawal of financial support is a common tactic to gain compliance to U.S. interests. Asset forfeiture is a major feature of RICO laws developed in the 1980s to combat criminal enterprises (e.g., organized crime).[37] Under these laws, legal businesses that materially benefit from organized crime activities (e.g., banks that launder drug money) are subject to monetary fines and the forfeiture of their assets. As another type of modern economic sanction, *qui tam* lawsuits are now being filed by private citizens against companies that defraud the government (e.g., overbilling for services, falsifying time reports). Under these "false claims" acts, offending companies often pay both compensatory and punitive damages for their misconduct. Financial recoveries and fines under these lawsuits over the past two decades amounted to billions of dollars.[38]

Under the principle of retaliation, the use of economic sanctions for many types of organizational misconduct is a logical punishment. Unfortunately, there is little conclusive evidence that such economic sanctions have been effective in changing corporate or organizational misconduct.[39] For many organizations in modern American society, economic fines are considered just part of the "cost of doing business."

Incapacitative Sanctions

Similar to economic sanctions, the nature and frequency of various types of incapacitative sanctions have changed in relationship to social changes in the wider society. Technological advances have served as the genesis for new devices for incapacitating and monitoring convicted offenders within their home and community (e.g., video cameras, electronic monitors that restrict physical movement).

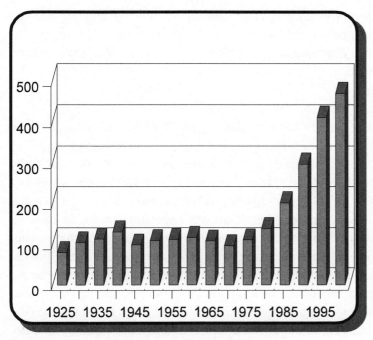

Figure 4.5. U.S. Incarceration Rates in the Twentieth Century
Data Source: U.S. Dept. of Justice (NCJ-85861, NCJ-198877)

Different levels of supervised probation have also been developed over the twentieth century, ranging from largely unsupervised release to intensive supervision programs. Institutions of confinement have changed in both their nature and type. Separate facilities have been more fully established for different groups of offenders (e.g., juvenile vs. adults, male vs. female institutions) as well as for different levels of offenders (e.g., minimum-, medium-, and maximum-security facilities). A wide range of specialized facilities have also been constructed within the past few decades, including "boot camps" and residential treatment facilities.

According to national data on correctional practices in 2002, there were over 2 million people in local jails and prisons in the United States.[40] The majority of these inmates are in state prisons (1.2 million). When incarceration rates are compared over time, it is evident that the use of imprisonment has dramatically increased in the mid-1980s and has not subsided (see Figure 4.5). The rise in incarceration rates can be attributed to several factors, including rising crime rates, the growth in mandatory sentencing policies and the growth of private prisons and the "prison industrial complex."[41] Drug offenses in particular have disproportionately contributed to the rising incarceration rates in this period.

Corporal Punishment

Legally accepted forms of corporal punishment for criminal behavior have been increasingly restricted to capital punishment in contemporary American society. Corporal punishment is still used in an unofficial capacity by law-enforcement officials to extract confessions and administer "street justice" to suspected criminals and inmates within institutions. However, capital punishment remains the only legitimate state-sponsored form of corporal punishment. Even for this punishment, the physical pain and disfigurement associated with death sentences have diminished over time, as states increasingly move toward lethal injection as the sole method of its implementation.

The number of recorded executions in the United States has fluctuated over the twentieth century. Executions increased from the 1910s through the 1930s before dropping in the 1940s until the end of the temporary moratorium in the 1970s, and then increasing again for the subsequent decades of the 1980s and 1990s (see Figure 4.6).

The high number of executions in the 1930s appears to be associated with a combination of distinct historical factors. High numbers of homicides in the decade were connected with Prohibition, violent acts between organized-crime syndicates (e.g., the Saint Valentine's Day massacre), and economic despair followed by a period of relative deprivation that may have contributed to relatively high levels of robbery-homicides and other serious crimes with a primarily economic motive.[42] Extrajudicial executions associated with lynching were also relatively high in this period.

During the last half of the twentieth century, there has been unprecedented changes in U.S. practices in the use of the death penalty. The decline in the 1960s was especially fueled by the social unrest of the times. Antiwar protests heightened people's "moral sensitivity to killing in general," leading many to question the government's rationale for doing so, either in war or through legal executions.[43] The civil rights movement focused attention on various domains of differential treatment, including minority overrepresentation in capital punishment. Inconclusive evidence about the deterrent effect of capital punishment added more doubts about the

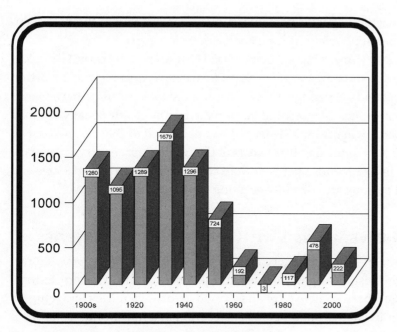

Figure 4.6. Executions in U.S. History (Twentieth Century)

Data Source: Espy File (1608–1990) BJS (1990–2002)

validity of this justification for lethal sanctions. Attorneys in this decade also began exploring the potential for legal challenges of the constitutionality of the death penalty. Public support for capital punishment was also declining, reaching a low in 1966 of 42 percent in favor of the death penalty for murder.[44]

The U.S. Supreme Court placed a legal moratorium on capital punishment as a result of its ruling in the case of *Furman v. Georgia* (1972). Specifically, the Court ruled that the death penalty, as it was then being administered, was "cruel and unusual punishment in violation of the 8th and 14th amendments." The immediate consequence of this decision was that over 600 death-row inmates in thirty two states had their sentences commuted to life imprisonment.[45]

Following the *Furman* decision, state legislatures introduced new and revised bills to devise death penalty procedures that could be considered constitutional. The Supreme Court has continued to rule on various aspects of the death penalty, including issues surrounding expedited federal review procedures, the use of scientific evidence to demonstrate discriminatory treatment, victim impact statements, and the applicability of the death sentence for special populations (e.g., juveniles, insane persons).

Capital punishment has again increased in use since the early 1980s. Rising crime rates and new social problems (like drug trafficking and terrorism) have precipitated the passage of new federal and state legislation that expands the scope of capital offenses. Public support for the death penalty climbed above 80 percent in the mid-1990s, but had decreased to about 66 percent by the year 2000.[46] In the first three years of the twenty first century, an average of seventy five executions per year were carried out in the United States and over 3,500 persons are currently awaiting execution on death row.[47]

COMPARATIVE ANALYSIS WITH OTHER WESTERN SOCIETIES

Punishments in America society derive from its unique developmental history and the historical philosophies and practices within Western Europe. The early European settlers were an assorted lot of adventurers and refugees who sought freedom from religious persecution in a new world. As mostly a British colony, America's early history was shaped by policies and practices of Mother England. The content of the law and types of punishments are based on the general traditions of Western Europe, but they also reflect the unique problems of this new world. These sources of similarity and difference are described below.

SIMILARITIES WITH WESTERN EUROPEAN TRADITIONS

For most of American history, punishment philosophies and practices in England and Western Europe dramatically affected the nature of punishment in the United States. The punishments included in the early legal codes of Colonial America were directly tied to Judeo–Christian values that were spread throughout Western Europe in the Crusades of the Holy Roman Empire and various inquisitions on the continent. For example, almost all capital crimes in the Puritan colonies of New England contained explicit references to biblical scripture.

The specific methods of corporal punishment used in Colonial America, as well as their specific symbolic and manifest function, are traceable to early Western civilization. These methods of punishment that were immortalized in the medieval period in Western Europe and transported to the early American colonies include the stocks and pillory for physical restraint and public humiliation, branding as a specific and general deterrent, and burning for inflicting physical and spiritual pain by preventing a proper Christian burial.

Another parallel between American history and that of Western Europe involved the enactment and application of numerous "bloody codes" to deal with specific social problems in their respective contexts. These "bloody codes" in England involved a dramatic escalation in the number of capital statutes in the mid-seventeenth and eighteenth centuries.[48] The additional capital codes were directed primarily at property offenses, ostensibly to protect the economic interests of the Crown and the propertied gentlemen of Parliament. The executions by guillotine of thousands during the "reign of terror" period (1794–5) of the French Revolution is a vivid example of similar practices in other parts of Western Europe. A similar response to threat in America history involved the "Black Codes" in the nineteenth century and the extrajudicial lynchings of blacks in the Reconstruction era.

Changes in penal philosophy in American history are also tied directly to its Western European roots. The period of Enlightenment and the Age of Reason that strongly affected the writing of the early European reformers (e.g., Jeremy Bentham, Cesare Beccaria, John Howard) were also influential in the movement toward more humane punishments in the early American republic. Subsequent reform practices in the United States regarding probation, parole, day fines, and a variety of intermediate sanctions are also derivative of ideas from Western Europe.

DIFFERENCES WITH WESTERN EUROPEAN PRACTICES
Although sharing a common legal and social history with much of Western Europe, the nature, magnitude, and prevalence of punishments in the United States are also unique to this particular context. These differences are most pronounced in punishment policies and practices within the twentieth century. They emanate from the confluence of various social, political, and economic conditions that have produced a greater reliance upon various types of sanctions in this country for purposes of both social control and social change.

Compared to other Western industrial countries in the last half of the twentieth century, the crime rate for serious offenses in the United States is unparalleled. It has one of the highest murder rates in the world, and its level of other violent crimes (e.g., robbery, rape) and serious property crimes (e.g., burglary, auto theft) is also markedly higher than other countries.[49]

The enormity of the crime problem in American society has led to a proliferation of various punitive measures to contain and deter it. This includes the wider use of incarceration and the death penalty. The incarceration rate far exceeds other Western countries. It is also the only Western industrial society that still retains and uses capital punishment for ordinary crimes.

The different response to crime in the United States is not only reflective of higher crime rates, but also a different orientation toward it. Take, for instance, the different responses in England and the United States to terrorist activity.

Acts of terrorism are capital offenses in the United States, whereas England does not have capital punishment for these crimes even though lethal bombings by members of the Irish Republican Army (IRA) have terrorized Great Britain's citizens and government officials for years. The British Parliament, however, has resisted public pressures to reinstate capital punishment for these offenders for several practical reasons (e.g., English jurors may acquit Irish terrorists in fear of reprisals, Irish citizens sentenced to death by English jurors would be considered martyrs). By generating either martyrs or feelings of immunity, the safest compromise response by British Parliament has been to simply give long periods of confinement to convicted terrorists. This example illustrates why an understanding of punishments must focus on its comparative historical context.

The United States also differs from other Western countries in its use of particular types of economic sanctions, especially civil litigation. Although it is difficult to estimate the volume of civil ligation practices in this country, most people agree that the United States has experienced unparalleled and unprecedented growth in litigation in the last half century. Its distinctiveness also is found in the widespread use of other economic sanctions, including injunctions, restraint of trade practices, asset forfeitures, denial of benefits, and certification and licensing practices.

When all forms of economic, incapacitative, and corporal punishments are considered, there is little question that the United States in the twenty first century is the most punitive country of the Western industrialized world. This statement is ironic given its global reputation as one of the most economically advanced and free societies of the modern world.

ESTIMATES OF CIVIL LITIGATION RATES PER 100,000 POPULATION IN SELECT COUNTRIES:

France (1999):	2,731
Japan (1999):	382
Finland (1999):	4,176
United States (1999)	4,800

Source: Authors' calculations from various Web sites, including www.stat.fi., www.justice.gouv.fr., www.ncsonline.org., www.stat.go.jp.

SUMMARY

Economic, incapacitative, and corporal sanctions have been used for purposes of social control and social change throughout American history. These sanctions have been justified on various grounds, including retribution, specific deterrence, rehabilitation and treatment, and restoration.

Particular historical periods are distinct in terms of their use of different types of sanctions. Both lethal and nonlethal corporal punishment were especially popular in Colonial America prior to the 1800s. These punishments were most common in the Puritan colonies of New England and less prevalent in the Quaker settlements in Pennsylvania. The reform era of more humane punishments began in the new republic in the 1800s and continued throughout the century with more restrictive contexts for corporal punishment, the establishment of probation, and individualized treatment of offenders. Capital punishment, however, continued throughout American history, involving both state authorized executions and extrajudicial practices by vigilante groups. All forms of sanctions have been used extensively in contemporary American society to deal with rising crime rates.

When compared to historical patterns throughout Western Europe, it is clear that the American history of punishment is rooted in the penal philosophies and practices of England and Western Europe. Over the last half of the twentieth century, however, the nature, magnitude, and frequency of various types of punishment depart substantially from contemporary practices in Europe. This includes high rates of civil litigation and other economic sanctions, unparalleled growth in incarceration rates, and the retention and use of capital punishment. As a response to high crime rates and other social problems, the United States has become the most punitive nation among Western industrial societies of the modern world.

Notes

1. A full enumeration of the population, including the number of illegal migrants from Latin American countries who enter through the southern borders, would increase even further the relative size of the Hispanic population in the United States.
2. See Central Intelligence Agency. 2003. *The World Factbook – The United States*. Web site location: www.odci.gov/cia/publications/factbook/geos/us.html.
3. The bottom class in this system suffer from an increasingly cumulative disadvantage through the denial of pay raises, health insurance coverage, and other work-related

benefits. See Central Intelligence Agency. 2003. *The World Factbook–The United States.* Page 8.

4. For general discussions of the social and legal histories of Colonial America, see Kai Erickson. 1966. *Wayward Puritans.* New Haven, CT: Yale University Press; Roger Lane. 1997. *Murder in America: A History.* Columbus: Ohio State University Press; Eric H. Monkkonen. 1991. *Crime and Justice in American History: Historical Articles on the Origins and Evolution of American Criminal Justice. The Colonies and Early Republic.* Volumes 1 and 2. London: Meckler.

5. See Kai Erickson. 1966. *Wayward Puritans.* New Haven, CT: Yale University Press.

6. For a discussion of the functions of the "dramatization of evil," see Frank Tannenbaum. 1938. *Crime and the Community.* Boston: Ginn and Company. Pages 156, 202–3.

7. Most victims of witch-hunting in this time period were women, especially women over the age of forty. The wider prosecution and persecution of women as witches has been attributed, in part, to efforts at reaffirming male authority at a time when some women were testing these gender barriers (e.g., the charismatic spiritual leader Anne Hutchinson) and other women were gaining a degree of economic independence through the inheritance of property. See David D. Hall. 1999. *Witch-Hunting in Seventeenth-Century New England: A Documentary History, 1638–1693.* 2nd ed. Boston: Northeastern University Press. Page 7.

8. For a general study of deviance in these early colonies, see Kai Erickson. 1966. *Wayward Puritans.* New Haven, CT: Yale University Press.

9. See William H. Whitmore. 1890. "The Body of Liberties, 1641." *A Bibliographical Sketch of the Laws of the Massachusetts Colony from 1630 to 1686.* Boston: Rockwell and Churchill. Page 55.

10. Roger Lane. 1997. *Murder in America: A History.* Columbus: Ohio State University Press. Pages 47–8.

11. See Kai Erickson. 1966. *Wayward Puritans.* New Haven, CT: Yale University Press.

12. For the original source of these data, see Linda Kealey. 1991. "Patterns of Punishment: Massachusetts in the Eighteenth Century." In Eric H. Monkkonen (ed.), *Crime and Justice in American History: Historical Articles on the Origins and Evolution of American Criminal Justice. The Colonies and Early Republic.* Volume 1. London: Meckler. Pages 344–67.

13. See Linda Kealey. 1991. "Patterns of Punishment: Massachusetts in the Eighteenth Century." In Eric H. Monkkonen, *Crime and Justice in American History: Historical Articles on the Origins and Evolution of American Criminal Justice. The Colonies and Early Republic.* Volume 1. London: Meckler. Page 356 (footnote 16).

14. For example, fines were imposed in 61 percent of the offenses against the person and 49 percent of the crimes against public order that were processed in the Philadelphia courts from 1791 to 1810. See A. B. Hobbs. 1991. "Criminality in Philadelphia: 1790–1810 compared with 1937." In Eric H. Monkkonen (ed.), *Crime and Justice in American History: Historical Articles on the Origins and Evolution of American Criminal Justice. The Colonies and Early Republic.* Volume 1. London: Meckler. Pages 339–43.

15. From a deterrence perspective, the public humiliation and shaming associated with being confined in stocks and the pillory also served as a potential deterrent for the wrongdoer and a general deterrent for other potential offenders in the community. As

a form of public degradation, community solidarity was also sometimes enhanced by these ritualist forms of incapacitation.

16. Todd R. Clear and George F. Cole. 2000. *American Corrections.* 5th ed. Belmont, CA: Wadsworth. Page 39.

17. Ibid. Page 40.

18. See Dario Melossi and Mark Lettiere. 1998. "Punishment in the American Democracy: The Paradoxes of Good Intentions." In Robert P. Weiss and Nigel South (eds.), *Comparing Prison Systems: Toward a Comparative and International Penology.* Amsterdam: Overseas Publishers Association. Page 23.

19. Under the Quaker Code of Pennsylvania, capital punishment was reserved for premeditated murder. The other colonies included numerous offenses as capital crimes. The Quaker Code remained until 1718. The revised Pennsylvania laws considered all felonies to be capital crimes with the exception of larceny. See Todd R. Clear and George F. Cole. 2000. *American Corrections.* 5th ed. Belmont, CA: Wadsworth. Page 37.

20. See Kathryn Preyer. 1991. "Penal Measures in American Colonies: An Overview." In Eric H. Monkkonen (ed.), *Crime and Justice in American History: The Colonies and Early Republic.* Volume 2. London: Meckler. Pages 492, 497.

21. The most comprehensive data on executions in American history were originally compiled by M. Watt Espy and further refined through grants through the University of Alabama Law Center and the National Science Foundation. This Espy File contains summary records of 14,570 executions in this country from 1608 to 1991. See M. Watt Espy and John Ortiz Smykla. 1991. *Executions in the United States, 1608–1991: The Espy File.* [Data File]. Inter-University Consortium for Social and Political Research. Ann Arbor: University of Michigan.

22. Estimates of the base population in these historical periods were derived from census data. An estimated 4 million people were used in the calculations for the 1780s and an estimated 270 million for the 1990s.

23. See William E. Nelson. 1991. "Emerging Notions of Modern Criminal Law in the Revolutionary Era: An Historical Perspective." In Eric H. Monkkonen (ed.), *Crime and Justice in American History: The Colonies and Early Republic.* Volume 2. London: Meckler. Pages 429, 441.

24. Ibid. Page 438.

25. See Todd R. Clear and George F. Cole. 2000. *American Corrections.* 5th ed. Belmont, CA: Wadsworth. Page 42.

26. For the historical development of probation, see Edward J. Latessa and Harry E. Allen. 1999. *Corrections in the Community.* 2nd ed. Cincinnati, OH: Anderson Publishing. Pages 105–45.

27. U.S. Department of Justice. *Prisoners 1925–81.* Bureau of Justice Statistics. Bulletin NCJ-85861. Washington, D.C.: U.S. Government Printing Office.

28. We emphasize that our findings are based on reported incidents of executions rather than the actual level of executions in this historical period. As we have mentioned earlier, our estimates of the actual number of executions in any given country or time period are influenced by the availability of data (e.g., comprehensive and systematic data on all U.S. executions in the 1800s are not available) and the specific definition of executions that we employ in our analysis (e.g., are extrajudicial executions by civilian

groups counted as executions?). We use the Espy data only to give a general impression of what groups might be more predisposed to capital punishment.

29. C. Spear. 1844. *Essays on the Punishment of Death.* Boston: John Green. Pages 227–31. Cited in William J. Bowers. 1984. *Legal Homicide: Death as Punishment in America, 1864–1982.* Boston: Northeastern University Press. Page 140.

30. The penalty for rape by a white person of a black woman was further reduced to a fine and/or imprisonment at the discretion of the court. See William J. Bowers. 1984. *Legal Homicide: Death as Punishment in America, 1864–1982.* Boston: Northeastern University Press. Page 140.

31. See William J. Bowers. 1984. *Legal Homicide: Death as Punishment in America, 1864–1982.* Boston: Northeastern University Press. Page 54. The number of hidden or undocumented lynchings in the South appeared to be especially high from 1865 to 1875, a period in which whites, fearful of intervention by the federal government, often buried or burned the bodies of lynching victims. See George C. Wright. 1997. "By the Book: The Legal Execution of Kentucky Blacks." In W. Fitzhugh Brundage (ed.), *Under Sentence of Death: Lynchings in the South.* Chapel Hill: University of North Carolina Press. Page 250. As an illegal act, secret and unrecorded lynchings have also taken place in later decades as well.

32. In contrast to the inverse relationship between legal and extrajudicial executions displayed in Figure 4.4, James Massey and Martha Myers found no substantial relationships between lynchings, legal executions, and imprisonment rates for black males in Georgia from 1882 to 1935. These authors call for future research in other states and during longer time periods to better assess the relationship between different forms of social control. See James L. Massey and Martha A. Myers. 1989. "Patterns of Repressive Social Control in Post-Reconstruction Georgia, 1882–1935." *Social Forces* 68(2): 484.

33. See James M. Denham. 1997. *A Rogue's Paradise: Crime and Punishment in Antebellum Florida, 1821–1861.* Tuscaloosa: University of Alabama Press. Page 203.

34. Within this context, it is important to note that it has been estimated that anywhere between one-half and two-thirds of threatened lynchings in the early twentieth century failed, largely because of intervention by the authorities. See Larry J. Griffin, Paula Clark, and Joanne C. Sandburg. 1997. "Narrative and Event: Lynching and Historical Sociology." In W. Fitzhugh Brundage (ed.), *Under Sentence of Death: Lynchings in the South.* Chapel Hill: The University of North Carolina Press. Page 26. Such a reconsideration or at least temporal stoppage of lynchings because of the possible innocence of the accused or direct intervention by civil authorities appeared to be less common in the nineteenth century.

35. See William J. Bowers. 1984. *Legal Homicide: Death as Punishment in America, 1864–1982.* Boston: Northeastern University Press. Page 142.

36. For a discussion of these cases and other types of white-collar crimes, see Jay S. Albanese. 1995. *White Collar Crime in America.* Upper Saddle River, NJ: Prentice-Hall; David O. Friedrichs. 2004. *Trusted Criminals: White Collar Crime in Contemporary Society.* 2nd ed. Belmont, CA: Wadsworth.

37. RICO stands for racketeering influenced and corrupt organizations.

38. For a review of *qui tam* lawsuits as a way of controlling organizational misconduct, see Terance D. Miethe. 1999. *Whistleblowing at Work: Tough Choices in Exposing Fraud,*

Waste, and Abuse on the Job. Colorado Springs, CO: Westview Press. The original "false claims" laws were developed in the mid-1800s. Called "Lincoln laws" after Abraham Lincoln, they were used to punish individuals who were defrauding the government in the period of reconstruction after the Civil War.

39. See Sally S. Simpson. 2002. *Corporate Crime, Law, and Social Control.* New York: Cambridge University Press; Charles A. Moore. 1987. "Taming the Giant Corporation: Some Cautionary Remarks on the Deterrability of Corporate Crime." *Crime and Delinquency* 33: 379–402.

40. U.S. Department of Justice. 2003. *Prison and Jail Inmates at Midyear 2002.* Bureau of Justice Statistics. Bulletin NCJ-198877. Washington, D.C.: U.S. Government Printing Office. April 2003.

41. See Nils Christie. 2000. *Crime Control as Industry: Toward Gulags, Western Style.* 3rd ed. New York: Routledge.

42. It took until the late 1960s to find a period of U.S. history with more recorded homicides than occurred in the early and mid-1930s. See Terance D. Miethe and Wendy C. Regoeczi. 2004. *Rethinking Homicide: Exploring the Structure and Process Underlying Deadly Situations.* Cambridge, UK: Cambridge University Press.

43. See Roger E. Schwed. 1983. *Abolition and Capital Punishment.* New York: AMS Press. Page 94.

44. For a review of public opinion surveys on the death penalty, see Robert M. Bohm. 1991. "American Death Penalty Opinion, 1936–1986: A Critical Examination of the Gallup Polls." In Robert M. Bohm (ed.), *The Death Penalty in America: Current Research.* Cincinnati, OH: Anderson Publishing; Death Penalty Information Center. 2004. *Summaries of Recent Poll Findings.* See Death Penalty Information Center Web site: http://www.deathpenaltyinfo.org.

    It is important to note that the attack on the death penalty in the United States in the 1960s was directed at multiple issues and concerns. California Governor Edmund G. "Pat" Brown in a 1960 address to the California legislator captured some of the major concerns surrounding the death penalty in this time period with the following comment: "The death penalty is invoked too randomly, too irregularly, too unpredictably, and too tardily to be defended as an effective example warning away wrong-doers." Quoted from Bryan Vila and Cynthia Morris. 1997. *Capital Punishment in the United States: A Documentary History.* Westport, CT: Greenwood Press. Page 117.

45. See Bryan Vila and Cynthia Morris. 1997. *Capital Punishment in the United States: A Documentary History.* Westport, CT: Greenwood Press. Pages 140–1.

46. Ibid. Page 230; Gallup Poll Release. 6/30/00. Cited in Death Penalty Information Center. 2004. *Summaries of Recent Poll Findings.* See Death Penalty Information Center Web site: http://www.deathpenaltyinfo.org.

47. See Bureau of Justice Statistics. 2002. *Capital Punishment 2001.* Washington, D.C.: U.S. Department of Justice. December 2002. NCJ 197020.

48. According to Radzinowicz's historical account of criminal law, capital punishment was restricted to a few serious offenses (like murder, treason, rape, and burning dwelling-house) under the English Common Law, and only six capital statutes were enacted between the mid-1300s and the early 1500s. An additional thirty capital statutes were added over the next 150 years. During the period between the mid-1600s and the first

quarter of the 1800s, nearly 200 capital statutes were passed. See Sir Leon Radzinowicz. 1948. *A History of English Criminal Law and its Administration from 1750*. London: Stevens and Sons Limited. Pages 4–5.

49. Differences between the United States and other countries are not as dramatic when the results from international victimization surveys are compared. However, even in victimization surveys, U.S. residents are estimated to have higher levels of fear of crime and victimization by burglary, auto thefts, and physical assaults than most countries in these surveys. See Pat Mayhew and Jan J. M. van Dijk. 1997. *Criminal Victimization in Eleven Industrialized Countries: Key Findings from the 1996 International Crime Victimization Survey*. The Hague: Ministry of Justice; Jan J. M. van Dijk, Pat Mayhew, and Martin Killias. 1991. *Experiences of Crime Across the World: Key Findings from the 1989 International Crime Survey*. 2nd ed. Boston: Kluwer Law and Taxation Publishers.

Suggested Readings

William J. Bowers. 1984. *Legal Homicide: Death as Punishment in America, 1864–1982*. Boston: Northeastern University Press.

W. Fitzhugh Brundage. 1997. *Under Sentence of Death: Lynchings in the South*. Chapel Hill: University of North Carolina Press.

Kai Erickson. 1966. *Wayward Puritans*. New Haven, CT: Yale University Press.

Roger Lane. 1997. *Murder in America: A History*. Columbus: Ohio State University Press.

Eric H. Monkkonen. 1991. *Crime and Justice in American History: Historical Articles on the Origins and Evolution of American Criminal Justice. The Colonies and Early Republic*. Volumes 1 and 2. London: Meckler.

Frank Tannenbaum. 1938. *Crime and the Community*. Boston: Ginn and Company.

CHAPTER FIVE

The History of Punishment in China

China represents an interesting case study for a comparative historical analysis of punishment. As one of the earliest civilization in the world, China has passed through several distinctive periods including its successive historical classification as a primitive commune, a slave and feudal system, a semicolonial and semifeudal system, and a socialist country. The Chinese legal tradition is a mix of primarily traditional Confucian and Legalist ideas, and the contemporary Marxism–Leninism and Maoism of the socialist legal ideologies.

Throughout its long feudal history and the current socialist period, China has employed various types of punishment to maintain order, eliminate both internal and external threats to this order, and to facilitate social change. China stands out as an interesting context for social science research because this transitional society represents a fundamental paradox: Major social and legal reforms driven by the capitalist market economy are taking place within a traditionally Asian, moralistic, and communitarian society. In other words, how has China been able to maintain its long and steady history of social control in the face of a dramatically changing socioeconomic environment?

Our examination of economic, incapacitative, and corporal punishment in China begins with a general overview of its demographic and structural characteristics. This general profile is followed by a more detailed historical account of major societal changes and events that influenced the nature, prevalence, and justifications for different types of sanctions. The chapter concludes with a brief comparative analysis of social control and punishment in China and other Asian countries (e.g., Japan and Singapore) as well as other socialist countries (e.g., the former Soviet Union, Cuba).

OVERVIEW OF STRUCTURAL FEATURES

China's evolving history dates back to the early twenty-first century B.C. and spans over 4,000 years. For centuries, China stood as a leading civilization in the world in areas of the arts and sciences. Foreign invasions, civil unrest, and corrupt governments in the nineteenth and early twentieth centuries led China into a semicolonial and semifeudal society. Since 1949, China embarked on its socialist construction after Mao's People's Liberation Army defeated Jiang's Nationalist Army.

The country covers a landmass of over 9 million square kilometers, comparable in size to the United States. Its terrain is diverse with mostly mountains in Xinjiang; high plateaus in Tibet; deserts in the western provinces; and plains, deltas, and hills in the eastern regions. The climate covers a wide range, from tropical zones in the southern regions to subarctic conditions in northern parts of China.[1]

An estimated 1.3 billion people now legally reside in China. Its population is relatively homogeneous, with Han Chinese comprising about 92 percent of the population. Racial and ethnic minorities include Zhuang, Uighur, Hui, Yi, and Tibetan.[2] The disparate treatment of ethnic and religious minorities in China (e.g., Muslim Uighurs, Falun Gong) has been a recent concern of international human rights groups.

Economically, China is moving from a socialist central-planned economy to a more capitalist market-driven system. Since the economic reforms and advent of the open-door policy in 1978, China's per capita gross domestic product (GDP) has quadrupled. Despite representing one of the largest economies in the world (the United States is the largest), however, China remains a developing country with a per capita GDP of just $4,400 [USD].[3] As measures of the quality of life, China is ranked lower than developed countries in life expectancy at birth, educational attainment, disposable income, and purchasing power. However, its relative

---

CHINA'S STRUCTURAL PROFILE:

- Former leading civilization of the world
- Geographically diverse
- 1.3 billion residents
- Homogeneous population
- Low economic development
- Transitional economy from planned to market economy
- Growing disparity in class, gender, urban–rural, intellectuals and laborers
- One-party political system
- Executive, legislative, and judicial branches of government separate in function, but all led by the communist party
- Hierarchy of four-tiered court system
- "Socialist law" legal tradition
- Relatively low crime rates and levels of civil litigation

Source: Central Intelligence Agency (2003)

economic position to other countries has increased dramatically in recent decades.[4]

The economic reforms have been somewhat of a "mixed blessing" in China. In particular, the new economic reforms have enhanced the living standards for the Chinese significantly. However, these same reforms have further widened the gap between urban and rural, intellectuals and laborers, men and women, and rich and poor.[5]

China's political structure is organized as a unitary, multinational socialist country with thirty-one provinces, autonomous regions, and municipalities. Each of these geographical units is under the direct control of the central government, located in the capital city of Beijing. Members of three branches of government are either elected (e.g., legislators), appointed (e.g., judges), or elected and nominated (e.g., members of the executive branch). The Chinese Communist Party (CCP) is the leading political party. No substantial political opposition groups currently exist in China.[6]

Chinese courts are hierarchically structured at four levels, ranging from the highest to lowest courts. The Supreme People's Court handles cases of national importance and appeals brought from the Higher Courts. Higher People's Courts, which are found in each province and autonomous region and municipality, handle significant cases of initial jurisdiction (e.g., a high-ranking public official's corruption case that carries a death sentence) and appeals from lower courts. Intermediate People's Courts are similar to "district courts" in some Western societies (e.g., United States). They handle other major cases in the initial jurisdiction (e.g., murders, robberies) as well as appeals from the lower courts. Found in local jurisdictions, Primary People's Courts handle minor cases.[7]

The current Chinese legal tradition is socialist. Following the general principles of the civil law tradition in organizing its legal structure, the socialist legal tradition is guided by Marxist ideology. In contrast to elaborate systems of codification in other legal tradition, Chinese laws are codified only in principle. Its legal codes are brief, general, and succinct in nature. An inquisitorial system is preferred in fact-finding and trial, in contrast to an adversarial system in the common law tradition. Ideologically, laws are viewed as an instrument for the proletarian ruling class, and their primary functions are seen as repressive and coercive rather than conciliatory and restitutive.[8]

The Chinese socialist legal tradition represents to some extent a continuation of the feudal legal tradition of Confucianism and Legalism. Embedded in a communitarian and moralistic ideology, the traditional Chinese society denounced the role of law in promoting the goodness in society. Instead, law was used as a last resort when all other measures failed. Laws remained primarily penal in their orientation throughout much of Chinese history. The recent legal reforms associated with the changing economic system are viewed by some analysts as transforming the Chinese legal tradition from a socialist system that resembled the civilian tradition to a system that incorporates characteristics of a civil law tradition.[9]

Based on available national data on criminal offenses and victimization, China is often characterized as having low rates of serious crimes compared to other Asian countries (e.g., India, Singapore, Thailand) and Western developed countries (e.g., United States, England). Its level of civil litigation is also relatively low compared to Western developed countries. Crime rates in China, however, have increased dramatically in the past two decades.[10] As described in the next section, economic, incapacitative, and corporal punishment are some of the types of sanctions used to control crime and deviance throughout Chinese history.

HISTORICAL CONTEXT FOR SANCTIONS

Our historical review of various sanctions focuses on three periods of China's history: (1) the feudal tradition (from the earliest Chinese civilization until the mid-nineteenth century), (2) the semicolonial and semifeudal era (from the 1840s to the 1940s), and (3) the socialist period (from 1949 to the present). In each of these periods, major events that fundamentally changed the social structure are highlighted and their impact on social control and punishments are discussed.

THE FEUDAL TRADITION UP TO THE LATE QING DYNASTY

Similar to other civilizations in the world, China's early historical evolution is characterized by an initial primitive or tribal society (pre-1700 B.C.), a slave period (1700–221 B.C.),[11] and a long period of feudal dynasties (221 B.C.–1911 A.D.).[12] Discussions in this section cover the period from ancient China until 1840, before the Opium War in the late Qing Dynasty.

China's early history was widely characterized by periods of war, riots, and massive social and political change. The earliest available records indicate that the Shang Dynasty (1700–1027 B.C.) and the subsequent Zhou Dynasty (1027–771 B.C.) were slave-based societies, rooted in patriarchal and aristocratic orders.[13] The decline of the slavery system and the rise and fall of small kingdoms during the Spring–Autumn period (770–476 B.C.) caused enormous social unrest and upheaval. The feudal lords and the populace, with little political power and privilege in the patriarchal and aristocratic slave system, demanded social and legal reforms.

The subsequent Warring States period (475–221 B.C.) was even more turbulent, with numerous small kingdoms at war against each other. Shi Huang Di, First Emperor of the Qin Dynasty, conquered the six states, put an end to the independent and warring states that lasted for over 800 years, and founded the first centralized and autocratic feudal empire in China in 221 B.C.[14] The emperor promoted economic development through land reform, but he also maintained order through strict control of the populace by destroying their weapons and burning books thought to promote old aristocratic culture and ideas.[15]

TIMETABLE OF CHINESE DYNASTIES
* Primitive society: pre-1700 B.C.
* Slave society: 1700–221 B.C.
Shang Dynasty: 1700–1027 B.C.
Zhou Dynasty: 1027–771 B.C.
Spring–Autumn period: 770–476 B.C.
Warring States period: 475–221 B.C.
* Feudal society (221 B.C.–1911 A.D.)
Qin Dynasty (221–206 B.C.)
Western Han Dynasty (206 B.C.–24 A.D.)
Sui Dynasty (581–618)
Tang Dynasty (618–907)
Five Dynasties (907–960)
Ten States (902–979)
Song Dynasty (960–1279)
Yuan Dynasty (1279–1368)
Ming Dynasty (1368–1644)
Qing Dynasty (1644–1911)
Source: Bozan, Shao, and Hu (1981)

The subsequent feudal dynasties such as the Western Han (206 B.C.–24 A.D.) and the Sui Dynasty (581–618) continued to struggle with conflicts between nobles and peasants and to maintain a unified China.[16] The establishment of the Tang Dynasty in 618 marked the beginnings of the most prosperous and powerful period in feudal China.[17] The Tang Dynasty, along with the Song (960–1279), Yuan (1279–1368), Ming (1368–1644), and early centuries of the Qing Dynasty (1644–1911), continued land and taxation reforms, developing vital technical and production skills in areas as diverse as textiles, ship-building, manufacture of bronze mirrors, brocade and salt, porcelain, brasswork, mining, and handicrafts. Its influence and power extended to most of Asia and Europe.[18]

During this long historical period, Confucianism served as the dominant philosophy. Born in a time of chaos and moral decline (around 551 B.C.), Confucius advocated "*li*" (propriety) and "*ren*" (benevolence or humaneness) to regain control of order.[19] Rituals of major events in life (e.g., marriage, death) were enormously important to Confucius. By being careful and attentive in the observance and practice of rituals in these major life events, Confucius believed, individuals would be trained to abide by the broader conventions of public morality. *Ren* was crucial for individuals to understand the importance of rituals. In fact, the virtuous qualities embodied by *ren* went beyond merely being kind or compassionate to being loyal, upright, filial, and loving and respecting one's parents and the elderly.[20]

If individuals were taught to internalize the values of piety and benevolence (and were led by these virtuous beliefs), Confucius argued, people would abide by societal rules voluntarily. However, if individuals were led only by fear of punishment, they would obey the rules but not develop a sense of shame.[21] More importantly, good people, not good laws, were critical to Confucius in maintaining an orderly society.[22] Leading by exemplary behavior would be more effective than by rigid rules.

Emperors throughout the history of feudal China understood the power of the Confucian *li* to rule the country when it was peaceful and orderly, but they also needed the Legalists' concept of *fa* (stern punishment) to suppress crime and deviance, particularly during tumultuous and rebellious historical periods. The "Confucianization" of the legal system resulted in some of China's distinct and hallmark principles of punishment in the areas of differential treatment (e.g., public officials receive harsher punishment for failing to meet higher moral standards) and thought reform (e.g., Confucians were strong believers in the transformability of human behaviors through the change of thought).

For Confucian practices of thought control to be effective in generating conformity, strict controls of the body were also necessary. Such control over the body (e.g., control over population movement) was facilitated and accomplished in Imperial China in several ways. First, adult children, particularly sons, could not move far away from home while their elderly parents were still alive because this practice would violate the principle of filial piety, a central aspect of Confucian belief. Second, China was an agrarian state during feudalism. Individuals relied on land and farming to survive, further limiting their mobility. Third, during most periods of ancient China, there was an elaborate and bureaucratic network of the *Baojia* system, involving elements of a household registry, collective responsibility, and communal vigilance.[23] Within this system of *Baojia*, individuals and families were effectively controlled by the clan, the village, and the state, not only for economic reasons (i.e., taxation), but more importantly, for social-control purposes (i.e., crime prevention and mediation).[24]

The first comprehensive legal code was the Tang Code promulgated in the Tang Dynasty.[25] Criminal motivation, circumstances surrounding the case, the relationship between offender and victim, and the offender's and victim's status (e.g., a father vs. a son or a gentleman vs. a commoner) were all legal factors in sentencing. The Tang Code included special treatment for people of higher social standing (e.g., a son who beats a parent receives decapitation, irrespective of whether or not injury results, but a parent who beats a son receives no punishment unless the son dies)[26] and people with certain characteristics (e.g., being a minor and/or disabled were mitigating factors).[27]

Criminal cases under the Tang Code were channeled into the legal system by following a clearly defined process. Minor cases were tried by the lowest-level courts and typically sanctioned by beatings. More serious cases, punishable through penal servitude or exile, were processed in provincial courts. These cases were reviewed and confirmed by the governor's court and the Board of Punishments. Capital cases required the confirmation by three High Courts and the emperor.[28]

Inquisitorial proceedings were largely used in criminal investigation and trial. The responsibility for truth-finding was vested with the judicial officer (e.g., the police, the prosecutor, and the judge) and defendants shouldered the responsibility of proving their innocence. Confessions through physical torture were justified and legalized throughout most of this feudal era in China's history.

LEGAL STRUCTURE AND PUNISHMENTS IN FEUDAL CHINA:

* Penal codes with elaborated scales of crime and punishment.
* Judicial structure with courts of first instances and courts of appeals.
* Punishments transformed from body mutilation in earlier dynasties to infliction of pain by beating, penal servitude, life exile, and the death penalty.
* Monetary redemption (for both minor and serious crimes) popular in later dynasties to strengthen the state's economy.

Economic Punishment

Fines as a separate sanction for misconduct did not exist in China throughout its feudal period. Monetary redemption was provided under the Tang Code. However, fines would become more widely recognized as punishments in subsequent dynasties.[29] In earlier dynasties, the law on monetary redemption was specific and narrow. For example, monetary redemption was allowed only in cases involving accidental injury or death in the Tang Code, with the benefit paid directly to the family of the victim.[30]

Toward the later period of feudal China, monetary redemption was still primarily reserved for specific offenses (e.g., accidental killings) or special offenders (e.g., women, children under fifteen, and public officials). However, its scope was widened at this time to include anyone who could afford the payment.

Expanding the scope of monetary redemption in China's feudal period did not necessarily benefit the victim's family. Instead, monetary redemption became viewed more as a resource for the state. For example, money collected from criminals in the Ming Dynasty was used to stockpile goods for use in emergencies, to help finance the construction of Imperial palaces, and to help run government departments.[31]

The use of redemption also expanded in later dynasties to include a variety of other forms such as labor and goods. For the growth of redemption across different types of offenses, the Ming Dynasty came up with a tripartite classification of offenders based on their resources (i.e., those who have resources, those with some resources, and those with no resources). Rice was the preferred method of payment. However, for those who did not have rice but could offer money or labor, the amount of monetary payment or labor was calculated in equivalent units of grain for government storage. Offenders who did not have any resources would serve their punishment.[32] During harsh economic times, monetary redemption was required for all offenders who had the ability to pay.[33]

As a type of monetary redemption, asset forfeiture (in the amount of stolen property, or all property) was used in both minor crimes and serious offenses. For

---

A woman in the Qing Dynasty who forced several other women into prostitution was allowed to pay a redeeming fine for her sentence of military exile.

A public official in the Qing Dynasty, upon discovery of his son committing a capital offense, beat the son to death and secretly buried the body. The official was permitted to redeem the penalty of eighty blows with monetary payments and a three-degree reduction in official rank.

Source: Bodde and Morris (1973:214)

It was common in the late Qing Dynasty for household slave girls to be subject to cruel treatment by their masters through means of scalding water and fire and beating to death. The head of the household usually attributed the offense to his wife, who, under the shield of Confucian *li*, could redeem the punishment.

Source: Meijer (1980)

Civil law in the Qing Code stipulated that merchants must register with the local government; failing to do so would subject them to sixty blows and forfeiture of their profits.

Source: Brockeman (1980)

example, public officials guilty of misdeeds could have illegally acquired properties confiscated and their penalties converted to forfeiture of one year's salary. In the case of serious crimes like treason, the official or the military general might have all property confiscated in addition to other punishments (e.g., decapitation of the offender, death or exile of the entire family).[34]

Overall, however, economic sanctions were less emphasized and applied than corporal punishment during this period of ancient and Imperial China. The unique social and cultural conditions of the times (e.g., most peasants lived in poverty with little personal property to redeem their punishments) rendered monetary redemption less practical. The confiscation of property was thus primarily applied to serious offenses committed by the gentry class, military, and public officials. Aside from its immediate impact on the status of these individuals, asset forfeiture and other types of monetary redemption also served to minimize the possibility that offenders' offspring would ever regain prominence in the future.

Another reason for the limited use of monetary punishments in this period is more ideologically rooted. In particular, economic sanctions were not compatible with Confucian ideology that thought affects deeds, and that only the reformation of the thought could correct future deeds. More importantly, for righteous reasons, paying for one's wrongdoings was simply inconceivable in a Confucian society in which order was largely maintained by virtue, not by economic power.

Incapacitative Punishment

Incapacitative sanctions were codified as legal punishment starting in the Sui Code (581–3). Specific types of incapacitative sanctions (e.g., penal servitude, banishment or exile for life) were also contained in the legal codes of the Tang and Qing dynasties of Imperial China.[35]

Penal servitude in its early form included both hard labor and the removal of offenders from their place of origin for a fixed term of years. Offenders were typically sent to salt or iron mines in other provinces to perform hard labor in the Ming Dynasty. However, offenders in the Qing Dynasty remained in their location of residency to serve their sentence in the government post service.[36] Public incapacitation often involved the attachment of

An offender was given 100 blows from heavy bamboo and three years of penal servitude for manufacturing and selling gunpowder privately in the Qing Dynasty.

Source: Bodde and Morris (1973:279).

---

* During the Qing Dynasty, Li was sentenced to life exile for inciting shopkeepers to close their shops to petition the release of a fellow shopkeeper. The usual legal punishment was immediate decapitation for this offense, but because the strike was not completed (only eight out of 300 shops actually closed), the life exile sentence was given as a one-degree reduction from the legal punishment.

** In 1806, Liang, a treasury janitor, stole 299 silver taels from the provincial treasury. According to law, he should be punished with 100 blows of the heavy bamboo and banishment. Based on the same law, Liang's punishment could be exempted if the embezzled money was returned in a year, which he did.

Source:
* Bodde and Morris (1973:278)
** Fu-mei Chang Chen (1980:197)

offenders to some sort of restraining device such as iron chains or cangue (i.e., pillory or stocks). Throughout this period, penal servitude was often, but not always, used in combination with corporal punishment (e.g., flogging).

The punishment of "life exile" differs from penal servitude in that it involves permanent banishment of the offender from the community. Life exile was the most serious punishment other than the death penalty because of the social stigma and the harsh living conditions in the exiled land. Although all offenders sentenced with life exile would be forced to relocate, the distance of the place to be exiled was determined by a complicated scheme largely dependent on the severity of the offense. In previous dynasties, the wife was forced to accompany the husband in exile and military exile was the most severe form of banishment. Under the Qing Dynasty, these practices were abolished.[37]

Corporal Punishment

Corporal punishment had been for centuries the dominant sanction under the Chinese penal system because of its presumed deterrent value and cost-effectiveness for the state. Over the entirety of China's feudal period, corporal sanctions shifted from their early emphasis on bodily mutilation to punishments that inflicted severe physical pain without permanent disfigurement. Death sentences remained a lethal corporal punishment across China's history.

The earliest available legal documents revealed the codification of the Five Punishments for criminal wrongdoing in the Shang Dynasty (1700–1027 B.C.). These punishments included *mo* (permanent branding on the offender's face), *yi* (amputation of the offender's nose), *fei* (feet amputation), *gong* (amputation of a male's reproductive organ or locking a woman up for life), and *da pi* (the death penalty).[38] In the *Book of Historical Document* in Zhou (1027–221 B.C.), it was recorded that "the great punishments use armor and soldiers; the next lower level uses the ax (for executions). The medium punishments use knives and saws (for amputation); their next lower level uses awls and presses. The minor punishments use whips and rods."[39] These early punishments all involved some form of body mutilation, and nothing else.

> **THE FIVE PUNISHMENTS IN THE SHANG DYNASTY:**
> - Face tattooing
> - Nose amputation
> - Feet amputation
> - Castration
> - Death penalty
>
> *Source:* Fu (1996:57).

Body mutilation was gradually reduced in the Qin Dynasty (221–206 B.C.) because it was technologically possible and economically attractive to exploit convicts' labor for the state's economy. Qin convicts wore distinctive clothing, had their heads shaved, wore a tattoo, and might also have their nose or foot (or both feet) cut off.[40] However, the practice of body amputation also diminished out of humanitarian reasons. In 167 B.C., Emperor Wen abolished all mutilating punishments by remarking that "once a limb was cut off, it could not grow again."[41] In the Han Dynasty, beatings and wearing of foot irons replaced the amputation of the nose and feet. With the exception of body tattooing and the death penalty, other forms of physical amputation became rare after the Han Dynasty.[42]

As the "new" Five Punishments emerged, they were codified in the Sui Code (581–3) and continued with few modifications in subsequent dynasties. These new punishments included beating with a light stick, beating with a heavy stick, penal servitude, exile for life, and the death penalty.[43] The later dynasties clearly had moved away from bodily amputation to physical punishment. Beatings became the most prevalent way of inflicting pain without causing permanent damage to the body.

The nature and magnitude of the corporal punishment in this period depended primarily on the severity of the offense. In the case of flogging, for example, the severity of the offense could influence the number of lashes, the body part to be whipped (e.g., the back or the buttocks), and even the weight of the bamboo stick (i.e., large sticks inflict more severe punishment). In the Song Dynasty, beatings were widely used as a single

> **"NEW" FIVE PUNISHMENTS IN SUI CODE (581–618 A.D.)**
> - Beating with a light stick
> - Beating with a heavy stick
> - Penal servitude
> - Lifetime exile
> - Death penalty
>
> *Source:* Johnson (1979)

punishment for minor offenses such as thefts, public drunkenness, and disorderly conduct.[44] It could also be used as a supplementary punishment with penal servitude for more serious offenses.[45]

Beatings with a stick were the favored method of punishment in Imperial China because of the presumed deterrent effect on both the individual and the wider society. This punishment was swift, humiliating, and painful without necessarily leaving physical scars or permanent damage on the body. As a specific deterrent, recipients of beatings could still be rehabilitated and reintegrated back into society. Compared to a death sentence, it was even possible to consider beatings to be a more humane and benevolent punishment.

The death penalty was widely used throughout this period of Chinese history. Capital offenses included a wide range of violent crimes, property crimes, and offenses against the family. For example, the Ten Abominations were capital offenses under the Tang Code.[46] These offenses involved the most heinous offenses in feudal China, including acts against the emperor, the state, and the family, and those of great depravity.

Capital crimes against the emperor included not only plotting or carrying out a rebellion, but also incompetence or malpractice (e.g., failure of a physician or chef to follow proper formulas in preparing the emperor's medicine or meals). Such crimes against the state might include switching allegiance to a foreign ruler or killing a superior civil or military official.[47] Capital crimes against the family included behaviors inconsistent with Confucian teachings in filial piety such as beating, murdering, or lodging accusations against elderly family members, failure to provide elders with adequate support, and incest.[48] The official category of "depraved crimes" included the killing of three or more members of a household, dismembering or burning a body in the process of murder, and sorcery with special reference to gu poison[49] and other black magic.[50]

Other capital offenses in this period included bribery as well as more conventional violent and property crimes (e.g., murder, rape, robbery, theft, and arson).[51] During the period of rapid economic growth, the government was increasingly desirous of controlling economic offenses and employed especially stiff sanctions for illicit manufacturing and selling of government goods.[52] Similarly, toward the latter half of the Qing Dynasty, the government imposed tighter controls and harsher sanctions to confront internal conflicts and foreign invasions. The following cases illustrate the use of the death penalty within this context:

- During a strike for better wages in 1778, a sailor injured a lieutenant who was stationed to suppress any disturbances. The sailor was sentenced to immediate decapitation and his head was left exposed on the bank of the Grand Canal.[53]

- To appease foreign governments and maintain order, the Qing government apprehended eleven men and sentenced five of them to immediate decapitation and exposure of the head for the killing of seven American seamen aboard an American opium ship in 1817.[54]

- A total of seventeen defendants were convicted of the crime of premeditated murder for profit in the killing of thirteen French sailors and looting their $60,000 cargo in 1828. Among them, sixteen offenders were sentenced to immediate decapitation and exposure of the head. The principle offender was sentenced to death by slicing.[55]

Based on the surviving written records of legal codes, the major dynasties in feudal China differed widely in the number of legally proscribed capital offenses. The Tang Code stipulated a total of 233 capital offenses. The lethal method was strangulation for 144 offenses and decapitation for the remaining eighty-nine offenses. The Song Dynasty (960–1279 A.D.) retained all capital offenses from the Tang Dynasty and gradually added sixty other offenses, making a total of 293 capital offenses. The number of separate capital provisions then dropped dramatically to a low of 135 offenses in the Yuan Dynasty (1279–1368).[56] This sharp decline corresponds to the period of Mongol rule (e.g., Genghus Khan) and Mongolian customs that conflicted with the use of a formal legal code.[57] The number of separate capital codes increased again during the Ming Dynasty (1368–1644) and then skyrocketed to over 800 separate offenses in the Qing Dynasty (1644–1911).

NUMBER OF CAPITAL OFFENSES IN DYNASTIES OF FEUDAL CHINA:	
Tang (681–907 A.D.)	233
Song (960–1279)	293
Yuan (1279–1368)	135
Ming (1368–1644)	282
Qing (1644–1911)	813
Data Source: Bodde and Morris (1973)	

Decapitation and strangulation remained the major legal methods of execution. Strangulation under the Tang Code was applied to various crimes (e.g., logging a complaint with a magistrate against grandparents or parents, scheming to kidnap and sell a person into slavery, opening a coffin while desecrating a tomb).[58]

Strangulation, though more physically painful, was considered a less severe punishment than decapitation because of the Chinese belief that it would be disrespectful to the ancestors if a person died without having his or her body intact. Other methods of execution included slicing of the body, chopping the body into pieces (truncation), beating to death, and burning. These latter methods were legally accepted forms of executions in some dynasties but considered extralegal methods in other dynasties within this historical period.

LEGAL METHODS OF EXECUTION:
- Decapitation
- Strangulation

OTHER METHODS OF EXECUTION:
- Body Slicing
- Truncation
- Beating to Death
- Burning
- Poisoning

Regardless of the time period in feudal China, all death sentences were required to undergo a review process within the court system, and some were checked and personally approved by the emperor. During the Song Dynasty, it has been reported that capital offenders had a final opportunity to plead their innocence at the marketplace where the execution was to take place. Upon an offender proclaiming innocence in this context, a retrial had to be conducted, focusing exclusively on the facts of the case.[59]

NINETEENTH CENTURY AND EARLY TWENTIETH CENTURY (1840S TO THE 1940S)

During the last hundred years of rule under the Qing Dynasty, the government implemented a closed-door policy on international relations. It largely prohibited free trade, open diplomatic communication, and even the learning of new technological advances from Western European nations.

Eager to cash in on a newfound commodity (i.e., opium) and frustrated with the uncooperative attitude of the Qing government, the British government started the Opium War in 1840 to open up China's trade markets. What followed was similar inequitable treaties between China and the American, French, and Japanese governments that colonized parts of China.

A string of military defeats exposed the corrupt, incompetent, and isolated regime of the Qing government and "led to China's descent from the rarified heights of the Celestial Court to a terrestrial nadir as the 'Sick Man of Asia.'"[60]

In addition to external forces, the late Qing government also faced internal turmoil and social conflict. Although the Chinese population grew dramatically during this period, limited technological advances in farming and other areas of industry coupled with heavy taxation and corruption led millions of peasants to near-starvation in the late nineteenth century. The Taiping Tianguo Rebellion movement (1851–6) erupted largely from frustrated and idle peasants who roamed around the country as bandits.[61] Although ultimately suppressed by the Qing government, this movement inspired more revolutions to follow, such as the Boxer uprising (1899–1901), the 1911 revolution led by Sun that overturned the Qing government, and the May 4th movement that led to the communist revolution in the early twentieth century.

Between the 1850s and the 1940s, China was a "half feudal and half colony" society, characterized by foreign occupation and civil wars.[62] It experienced the fall of the last feudal dynasty (i.e., the Qing government), the rise and the fall of the Nationalist government, and the emerging communist revolution.

To respond to these social changes and the internal and external demands, a series of political, economic and legal reforms were undertaken by the Chinese government. These reform efforts included adopting European models of government, opening its borders, establishing more routine diplomatic exchanges, encouraging technological innovations, enacting new legal codes, and reforming the legal system.[63] More importantly for our purposes, the Chinese government drastically transformed its traditional penal system that had lasted for thousands of years.

The most profound change in punishment was the complete abolition of physical amputation in 1905. Practices such as tattooing, body amputation, beheading of the corpse, and the public display of heads

> **MAJOR GOVERNMENTS AND EVENTS, 1840–1949:**
>
> * Late Qing Dynasty (1840–1911):
>   Opium War (1840–2)
>   Second Opium War (1856–60)
>   Taiping Tianguo Rebellion (1851–6)
>   Sino-Japanese War (1894–5)
>   Boxer Rebellion (1899–1901)
> * The Nationalist Government (1911–49):
>   Bourgeois Revolution (1911)
>   Oppression of Imperialists and Warlords (1912–19)
>   Anti-Imperialist May 4th Movement (1919)
>
> *Source:* Bozan, Shao, and Hu (1981)

> Major forms of punishment in the Nationalist government (1911–49) included fines, incarceration, and the death penalty.

were banned. Beatings with bamboo were gradually replaced with fines.[64] In the 1908 new Penal Code, legal forms of punishment included only fines, incarceration, and the death penalty.[65]

Economic Sanctions

In the late Qing Dynasty, fining became even more popular as a way of collecting money to pay for demands that emanated from treaties with foreign governments. Judicial corruption became rampant in this period. Legal proceedings were extremely expedited when defendants could afford to bribe officials, whereas cases could drag on for years for those who could ill afford to pay the bribes.[66]

Since the turn of the twentieth century, fines were widely applied to criminals, particularly those who committed thefts and other petty crimes. National crime data in 1918 revealed that about a quarter of the convicted criminals (a total of 41,911) received fines.[67] Similar rates of fines were found in the capital city of Beiping (changed to Beijing after 1949) during this same time period. These criminals were primarily convicted of thefts, opium-related crimes, and gambling. Offenders who committed these minor offenses were typically lower-class citizens who were poor, idle, and ignorant of the law, based on official interpretations of the cause of their crimes.[68]

Corporal Punishment

Corporal punishment was officially abolished in 1908, with the exception of the death penalty. However, to respond to growing violence and disorder, the Yuan Shikai regime brought back beating with a bamboo stick as a legal punishment between 1914 and 1916. Because it was believed that rehabilitation alone might be insufficient to curb crime, beating was considered necessary to instill fear to deter criminals. Those criminals receiving a sentence of beating typically were given a set number of blows ranging from thirty to 120. Beatings were primarily decreed for petty offenses such as theft, moral offenses, and cheating, and only applied to criminals sentenced to short-term incarceration (e.g., less than three months).[69] To be consistent with the rules of modern prisons, medical officers were required to assess the criminal's physical condition and authorize the beatings.

In addition to the judicial sentence of beatings during this brief period of time, prison authorities were also authorized to use beating to discipline inmates and reinforce prison rules. Prisoners who exhibited unruly and aggressive behavior, uttered abusive language, failed to follow prison rules, and disrespected the authorities could all face beating. Other forms of punishment, such as reduction of food, were also widely practiced in prisons during this time period.

Historical records also show that the rate of death in custody was high. Aside from possible beating and brutality in prison, a sizable number of deaths in custody were the result of poor living conditions and inadequate medical care. For example, scrofula (tuberculosis) was linked to three deaths and twenty other medical problems in Beijing Number One prison in 1914. It was also recorded that thirty-four prisoners died for unspecified reasons in that year.[70]

The extent of the death penalty in practice is difficult to determine in the absence of national data. However, various records show that massive executions were carried out immediately after the Taiping Tianguo Rebellion.[71] The methods of execution included decapitation and slicing. On the atmosphere at the execution of twenty-four bandits in Canton in 1851, an eyewitness wrote the following harrowing account[72]:

> A habitual thief in 1915, failing to reform himself and demonstrating unruly behavior in prison, received thirty blows with bamboo sticks. The beating was authorized by prison officials.
>
> *Source:* Dikotter (2000)

> **THE TIENTSIN MASSACRE IN 1870:**
>
> In the late 1800s, many Chinese resented the white Christian missionaries flocking to China. Amid rumors that children were being abused, kidnapped, or used for witchcraft, a French charitable orphanage in Tientsin (spelled as Tianjin in standard Pinyin in the mainland China) was surrounded by angry Chinese. Upon being fired at by the French guards, the Chinese stormed the orphanage, killing eighteen foreigners, including a French consul and ten nuns. Fearing reprisal by the foreign government, the Qing government executed sixteen Chinese involved in the incident.
>
> *Source:* Available online at www.onwar.com/aced/chron/

In this lane, not larger than the deck of a hulk, and almost surrounded by dead brick walls, upwards of four hundred human beings have been put to death during the past eight months of the present year. It is fetid with the stench of decomposing heads, and rank with the streams raised by the hot sun from a soil saturated with human blood . . . . The first time I entered the place I found four bodies so left, lying in various attitudes as they had fallen, their heads near them, and two pigs moving among them, busily feeding in the pools of blood . . . at the distance of about seven yards, and facing this scene, a woman sat at the floor of one of the pottery workshops, affectionately tending a child on her knees, of one or two years old; both stared hard, not at a sight so common as pigs feeding among human bodies on human blood, but at the strangely-dressed foreigners.

When describing the execution process, this observer noted that, within three minutes, a single executioner had executed thirty three men with their knees down and head extended, pulled forward, and severed. The ringleader was then sliced with two cuts across the forehead, a cut on the left breast, cuts from the front of the thighs, and cuts across the body, and then decapitated, in four or five minutes.

After the fall of the Qing government and judicial reform in the 1910s, the recorded number of death sentences reduced drastically. For example, in the capital city in 1918, only six people among over 6,000 convicted criminals were sentenced to death.[73] Although relatively fewer criminals were judicially executed at the turn of the twentieth century, more than 1 million soldiers and civilians were killed through military tribunals, extrajudicial executions, and in both civil wars and wars against foreign intruders in this time period.

Incapacitative Punishment

The major transformation of the penal system in China during this period of civil unrest and social change was the introduction of a modern prison system and the re-articulation of humanity and education (the system of *gan hua*) in the treatment of the offenders.

Shen Jiaben (1840–1913), the appointed legal expert responsible for laying out the plan for prison reform in the late Qing Dynasty, drew up four principles to guide prison reform. First was the construction of model prisons. He envisioned that to effectively use limited financial resources, model prisons should first be set up in major cities and then spread down to the county level. Second, the training of prison personnel should emphasize discipline, education, and hygiene. Third, rules and regulations for modern prisons would be established, borrowing the best practices from other countries. The last principle involved the compilation of crime statistics using scientific methods.[74]

Grounded in Confucian teachings and exposed to Western ideas, Shen believed that ancient China and the modern West had at least one thing in common: the belief that reformation of criminals ought to be the primary goal of modern prison rather than the infliction of pain and humiliation.[75] Guided by these principles, Beijing Number One Prison opened in 1912. The new prison faced the challenge of housing a rising number of inmates as incarceration replaced corporal punishment as the primary punishment response for serious offenses.[76] For example, in the city of Beijing in 1918, about a third of the convicted criminals (2,153 offenders) received a prison sentence (while one-third received fines and the other third short jail sentences). Overcrowded and underfunded, the local prison nevertheless appeared to run largely in accordance with the reform ideals (i.e., different religious practices were tolerated; inmates were given individual attention; vocational training and moral education were daily routines; data on inmates and procedural matters were entered in prison logs; and punishment for violation of the prison rules primarily involved reproach, loss of pay, deprivation of the privileges of receiving visitors, exercise, reading, rationed food, and solitary confinement).[77]

Far from meeting the high expectations of humanitarian treatment and reform of offenders, however, a 1926 study found that Beijing Number One Prison was insufficient in providing education to successfully reintegrate inmates and offered little deterrence for habitual criminals. Others argue that the architectural design of the prison and the technology it used signified a shift of regime "away from conceptualizations centering on family-based criminality (in ancient China) toward the institutional surveillance and policing of the individual disciplinary subject."[78] In addition, prison violence and brutality, high death rates, and unsanitary conditions were constant reminders of the gap between the rhetoric and the reality of criminal justice reform efforts.[79]

SOCIALIST CHINA FROM 1949 TO THE TWENTY-FIRST CENTURY

Major changes in Chinese society after 1949 had profound effects on the nature and use of punishment. The post-1949 period is marked by two distinct developments: (1) the first thirty years of a socialist system with a state-planned economy and class struggle as its main political objectives, and (2) the post-1978 economic reforms that marked the transformation to a market economy and a more open political system operating under the framework of the rule of law.

Mao and his comrades established the People's Republic of China in 1949. The first thirty years of socialist China (1949–78) saw continued revolution and class struggle. Mao's political ideology was aimed at eliminating differentiations created under the feudal system (i.e., the rich and the poor, men and women, urbanites and peasants, and those who engage in labor and intellectual work) and bringing equality to contemporary Chinese society.

Under Mao's leadership, the communitarian value of self-sacrifice for the good of the community was promoted in this new China. The state-planned economy was the single dominant economic form. There was neither free market nor free trade. Major living necessities were rationed based on the number of people in a household, and housing, medical care, and educational opportunities were distributed through the workplace. Under these conditions, individuals and families were effectively managed and controlled within the community based on the traditional "household registration system," and at work because of their dependence on the government for their jobs and basic benefits.[80]

Following Mao's ideological positions about a "living law" and popular justice, China in this period had no formally codified body of law, few legal professionals, and no legally proscribed procedures.[81] People's Courts at various levels were merely political machines, in charge of carrying out political and party policies. Most cases were tried with summary judgment involving wide popular participation at trial and sentencing rallies. More serious cases were typically turned over to special revolutionary people's tribunals.

The lawlessness of popular justice was brought to a halt after 1978 when China officially embarked on nationwide economic reforms. The major themes of the Chinese economic reforms in the 1980s and the 1990s involved the transformation from the socialist state-planned economy to the market economy in both rural and urban sectors. The political leadership

---

MAJOR EVENTS IN CHINA, 1949 TO 2002:

* Socialist China under Mao (1949–78):

  Agrarian reform (1950)

  The Three Anti–Five Anti and Thought Reform Campaigns (1951)

  Great Leap Forward (1958)

  Cultural Revolution (1966–76)

  Popular justice and summary judgments in law

* Socialist China under reforms (1978 – present):

  Passage of criminal law in 1979

  Passage of criminal procedural law in 1979

  Revision of criminal procedural law in 1996

  Revision of criminal law in 1997

  Source: Bozan, Shao, and Hu (1981)

under Deng took several bold steps to transform China from a backward agricultural-based society into a modernized country in the areas of industry, agriculture, technology, and national defense.[82]

These economic reforms have had profound implications for Chinese society. Although the reforms have improved living standards and opened Chinese society to the outside world at an unprecedented rate, they have also created numerous social problems. These problems have included a growing number of the "floating population" (i.e., migrants), changes in cultural values from communitarianism that stresses self-sacrifice to individualism that glorifies materialism and individual success, a widening social disparity across different ethnic and religious groups, and surging crime rates.[83]

Economic Sanctions

The use of economic sanctions, particularly fines and asset forfeiture, varied dramatically during the socialist period. Although there were few legal stipulations and actual imposition of fines prior to the economic reforms in 1978, fines and other forms of economic sanctions have proliferated both in law and in practice since the reform.

No codified laws existed in the Mao era (1949–78). Instead, legal rules and regulations were made on an interim basis. Based on the 1956 Supreme People's Court summary, ten common punishments were applicable to criminals, including fines and confiscation of properties.[84] When used as a punishment, fines were most likely applied to minor offenses.

The use of fines as economic punishments was probably infrequent under Mao's rule because of the political climate at the time. Specifically, crimes were considered evil and a serious threat to the socialist society. Criminals were enemies of the entire proletarian class, and in this political climate it was inconceivable to allow offenders to pay for their evil acts.[85]

MAJOR ASPECTS OF CHINA'S LEGAL SYSTEM AND PUNISHMENT IN POST-MAO ERA:

* Legal codification proliferated after 1978.
* Legal system experienced a series of reforms.
* Dramatic increase in the number of offenses.
* Dramatic increase in offenses punishable by fines.
* Dramatic increase in capital offenses.
* Reform through labor and thought reform continue as major goals in Chinese corrections.
* Lethal injection in execution was legal after 1997.

NUMBER OF OFFENSES SUBJECT TO FINES IN CHINA OVER TIME:

Year	Number
1956	10
1979	20
1997	182

Source: Shaw (1998); Yu, Wang, and Ran (2003); Luo (1998)

* The highest-ranking governmental official, Cheng Kejie, was convicted of bribery in 2000 and sentenced to the death penalty, deprived of political rights, and had his entire personal property confiscated.
* A liquor manufacturer was convicted of manufacturing shoddy products and sentenced with a fine of $5,000 [USD], confiscation of $5,000 in profit from the sales, and compensation of $6,000 [USD] to the victim.
* Two defendants were convicted of child abduction, resulting in the death of the victim. The primary offender received the death penalty, deprived of political rights, and confiscation of $1,200 [USD] in personal property and the accomplice received ten years' imprisonment and a fine of $600 [USD].

Source: Judicial Document Selections of the People's Court, Zhejiang, (2000)

In contrast to fines, asset forfeiture was a major form of sanctions against landlords and the bourgeois class under the communist egalitarian principle. These economic punishments were also used in campaigns against corruption in this early period of the socialist China. For example, between 1959 and 1965, nearly 4,000 offenders were arrested for corruption-related offenses in Hubei province alone. Large amounts of money were recovered from these offenses.[86]

Since the beginning of the economic reforms of the late 1970s, fines and asset forfeiture have been stipulated in the criminal law for a growing number of offenses.[87] However, due to the traditional view that paying fines was "buying" freedom and contrary to socialist ideology, only a few criminal offenses (twenty articles out of about 100) were subject to fines based on the 1979 Criminal Law. The actual imposition of fines was even more rare.[88]

The further entrenchment into economic reforms has brought changes in China's views about crime and punishment. Economic sanctions have gained more recognition as an efficient way of disposing of criminal offenses. In fact, the revised Criminal Law in 1997 dramatically expanded the scope of fines and asset forfeiture. Under this law, about 50 percent of the criminal offenses (182 out of 375 articles) carry fines as part of the punishment. Numerous crimes, particularly instrumental crimes (e.g., property crimes, drug offenses, economic crimes, and corruption), have a legally stipulated punishment of fines and/or asset forfeiture. These punishments have been applied to major and minor offenses and the amount of fines diverges tremendously across cases.

Similar to patterns in Western countries like the United States, China in the past two decades has experienced a litigation "explosion." The number of civil litigations (i.e., lawsuits) in this time period has more than tripled, and the number of economic and administrative cases has increased by even a higher level.[89] Most of these lawsuits involve economic compensation or sanctions. The scope and magnitude of these sanctions is unprecedented.

Take, for instance, the following cases adjudicated in the People's Courts in recent years:

- In a malpractice lawsuit brought against a military hospital, the hospital was ordered to pay $12,000 [USD] to the victim.[90]

- In a wrongful use of one's image and slandering case, a television station was ordered to pay about $1,000 [USD] for damages and emotional distress suffered by the victim.[91]

- In a wrongful asset-freezing lawsuit, a local procuratory office was ordered to return $35,000 [USD] of the frozen currency to the plaintiff and pay $25,000 in financial losses as a result of the governmental action.[92]

- In a lawsuit involving copyright and patent right violations, an electrical company was ordered to apologize to and pay a research institute $12,000 [USD] for financial losses.[93]

- A nutrition company was sued in violation of the plaintiff's sole distributor agreement and was fined in the amount of about $250,000 [USD].[94]

NUMBER OF CIVIL CASES TRIED:	
1986	978,990
1990	1,849,728
1995	2,714,665
2000	3,418,481
NUMBER OF ECONOMIC CASES TRIED:	
1986	308,393
1990	598,317
1995	1,272,434
2000	1,315,405
NUMBER OF ADMINISTRATIVE CASES TRIED:	
1990	12,040
1995	51,370
2000	96,614

Source: Law Yearbook of China (1987–2001)

In other substantive areas, fines have traditionally been used as a tool to maintain order and to carry out certain governmental policies. For example, the one-child, family planning policy has been largely maintained by fines in the past three decades. According to the State Family Planning Commission, over $3 million in fines were assessed between 1985 and 1993 for children born outside family planning rules.[95] In large cities, the fine for violating family planning policy could be multiple times the couple's annual salary.[96] However, recently due to disparities in income and privatization of the economy, some argue that fines are no longer effective even in urban areas because more and more people are able to afford fines and work in the private sector.

> Parents are subject to fines if they have children outside the boundaries of the state family planning policy.

Fines have also been widely used to control the migrant population in recent years. Migrants who do not obtain temporary residency status (requiring a fee to register) may be fined and employers that hire workers who do not have a work permit are also subject to fines. Beijing has raised substantial amounts of money over the past decade through the imposition of fines relating to migrants.[97]

Migrants in China may be fined for not having appropriate residency registration cards and work permits.

Another area in which fines and other forms of economic sanctions have played a substantive role is the evolving regulation and sanctioning of computer-related crimes and Internet activities. For example, individuals and organizations are now subject to maximum fines of $600 and $2,000, respectively, for deliberately inputting a virus to damage a computer information system and for selling special safety-protection products for computer information systems without permission.[98] Owners of Internet cafés are subject to fines starting at $600 and forfeiture of their licenses if they offer sites featuring pornography, violence, gambling, superstitions, and other information harmful to government interests. The penalty for operating an Internet cafe without a license is a $4,000 fine and confiscation of computer equipment and income generated from the business.[99]

Businesses and individuals are subject to fines if they provide or access restricted Web sites (e.g., pornography, violence, gambling, superstitions).

Incapacitative Sanctions

Incapacitative punishments have long been a major form of sanctions in socialist China. While also changing with the current times in Chinese society, incapacitative sanctions have consistently focused on reform and education of offenders through thought reform and physical labor. As reflected in Mao's writings, the Chinese Communist Party considered it a historical mandate to reform criminals with the communist ideology to prepare their integration into the new China.

In the initial years of the socialist construction (1949–59), prison reform efforts primarily targeted prisoners of war, convicted criminals, bandits, gangsters, drug addicts, and prostitutes. Regarding these groups of people as evil and infected with the parasitic lifestyle and reactionary thoughts of the bourgeois class of the old society, the communist leadership tried to transform their minds through exposure to harsh environments (e.g., extreme cold or hot weather), hard labor, malnutrition, humiliating treatment, and physical torture to gradually cleanse their thoughts.[100]

Although it is difficult to obtain comprehensive data on the composition of prisoners and the relative severity of punishment in earlier periods of socialist China, Dikotter's analysis of 400 inmates detailed in a handwritten prison registry in the 1950s offers a glimpse into Chinese prisons under the communist rule.[101] It was recorded that about 30 percent of the prisoners in that particular prison facility were political prisoners, including military or government leaders left behind by the KMT (e.g., counterrevolutionaries, old-regime military and law enforcement officers, and members of secret societies). The remaining 70 percent of inmates were common criminals found guilty of corruption, theft, robbery, fraud, hooliganism, rape, murder, gambling, drug dealing, or sodomy. Most prisoners were serving over five years of imprisonment, nearly forty inmates served a life sentence, and four were on death row. More poor peasants and workers were serving life terms than landlords or rich peasants.

Compared to punishments in other countries, prison sentences were relatively long during the initial years of socialist China. The following examples illustrate this point:

- A postal worker in Beijing in 1957 was given seven years of incarceration for stealing a bicycle.

- A poor farmer was sentenced to ten years for stealing seven bicycles.

- A peasant in 1958 served twelve years in prison for stealing two pairs of trousers.

- A cadre in a public security office was given a fifteen-year sentence for stealing 700 Yuan (an average worker earned approximately 200–300 Yuan per year at the time).

- A college graduate working in a state bank was sentenced to twenty years for embezzling 3,000 Yuan.

- A man who caught his wife and another man in the act of committing adultery and killed both with a knife received a prison term of eleven years.[102]

Since the 1978 economic reforms, Chinese legal reform has been undergoing dramatic transformation. The first criminal law in socialist China was passed in 1979, which stipulated major forms of incapacitative sanctions. These punishments included supervision (i.e., offenders are subject to surveillance but are allowed to continue working and living in the community), house of detention (i.e., short-term incarceration in local jail between fifteen days and two years), reform through labor camp (i.e., offenders are forced to work in a remote farming area for a period of time, normally not exceeding three years), and prison (i.e., long-term incarceration in a state facility). For juvenile offenders, the work–study school and the juvenile reformatory are generally used for young offenders who committed minor offenses and serious offenses, respectively. Probation and community service are also available forms of sanctions during this period of time.

> **MANDATORY DRUG DETOXIFICATION PROGRAM:**
>
> Drug use reemerged in mainland China after 1980 due to its open-door policy and growing interaction with the outside world. To deal with the surging rates of drug use and drug-related crimes, the Chinese government mounted several campaigns, including the establishment of the compulsory detoxification and community drug rehabilitation camps. Hundreds and thousands of drug users were put into these rehabilitation camps for mandatory treatment. Those who fail the program and relapse are subsequently committed to long-term incarceration in labor camps.
>
> *Source:* Wang (1999)

Based on the 1997 Criminal Law, probation is applied only to offenders (1) who are sentenced with a short-term detention or less than three years of incarceration, (2) who are not a recidivist, and (3) who show remorse and pose little threat to society based on their actions and attitude.[103] The number of offenders who received probation relative to those who receive incarceration is unknown. However, based on provincial judicial reports, between 20 and 30 percent of convicted criminals received longer than five years of incarceration, life imprisonment, or death in recent years.[104] The remaining offenders received either short-term incarceration or probation.

Systematic annual data of incarceration rates (including those who are in the confinement of a labor camp and those who serve their sentence in prison) are not available. However, various sources reveal that China has had extremely low incarceration rates ranging from twenty-six per 100,000 in 1978 to 103 per 100,000 in 1995.[105]

The hallmark of the Chinese prison reform is productive labor and thought reform. Thought reform is both a process and a goal to achieve the ultimate reform of a criminal. Chinese philosophers and thinkers, both ancient and contemporary, generally believed in the goodness of human nature and the reformation of human behaviors. Confucius, in particular, believed that cultivating a sense of "shame" in the individual and letting virtue, not law, prevail would lead to a moral and orderly society.[106] Confucian shaming is engulfing because individuals in the context of conforming to collective norms are forced to lose individuality and independence.[107]

Thought reform in the socialist Chinese prisons largely followed this process of engulfing shame, through constant brainwashing, study sessions, criticism and self-criticism sessions with intense group and social pressure, and explicit and instant reward and punishment systems.[108] What differed in the socialist prison education program from previous practices was its content – that is, the communist political and ideological beliefs replaced the Confucian notion of virtue.

Productive labor is a major activity in prisons even though it is a secondary goal.[109] Several characteristics exist in reform through labor programs. For example, the program is modeled after military organizations and imposes stringent disciplinary requirements on offenders. Convicts engage in a variety of productive labor in groups, including working in factories, farms, and mining fields. Prison labor has recently contributed to the local economy significantly due to the increasing use of more technologically advanced tools within specialized factories.

Corporal Punishment

As China has moved toward modernization, corporal punishment for criminal behavior has been virtually eliminated in law.[110] The clear exception is the death penalty, which remains intact within socialist China.

The number of capital offenses stipulated in official decrees and criminal laws changed in the last half of the twentieth century. There were ten legally stipulated capital offenses in the early 1950s, increasing to twenty-eight capital offenses in 1979 (primarily counterrevolutionary offenses) and sixty-eight capital offenses in the revised 1997 Criminal Law (including major violent, property, economic, and corruption offenses).[111]

The growth in capital offenses in China in the last decade can be attributed primarily to the economic reforms and the consequential changes in political, social, and cultural institutions. The promotion of the market economy and the increasingly open-door policy facilitates a host of new activities, including criminal ones. During this transitional period, however, the new value system and subsequent development of informal control mechanisms have not yet been fully established to minimize value conflict and reduce criminal opportunities. Accordingly, China has used the evolving death penalty laws to deter both old forms of criminal behavior (like murder and theft) and newly emergent offenses (e.g., financial fraud and drug trafficking).

NUMBER OF LEGALLY STIPULATED CAPITAL OFFENSES IN CHINA:

Year	Number
1950	10
1979	28
1982	48
1990	60
1992	67
1995	75
1997	68

Source: Chen (1997)

The number of known executions in China has ranged between 1,000 and nearly 4,400 per year in the past two decades.[112] There is no uniform pattern in these executions over time (see Figure 5.1). For example, Amnesty International documented 1,791 executions in 1994, 4,367 executions in 1996, and 1,060 executions in 2002. The huge fluctuation in the number of state-sponsored executions might be the result of strike-hard campaigns that target certain groups of people and/or offenses in a specific time frame. For example, offenses such as train robbery, murder, causing explosions, drug trafficking, corruption, and religious cult practices have been at varying times the target of government crackdowns over the years, and the number of death penalty cases would be expected to increase in time periods of social threat.[113]

China appears to be developing more humane and less disfiguring methods of executing offenders. Although shooting with a single gunshot to the back of the head has been a long-standing legal practice, lethal injection was legalized in 1997 to provide an alternative means of execution. It was reported that lethal injection became a popular method of execution, especially in impoverished and inaccessible regions of southwestern China. For example, "mobile execution" vans are used in Yunnan province as facilities for conducting lethal injections. There are eighteen white-and-blue vans with flashing lights and sirens on their roofs and the word "court" on the sides. Death-row inmates are executed by lethal injection inside the van.[114]

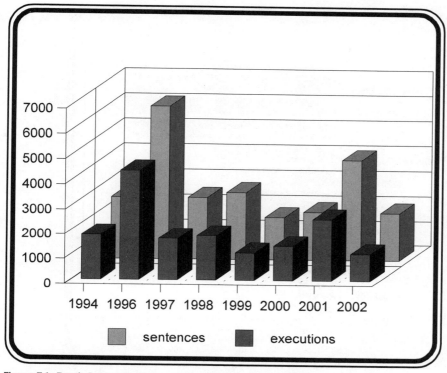

Figure 5.1. Death Sentences Given and Executions in Modern China
Data Source: Amnesty International Reports (1996–2002)

COMPARATIVE ANALYSIS WITH OTHER ASIAN AND SOCIALIST SOCIETIES

China is one of the oldest civilizations in the world. Its philosophies and religion have impacted many regions in Asia. The roots of Chinese punishments can be traced back to Confucianism, which gained immense popularity in Asian countries such as Japan and Singapore. Nonetheless, the socialist revolution based on Marxism provides China with a unique history among traditional Asian countries. The current Chinese legal system is a combination of the old (Asian culture), the new (the civil law and the popular justice approach), and an evolving legal context (i.e., a transformation from an inquisitorial to an adversarial system). The Chinese legal system has elements of both similarity and differences with other Asian and socialist legal systems.

The traditional Chinese legal system was paternalistic and inquisitorial, where legal "truth" was discovered by interrogators (e.g., law enforcement and

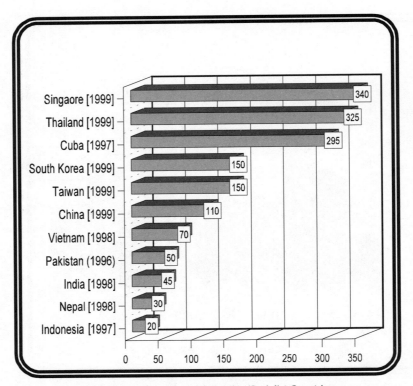

Figure 5.2. Prison Rates in China and Other Asian/Socialist Countries
Data Source: Walmsley (2000)

the presiding judicial officers). Ordinary citizens in the courtroom were afforded few rights. Torture was legally permitted for defendants and witnesses alike to extract confessions and corroborate testimony. Legal sanctions were harsh and typically involved corporal punishment.

Other legal systems in Asia share some of these characteristics. This is especially true of the emphasis on defendants' confessions (with little procedural safeguards) and the harshness of criminal sanctions (e.g., most Asian countries have retained the death penalty and use extrajudicial methods of social control).[115] However, differences across Asian cultures also exist in the use of corporal punishment. For example, Singapore still uses corporal punishment like flogging extensively and its execution rate is one of the highest in the world, whereas Japan rarely executes its offenders in recent years and most offenders are released without supervision by legal authorities immediately after their convictions. These practices are contrary to current trends in China. The estimated imprisonment rate in China is also lower than many Asian and socialist countries (see Figure 5.2).

The Chinese punishment system also has points of similarity and differences with its socialist counterparts. For example, popular participation is highly stressed in a socialist legal system. Similar to the People's Assessors in the Chinese judiciary, for example, the former Soviet Union employed a lay judge system to assist the professional judges in dispensing justice. Popular justice in socialist countries is intended to keep laws "alive" to reflect the wills of the populace and the changing conditions of the communist revolution.[116] China is also comparable to other socialist countries in that its legal sanctions are not only responsive to social threats, but they are also subject to the will of political leaders. When confronted with increasing social conflicts (e.g., political opposition) and surging crimes, more swift and severe sanctions that exceed legal limits are likely to be implemented. Such conditions characterize the "strike-hard" campaigns against crime and deviance in China in recent decades.

SUMMARY

This chapter reviews the historical developments of punishment in China. We classified the history of China into three major periods of time: the feudal, the semicolonial and semifeudal, and the socialist period. The major types of legal sanctions (i.e., economic sanctions, incapacitative sanctions, and corporal punishment) vary dramatically in these different historical periods.

Under a strong Confucian influence and constraints of socioeconomic conditions, no economic sanction was stipulated in laws in early times. Starting with the Tang Dynasty in the seventh century, monetary sanctions were legally permitted, but only as a redemption and not as a separate punishment. Through time, redemption by goods and services was permitted. The use of monetary fines as distinct punishments increased in the post-Mao era.

The primary forms of incapacitative sanctions during feudal China involved penal servitude (hard labor in a designated area) and life exile (permanent banishment). The first modern prison was established in the early 1900s. Although its incarceration rates have surged in recent years, the overall imprisonment rate in contemporary China remains in the middle range when compared with other Asian countries.

Lethal and nonlethal corporal punishment has been used throughout most of China's history. China uses capital punishment more than any other country in the world. Similar to other countries, it uses capital punishment and other legal sanctions for purposes of social control and the minimization of threats to the prevailing social order.

Notes

1. Central Intelligence Agency. 2003. *The World Factbook. China.* Washington, D.C. Web site location: www.odci.gov/cia/publications/factbook/geos/us.html.
2. Ibid.
3. Ibid.
4. Ibid.
5. John Knight and Lina Song. 2002. "Rural-Urban Divide: Economic Disparities in China." In Thomas Buoye et al. (eds.), *China: Adapting the Past, Confronting the Future.* Ann Arbor: University of Michigan Press. Pages 377–81; Margaret Y. K. Woo. 1994. "Chinese Women Workers: The Delicate Balance between Protection and Equality." In Christina K. Gilmartin et al. (eds.), *Engendering China: Women, Culture, and the State.* Cambridge, MA: Harvard University Press. Pages 279–98.
6. Central Intelligence Agency. 2003. *The World Factbook. China.* Washington, D.C. Web site location: www.odci.gov/cia/publications/factbook/geos/us.html.
7. Central Intelligence Agency. 2003. *The World Factbook. China.* Washington, D.C. Web site location: www.odci.gov/cia/publications/factbook/geos/cis/html.
8. Mao spoke about two types of social contradictions. For antagonistic contradictions between the people and the enemy, the exercise of proletarian dictatorship of repression or coercion was a must. Yet, persuasion and education should be the major means of solving the contradictions among the people. Within this framework, law (particularly criminal law) was viewed primarily as an oppressive measure of social control. See Harold M. Tanner. 1999. *Strike Hard!* Ithaca, NY: Cornell University Press. Pages 10–11.
9. See Albert H. Y. Chen. 1996. "The Developing Theory of Law and Market Economy in Contemporary China." In Wang Guiguo and Wei Zhenying (eds.), *Legal Developments in China: Market Economy and Law.* Hong Kong: Sweet & Maxwell. Pages 3–21.
10. See *Law Yearbook of China (1987–2003).* Beijing: Law Yearbook of China Publishing House.
11. This period involves several dynasties, including the Shang (1700–1027 B.C.), Zhou (1027–771 B.C.), Spring and Autumn (770–476 B.C.), and Warring States (475–221 B.C.).
12. This period includes Qin (221–206 B.C.), Han (206 B.C.–220 A.D.), Three Kingdoms (220–280), Jin (265–420), Southern and Northern Dynasties (420–589), Sui (581–618), Tang (618–907), Five Dynasties (907–960), Song (960–1279), Yuan (1279–1368), Ming (1368–1644), and Qing (1644–1911).
13. Shang and Zhou were a slave-based society in which offenders and prisoners of war could be sold and/or awarded to the nobles as slaves. Archeological evidence suggests that in the Shang Dynasty, hundreds of bodies were found in a single grave, obviously

buried as sacrifices to their master. Jian Bozan, Xunzheng Shao, and Hua Hu. 1981. *A Concise History of China.* Beijing: Foreign Language Press. Pages 9 and 13. "Patriarchal and aristocratic orders" refers to the hierarchical order in the society of Shang and Zhou. Patriarchal order required that the father be the head of the household and the right of succession fall on the eldest son. Aristocratic order established the superior status of the King, his royal kinship, and the class of the nobles over commoners and slaves.

14. Ibid.

15. Shi Huang Di replaced the system of private ownership of land by the nobles and replaced it by one of free trade in land. See ibid. Pages 20–5.

16. Ibid. Pages 45–6.

17. Ibid. Pages 47–50.

18. Ibid. Pages 55–84.

19. David Curtis Wright. 2001. *The History of China.* Westport, CT: Greenwood Press. Pages 20–4.

20. Heiner Roetz. 1993. *Confucian Ethics of the Axial Age.* Albany: State University of New York Press. Pages 123–45.

21. Derek Bodde and Clarence Morris. 1973. *Law in Imperial China.* Philadelphia: University of Pennsylvania Press. Pages 21–2.

22. Heiner Roetz. 1993. *Confucian Ethics of the Axial Age.* Albany: State University of New York Press. Pages 149–84.

23. Michael Dutton. 1992. *Policing and Punishment in China – From Patriarchy to "the People."* Cambridge, UK: Cambridge University Press. Pages 55–94.

24. The household registration system has lasted for centuries in China, encompassing not only the feudal society but also the Nationalist period, and into the socialist China. Although most commentators have argued that household registration was used for purposes of economic management and social control, others contend that household registration also helped pool resources, provide defense, and gain regional autonomy. See ibid. Page 64.

25. There were other codes of substantive and procedural rules throughout Imperial China. However, the Tang Code is the most widely known legal system at this time and thus is described here to illustrate the criminal justice system in Imperial China.

26. As another example of special treatment for high-status people, beatings could not be applied to people with certain ranks because it was considered degrading for the government. See Derek Bodde and Clarence Morris. 1973. *Law in Imperial China.* Philadelphia: University of Pennsylvania Press. Page 37.

27. Wallace Johnson. 1979. *The Tang Code.* Princeton, NJ: Princeton University Press. Pages 3–38.

28. Derek Bodde and Clarence Morris. 1973. *Law in Imperial China.* Philadelphia: University of Pennsylvania Press. Page 116.

29. As an example of economic sanctions in early times, men in the Zhou Dynasty who refused to go to war were subject to a fine. See Herrlee Glessner Creel. 1980. "Legal Institutions and Procedures during the Chou Dynasty." In Jerome Alan Cohen, R. Randle

Edwards, and Fu-mei Chang Chen (eds.), *Essays on China's Legal Tradition*. Princeton, NJ: Princeton University Press. Pages 26–55.

30. In order to redeem the punishment, the offender must pay the appropriate amount of copper to the victim's family. See Geoffrey MacCormack. 1990. *Traditional Chinese Penal Law*. Edinburgh, England: Edinburgh University Press. Page 105.

31. Ibid. Page 106.

32. Ibid. Pages 106–7.

33. Ibid.

34. Derek Bodde and Clarence Morris. 1973. *Law in Imperial China*. Philadelphia: University of Pennsylvania Press. Pages 79–80.

35. Ibid. Pages 76–7.

36. Geoffrey MacCormack. 1990. *Traditional Chinese Penal Law*. Edinburgh, England: Edinburgh University Press. Pages 100–5.

37. Ibid. Pages 103–5.

38. Zhengyuan Fu. 1996. *China's Legalists*. Armonk, NY: M. E. Sharpe. Pages 57–8.

39. Brian E. McKnight. 1992. *Law and Order in Sung China*. Cambridge, UK: Cambridge University Press. Page 329.

40. Ibid. Pages 330–1.

41. Geoffrey MacCormack. 1990. *Traditional Chinese Penal Law*. Edinburgh, England: Edinburgh University Press. Page 100.

42. Derek Bodde and Clarence Morris. 1973. *Law in Imperial China*. Philadelphia: University of Pennsylvania Press. Page 76.

43. Geoffrey MacCormack. 1990. *Traditional Chinese Penal Law*. Edinburgh, England: Edinburgh University Press. Page 100.

44. Brian E. McKnight. 1992. *Law and Order in Sung China*. Cambridge, UK: Cambridge University Press. Pages 338–43.

45. Ibid.

46. The Ten Abominations were regarded as the most heinous offenses in the Tang Dynasty and were separately listed from other offenses. The subsequent penal codes retained such stipulations. The Ten Abominations included plotting rebellion, plotting great sedition, plotting treason, contumacy, depravity, great irreverence, lack of filial piety, discord, unrighteousness, and incest. All crimes in this category were capital offenses (though the death sentence could be exempted with amnesties), and executions would be carried out immediately after the approval of the death penalty. See Wallace Johnson. 1979. *The Tang Code*. Princeton, NJ: Princeton University Press. Pages 17–22.

47. For example, thirty nine prominent officials were convicted of treason and executed in the aftermath of the largest peasant rebellion in the Tang Dynasty. The thirty-nine offenders were partisans initially trapped behind enemy lines who then accepted appointment to posts in the enemy's government. See Charles Benn. 2002. *Daily Life in Traditional China – The Tang Dynasty*. Westport, CT: Greenwood Press. Page 196.

48. Filial piety (*xiao*) was considered the "fundamental power on account of which the Chinese nation managed to persist continuously." It was the basic social duty and primary virtue in Chinese society. Filial piety generally refers to "a respectful and obliging attitude towards the elders of the family." More specifically, filial piety required respectful care of elderly family members (e.g., not making a long journey when the parents

are alive, caring for parents' physical and emotional well-being), obedience to parents and superiors (e.g., submission to the will of the elder family members), and moral vigilance when a son fulfills the wishes of the parents (e.g., be observant of the laws rather than unconditionally following the instruction of the parents). Heiner Roetz. 1993. *Confucian Ethics of the Axial Age*. Albany: State University of New York Press. Pages 43–52.

49. *Gu* poison was extracted from venomous creatures such as snakes, toads, scorpions, and spiders that were believed to be most noxious because of their survival in combat with other creatures. It was believed that the gu poison was extremely lethal, causing a victim to deteriorate, vomit blood, and die. See Charles Benn. 2002. *Daily Life in Traditional China – The Tang Dynasty*. Westport, CT: Greenwood Press. Page 197.

50. Other black magic includes cursing to cause misfortune and death, and stabbing the heart or nailing the eyes in a doll to inflict harm on the intended victim. See ibid. Pages 197 and 212.

51. See ibid. Pages 204–10; Brian E. McKnight. 1992. *Law and Order in Sung China*. Cambridge, UK: Cambridge University Press. Pages 82–109 and 469.

52. For example, 100 blows from heavy bamboo were applied for selling a single pound of illegal tea, and the death penalty was imposed on people who manufactured or sold twenty or more pounds of tea. Brian E. McKnight. 1992. *Law and Order in Sung China*. Cambridge, UK: Cambridge University Press. Pages 94–5.

53. The public display of the criminal's body parts (e.g., head) largely served as a deterrent to the general public and a further denunciation of the offender and the act. See Derek Bodde and Clarence Morris. 1973. *Law in Imperial China*. Philadelphia: University of Pennsylvania Press. Page 186.

54. R. Randle Edwards. 1980. "Ching Legal Jurisdiction over Foreigners." In Jerome A. Cohen, R. Randle Edwards, and Fu-mei Chang Chen (eds.), *Essays on China's Legal Tradition*. Princeton, NJ: Princeton University Press. Pages 222–69.

55. Ibid.

56. The Yuan Code was the first that codified death by slicing as a method of execution. Nine capital offenses were subject to this kind of execution. See Paul H. Chen. 1979. *Chinese Legal Tradition under the Mongols – The Code of 1291 as Reconstructed*. Princeton, NJ: Princeton University Press. Pages 42–3.

57. The low number of capital codes under the Yuan period does not necessarily mean that capital punishment was rarely used in this period. Although data on the actual number of legal and extrajudicial executions are unavailable for most of China's history, the Mongol reputation for harsh punishment would suggest that summary extrajudicial executions were extremely common in this time period. See Derek Bodde and Clarence Morris. 1973. *Law in Imperial China*. Philadelphia: University of Pennsylvania Press. Page 103. In contrast, other researchers have noted Mongolian rulers' lenient and cautious attitude toward punishment, suggesting that formal executions may have been relatively less prevalent in the Yuan period. Available records reinforce this alternative view in that there was a seventy- to eighty-year period during the Yuan Dynasty in which no executions were carried out. See Paul H. Chen. 1979. *Chinese Legal Tradition under the Mongols – The Code of 1291 as Reconstructed*. Princeton, NJ: Princeton University Press. Page 43–7.

58. See Charles Benn. 2002. *Daily Life in Traditional China – The Tang Dynasty*. Westport, CT: Greenwood Press. Pages 207–8.

59. Ichisada Miyazaki. 1980. "The Administration of Justice During the Sung Dynasty." In Jerome Alan Cohen, R. Randle Edwards, and Fu-mei Chang Chen (eds.), *Essays on China's Legal Tradition*. Princeton, NJ: Princeton University Press. Pages 56–75.

60. David Curtis Wright. 2001. *The History of China*. Westport, CT: Greenwood Press. Pages 102–5.

61. Ibid. Pages 107–10.

62. This view of China as "half feudal and half colony" is based primarily on the perspective of the government of the People's Republic of China.

63. David Curtis Wright. 2001. *The History of China*. Westport, CT: Greenwood Press. Pages 110–11.

64. Frank Dikotter. 2002. "The Promise of Repentance – Prison Reform in Modern China." *British Journal of Criminology* 42: 240–9.

65. Ibid.

66. For example, consider a 1898 case involving the repayment of a debt and accumulated interest. Upon taking bribes, the magistrate conducted a hearing the same afternoon the defendant was arrested and released the defendant the next day. See Kwan Man Bun. 2001. *The Salt Merchants of Tianjin – State-Making and Civil Society in Late Imperial China*. Honolulu: University of Hawaii Press. Pages 71–2.

67. For general and specific discussion of these crime data, see Frank Dikotter. 2000. "Crime and Punishment in Early Republican China: Beijing's First Model Prison, 1912–1922." *Late Imperial China* 21: 140–62.

68. Ibid.

69. Ibid.

70. Ibid.

71. The Taiping Rebellion represented one of the most destructive civil wars in Chinese history, killing 20 million or more people and nearly overthrowing the Qing government. See Derek Bodde and Clarence Morris. 1973. *Law in Imperial China*. Philadelphia: University of Pennsylvania Press. Pages 104–12.

72. Derek Bodde and Clarence Morris. 1973. *Law in Imperial China*. Philadelphia: University of Pennsylvania Press. Page 110.

73. Frank Dikotter. 2000. "Crime and Punishment in Early Republican China: Beijing's First Model Prison, 1912–1922." *Late Imperial China* 21: 140–62.

74. Frank Dikotter. 2002. *Crime, Punishment and the Prison in Modern China*. NY: Columbia University Press. Pages 43–52.

75. Frank Dikotter. 2000. "Crime and Punishment in Early Republican China: Beijing's First Model Prison, 1912–1922." *Late Imperial China* 21: 140–62.

76. Fines remained the primary punishment for minor offenses in the early twentieth century. See ibid.

77. Ibid.

78. Dutton argued that in ancient China punishment and control were primarily achieved through mutual policing and the involvement of the family. At the turn of the twentieth century, however, modernized prisons paralleled their design with Western military-like prisons. Individual isolation and discipline became the major

focus of prison protocols. See Michael Dutton. 1992. *Policing and Punishment in China – From Patriarchy to "the People."* Cambridge, UK: Cambridge University Press. Page 177.

79. Frank Dikotter. 2000. "Crime and Punishment in Early Republican China: Beijing's First Model Prison, 1912–1922." *Late Imperial China* 21: 140–62.

80. Victor Shaw. 1996. *Social Control in China.* Westport, CT.: Praeger.

81. C. W. Lo. 1995. *China's Legal Awakening.* Hong Kong: Hong Kong University Press.

82. The decade of the 1980s mainly saw reform efforts in the rural sector with privatization of the land and the responsibility system designed to stimulate agricultural productivity. In the 1990s, urban reforms became more widespread. These urban reforms followed the promotion of entrepreneurship in the 1980s and involved previously state-owned enterprises (e.g. policies on privatization of housing, pension, and medicare).

83. Dingjian Cai. 1997. "China's Major Reform in Criminal Law." *Columbia Journal of Asian Law* 11: 213–18; Dean G. Rojek. 2001. "Chinese Social Control: From Shaming and Reintegration to 'Getting Rich is Glorious.'" In J. Liu, L. Zhang, and S. Messner (eds.), *Crime and Social Control in a Changing China.* Westport, CT: Greenwood Press. Pages 89–104.

84. Victor N. Shaw. 1998. "Productive Labor and Thought Reform in Chinese Corrections: A Historical and Comparative Analysis." *The Prison Journal* 78: 186–211.

85. Zongquan Yu, Shuan Wang, and Rong Ran. Nov. 25, 2003. "On the Current Situation and Development of Fines." www.chinacourt.org.

86. Shuqin Zhong. 1995. *The Theory and Practice of Anti-Corruption in New China.* Beijing: China Procuratory Publishing House. Page 3.

87. The Chinese Criminal Law classifies punishments into two categories: main forms of punishment (including control, short-term detention, short-term incarceration, long-term incarceration, life imprisonment, and the death penalty) and supplementary punishment (including fines, deprival of political rights, and asset forfeiture). These supplementary punishments can also be used alone. See *Law Yearbook of China,* 1998. Criminal Law, Articles 33 and 34. Law Publishing House.

88. Zongquan Yu, Shuan Wang, and Rong Ran. Nov. 25, 2003. "On the Current Situation and Development of Fines." www.chinacourt.org.

89. *Law Yearbook of China,* 1987–2001. Law Publishing House.

90. *Judicial Document Selections of the People's Court.* Beijing. 2000. Law Publishing House. Pages 336–9.

91. Ibid. Pages 372–5.

92. *Judicial Document Selections of the People's Court.* Zhejiang. 2000. Law Publishing House. Pages 528–30.

93. *Judicial Document Selections of the People's Court.* Sichuan. 2000. Law Publishing House. Pages 696–703.

94. *Case Collections.* 1999. Beijing: The Chinese People's University Publishing House. Pages 170–5.

95. See U.S. Department of State. 1998. *China Country Report on Human Rights Practices for 1998: "Population Control"* at http://www.laogai.org/reports/stdept/sdpop.html.

96. Ibid.

97. For example, a total of $2,000 in fines were levied in 1993 on companies that employed workers without a residency card and/or work permit. In 1995, fines in the amount of $5,500 were collected in construction areas around eight public cemeteries in Beijing for violation of the regulation on housing rental by temporary workers. In 1997, Beijing levied fines worth about $500,000 on migrants for various violations (e.g., public sanitation, failing to register, working without a permit). See Human Rights in China. 2002, Nov. 6. Institutionalized Exclusion: The Tenuous Legal Status of Internal Migrants in China's Major Cities. Pages 53–79.

98. See David M. Lamb. 2003. "Regulations of the People's Republic of China on Protecting the Safety of Computer Information." Cited in *Cyber Crime: The Cyber Criminal Epidemic*. November 24, 2003 at http://www.geocities.com/chopshoptuning/paper.html.

99. Stephen Lawson. 2001. "China cracks down on internet cafes." CNN.com/sci-tech. April 19, 2001.

100. Jean Pasqualini. 1993. "Glimpses inside China's Gulag." *The China Quarterly* 134: 352–7. Other personal accounts documenting the gulag system under communist China include Pu Ning. 1994. *Red in Tooth and Claw: Twenty-Six Years in Communist Chinese Prisons*. New York: Grove Press; Harry Wu. 1994. *Bitter Winds: A Memoir of My Years in China's Gulag*. New York: John Wiley.

101. Frank Dikotter. 1997. "Crime and Punishment in Post-Liberation China: The Prisoners of a Beijing Gaol in the 1950s." *China Quarterly* 149: 147–59.

102. Ibid.

103. Gengsheng Mao. 1999. *Interpretation of the Chinese Criminal Law*. Beijing: Tong Xin Publishing House. Pages 144–51.

104. For example, 25.5 percent of the convicted criminals in Jiangxi province received severe sentences of more than five years in 2000; in Hebei province, the number was 24.6 percent in 2000. See *Law Yearbook of China*. 2001. Law Publishing House. Pages 811 and 871.

105. The estimated incarceration was 26 per 100,000 in 1978, 111 per 100,000 in the period between 1989 and 1992, and 103 per 100,000 in 1995. See George W. Crockett and Morris Gleicher. 1978. "Inside China's Prison." *Judicature* 61: 409–15; Marc Mauer. 1991. *American Behind Bars: A Comparison of International Rates of Incarceration*. Washington, D.C.: The Sentencing Project. Marc Mauer. 1992. *American Behind Bars: One Year Later*. Washington, D.C.: The Sentencing Project. David Biles. 1995. "Prisoners in Asia and the Pacific." *Overcrowded Times* 6(6): 5–6.

106. Heiner Roetz. 1993. *Confucian Ethics of the Axial Age*. Albany: State University of New York Press. Pages 165–84.

107. Scheff argued that secure social bonds that hold a society together involve a balance between closeness and distance – a bond that balances the needs of the individual and the needs of the group. It involves being able to maintain ties with others who are different from one's self. Where there is little differentiation in terms of the distance between individuals and other members of society, individuals are engulfed in such an environment because they must sacrifice their individuality for their loyalty to the group. See Thomas J. Scheff. 1990. *Microsociology: Discourse, Emotion, and Social Structure*. Chicago: University of Chicago Press. Page 4.

108. Michael R. Dutton. 1992. *Policing and Punishment in China – From Patriarchy to "the People."* Cambridge, UK: Cambridge University Press. Pages 308–18.

109. See Victor N. Shaw. 1998. "Productive Labor and Thought Reform in Chinese Corrections: A Historical and Comparative Analysis." *The Prison Journal* 78: 186–211.

110. In contrast to the formal law, human rights organizations have reported numerous instances of different types of corporal punishment in China in the last decade. These offenses involve police brutality and torture of prisoners, especially political dissidents and religious followers. Thus, nonlethal corporal punishment may be curtailed in theory but not necessarily in practice in contemporary China.

111. No documented number of capital offenses was available prior to 1979. Nevertheless, based on a number of published government decrees, we estimated about a dozen capital offenses may have existed between 1949 and 1978. See Stephen B. Davis. 1987. "The death penalty and legal reform in the PRC." *Journal of Chinese Law* 1: 303–34; Michael Palmer. 1996. "The People's Republic of China." In Peter Hodgkinson and Andrew Rutherford (eds.), *Capital Punishment – Global Issues and Prospects.* Winchester, UK: Waterside Press. Pages 111–12.

112. Amnesty International. 1996–2002. *Annual Reports: China.*

113. Although no number of death penalty cases is given in the annual reports by the courts published in *Law Yearbook of China* (1987–2001), the overall number of cases that received more than five years of incarceration (including life imprisonment and the death penalty) appears to be increasing over the years.

114. Straits Times. 2003. *China News Weekly.* Laogai Research Foundation. 05/05/03.

115. For example, Japan allows an extensive period of time for pre-charging and pretrial detention, stresses defendants' confessions, and ignores adequate legal representation, all in an effort to pursue societal justice. See Hong Lu and Terance D. Miethe. 2003. "Confessions and Criminal Case Disposition in China." *Law & Society Review* 37: 549–78.

116. For example, the Cuban legal system took the most drastic step by allowing lay judges to serve on the Supreme Court. See Marjorie S. Zatz. 1994. *Producing Legality – Law and Socialism in China.* New York: Routledge.

Suggested Readings

Derek Bodde and Clarence Morris. 1973. *Law in Imperial China.* Philadelphia: University of Pennsylvania Press.

Jerome A. Cohen, R. Randle Edwards, and Fu-mei Chang Chen (eds.). *Essays on China's Legal Tradition.* Princeton, NJ: Princeton University Press.

Frank Dikotter. 2002. *Crime, Punishment and the Prison in Modern China.* NY: Columbia University Press.

Michael Dutton. 1992. *Policing and Punishment in China – From Patriarchy to "the People."* Cambridge, UK: Cambridge University Press.

Wallace Johnson. 1979. *The Tang Code.* Princeton, NJ: Princeton University Press.

Yongping Liu. 1998. *Origins of Chinese Law – Penal and Administrative Law in Its Early Development*. Oxford, NY: Oxford University Press.

Geoffrey MacCormack. 1990. *Traditional Chinese Penal Law*. Edinburgh, England: Edinburgh University Press.

Brian E. McKnight. 1992. *Law and Order in Sung China*. Cambridge, UK: Cambridge University Press.

CHAPTER SIX

Punishment Under Islamic Law

Laws in many countries derive from religious tenets and principles. Confucian notions of filial piety and thought reform continue to influence the Chinese legal system. Biblical proscriptions in the Old Testament about the evils of murder, theft, adultery, and other sins are firmly entrenched in the case law and civil codes across Western Europe and the Americas. Hindu laws that were initially developed around 100 B.C. are still used in parts of India.[1] However, a recent historical pattern has been the growing separation of church and state. The clear exception to this secular trend involves the Islamic legal tradition and especially the resurgence of Islamic fundamentalism in several Muslim countries of the modern world.

This chapter examines the history and use of punishment under Islamic law. We begin with an overview of the nature of Islamic faith, its historical foundation, and variation in Islamic practices over time and place. Both substantive and procedural elements of the Islamic law and the allocation of criminal sanctions are discussed within the context of different types of wrongdoing (e.g., *Hudud, Qesas, Ta'azir* offenses). Saudi Arabia's practices in controlling crime and deviance are described as a case study of punishment under Islamic law. The chapter concludes with an examination of similarities and differences across Islamic countries in the nature and scope of sanctions and other mechanisms of social control.

OVERVIEW OF ISLAMIC FAITH AND LAW

The principles of Islamic faith derive from the teachings of the Prophet Muhammad, the messenger of Allah. The "Five Pillars of Islam" are faith (i.e, the belief that there is no god except Allah), prayer, alms-giving for the needy, fasting, and pilgrimage.[2] Muslims are obligated to care for all other creations of God and assume that all needs, benefits, and protections will be provided if everyone performs their duties properly. Islamic law is known as the *Shari'a* ("the path to follow") and it prescribes what should be done to those who neglect their duties, abandon their faith, or break the law of the community. However, different interpretations of Islamic law exist among different sects of Muslims in terms of when and how the law should be applied.

STRUCTURAL PROFILE OF ISLAM AND MUSLIMS:

- Islam is the second-largest religion in the world.
- There are over 1.2 billion Muslims in the world today.
- Muslims are found on all major continents.
- The *Qur'an* and the *Sunnah* of the Prophet Muhammad are the two primary sources of the basic corpus of Islam.
- Islam covers all aspects of human existence.
- Islamic practices and principles vary across different sects and schools of thought.

Islamic law involves codes of conduct based on Allah's commands that "have an existence independent of society imposed upon society from above."

Source: Goitein and Shemesh (1961:9)

When compared to Western legal traditions (e.g. common law, civil law), Islamic law is often viewed as relatively inflexible to changing social conditions in a society and as far more inclusive of all aspects of social and economic life of the individual. In fact, the *Shari'a* seeks to regulate the entirety of human existence, addressing such religious matters as religious ritual and prayer, fasting, alms-giving, and pilgrimages and extending its proscriptions and prescriptions to personal hygiene, diet, sexual conduct, responsibilities, and child- rearing, as well as the citizens' relationship to the ruler.[3] Some Muslim jurists contend that the solution to every contemporary problem is found in the texts of Islamic law. However, it is important to note that the Western notion of "hyperlexis" (i.e., the overextension of law in modern industrial societies) also suggests that legal attempts to regulate all aspects of social life are not exclusively reserved to Islamic legal systems.[4]

The content of Islamic law emanates from several different sources. The primary sources are the *Qur'an* (the Muslim Holy Book) and the *Sunnah* (Muhammad's traditions). Of the over 6,000 verses in the *Qur'an*, an estimated 200 verses in a broad sense deal with legal issues, including matters of family and civil law (seventy verses), penal law (thirty), international relations (twenty-five), legal jurisdiction and procedures (thirteen), economic and financial order (ten), and constitutional law (ten verses).[5] The *Sunnah* explains and clarifies the *Qur'an*. The *Qur'an* and the Prophet's *Sunnah* were the sole authority for Islamic law, government, and religion during the early stages of the development of Islam (i.e., before the death of Muhammad in 632 A.D.).

Depending on sectarian and denominational traditions, additional sources of Islamic law were recognized to resolve conflicting guidance in the *Qur'an* and *Sunnah*. These include the *Hadith* (Muhammad's sayings), *Ijma* (consensus), *Qiyas* (analogy), *Ijtihad* (independent judgment), *Istislah* (public good), *Ravayat* (Imams sayings), and *Urf* (custom or usage). For example, consensus by scholars or the community at large on a particular interpretation of the *Qur'an* and *Sunnah* became a source of law similar to the notion of precedent in common law systems. Both the passage of legislation and criminal penalties for actions and circumstances in which direct spiritual guidance was not available from the *Qur'an* were often justified on the authority of consensus. However, some sects of Islam (e.g. *Shi'a*) do not approve of consensus as a source of law or use a different definition of it. Other sects have closed the "gates of *ijtihad*," restricting the authority to find laws based on consensus.[6] Similarly, analogical reasoning (*qiyas*) provided jurists with a method to broaden an existing rule to similar situations. For example, some Islamic jurists have imposed the penalty of stoning for the crime of sodomy, reasoning that sodomy is similar to the offense of adultery and thus should be punished by the same penalty as dictated by the *Qur'an* for adultery.[7]

As a response to changing social conditions, several additional sources have been incorporated within the Islamic legal system. These include customs of a given area, the requirement of public interests and a jurist's preference for a rule other than the one normally followed to achieve an equitable result, and the emergence of non-*Shari'a* courts.[8] These alternative courts allow the ruler to administer law in the public interest. These rules involve criminal, commercial, and constitutional laws that were adopted from the pre-Islamic societies (e.g., Byzantines, Persians) and more recently from Western cultures.

Although Islam and Islamic law are not monolithic (because their local character is a reflection of the particular culture, customs, language, economic structure, and political ideology in the prevailing historical context), some fundamental features of this type of theocracy hold across different contents. Basic characteristics of *Shari'a* law include the following[9]:

- It is not given by a ruler but has been revealed by God.

- It has been amplified by leading Muslim jurists like Abu Hanafi, Shafi, and Malik in the respective legal schools.

- It remains valid whether recognized by the state or not.

- It originates not in customs and traditions but in divine revelations only.

- It is so comprehensive and all-embracing that it covers every aspect of a legal system – personal law, constitutional law, international law, criminal law, mercantile law, and so on.

- It is not in the nature of "should be" but lays down what the law is.

HISTORICAL DEVELOPMENT OF ISLAM AND ISLAMIC LAW

All legal systems, even those derived from divine revelations, are shaped by the prevailing social, political, and economic forces of the times. Accordingly, the development of Islam and the Islamic legal tradition is a reflection of particular historical patterns and events.

Islamic faith and law emerged from the region of the Middle East in the mid-seventh century and spread within the next several centuries to North Africa and Central Asia. There are an estimated 1.2 billion Muslims in the world's population today, residing in all major regions of the world. Muslims represent a majority of the population in over fifty countries.[10]

THE EARLY HISTORY OF ISLAM

Social order in pre-Islamic times in the region known as Arabia was based on family ties, customs, and traditions. This area was inhabited by nomadic tribes who traveled traditional circuits for worship and trade. Retaliation in the form of blood feuds within and between tribes was the primary response to personal injury. However, because of traditional notions of collective responsibility, feuds persisted over time as perpetual retaliatory acts against offended parties on both sides of the initial dispute.

During this time period, Mecca was the most important town in Arabia, serving as both a religious center for neighboring tribes and a major commercial center for local merchants to trade with the Byzantines and Persians.[11]

The Prophet Muhammad was born in Mecca in 570 A.D. as a member of the Quraysh tribe. When he was twenty-five years old, Muhammad acquired wealth and position through marriage to the widow of a rich merchant. After a short career as a trader, the Prophet is believed to have started receiving divine revelations at the age of forty, whereupon he began propagating his message of religious and social reforms.[12]

Many of the religious and moral precepts of the Prophet Muhammad were not well-received in Mecca because they conflicted with various pagan beliefs and prevailing economic interests.[13] In fact, the ruling families were especially fearful that this new religion would seriously harm Mecca's unique position as a center of pilgrimage and commerce. In the face of mounting and increasingly violent persecution, Muhammad and his followers left Mecca and eventually settled in Medina, a mainly agricultural community in western Arabia.[14] This migration to Medina in 622 A.D. (called the *hijra*) was a turning point for Muhammad and his followers and remains a major milestone as the beginning date of the Muslim calendar.

The migration to Medina was significant in the development of Islam and Islamic law in a variety of different ways. Through the support of local residents and Muhammad's growing power and prestige as an arbitrator to settle disputes and restore peace among rival Arab tribes, the Muslim community grew larger and was able to effect changes in prevailing practices. For example, through Muhammad's teachings and deeds, faith replaced blood as a social bond, thus allowing the suppression and control of the blood feuds customary in pre-Islamic Arabia by the alternative means of individual responsibility and arbitration.[15] During the Medina period, it has also been noted that the content of the messages in the *Qur'an* and *Sunnah* shifted toward specific political and legal norms, presumably because Muslims needed more detailed instruction and guidance when they had the freedom to develop their own institutions and apply the norms of their new religion.[16]

From the perspective of law and social control, Muhammad's settlement in Medina is important because of its implications for the subsequent development of a type of theocratic state. Specifically, religious doctrines became codes of conduct for its followers and the expression of political and legal norms. As the apostle who had divine authority, political authority that resonated with the tribal spokesman (*shaykh*) was now transferred under Islamic precepts to the Prophet and his successor.[17] Thus, the consolidation of the religious and political authority provided a unified front for purposes of social control and regulating all aspects of human existence.

Throughout the remaining ten years of his life after *hijra*, Muhammad concentrated on consolidating the Muslim community's influence over Medina and the surrounding Arab tribes. This was accomplished by agreements, contracts, tributes, and military force. The military might of the Muslims was ultimately revealed in the unopposed march into Mecca in 630 of Muhammad and his followers. By the time of his death in 632, Muhammad had established Muslim rule throughout Arabia and converted most of its population to Islam.

ISLAMIC RULE AND LAW, 632 A.D. TO THE MID-TWENTIETH CENTURY

The period following Muhammad's death and lasting through the mid-twentieth century marks a time of both increasing influence and decline in Islam. The first three centuries of Islam (seventh to ninth century) were an especially important period of expansion of Islam, involving the religious conversion of a wide diversity of ethnic and cultural groups. This was also the formative period of the Islamic legal system (*Shari'a*), as its divine principles and concepts were interpreted and applied in an evolving historical context characterized by major social, political, and economic changes. By the end of this period, Islam had spread to all major continents of the world. However, the power and nature of Islamic faith and law exhibited enormous variability across place and time during this long historical period.

The earliest successors to Muhammad as the religious and political head of the community (called the Caliphs or deputies) embarked on an enormous conquest of territory beyond the boundaries of Arabia and an expansion of Muslim rule in only a few decades. By the end of the Ummayyad Dynasty in 750 A.D., the Muslim empire was firmly entrenched throughout the Middle East (including the states and territories of Syria, Palestine, Iraq, Persia [Iran], Egypt, and Turkey), and had reached as far west as Spain and to northern India in the east. Territorial expansion continued under the 'Abbasid Dynasty (750–1258), during which time the capital of the Muslim empire transferred from Damascus (Syria) to Baghdad (Iraq). It was during the 'Abbasid dynasty that the "Golden Age" of Arabic science, mathematics, medicine, and theology developed and flourished.[18]

It is important to note that the social and political conditions surrounding the expanding Muslim empire during this period are the very types of external forces that pose a severe threat to social order. The problem with social order was exacerbated by the enormous ethnic and cultural differences of those conquered, the existence of prevailing governments and laws in many of these lands that derived from ancient and sophisticated civilizations, and class struggles rooted in Arab hegemony over non-Arab Muslims.

The primary solution to social order in the early Muslim empire in the face of unparalleled diversity involved a process of consolidation and assimilation called Islamization. From this perspective, disparate groups became a coherent and integrated Islamic "whole" through the adoption and adaption of pre-Islamic norms and institutions of both Arab and non-Arab segments of the Muslim population.[19] Although its immediate acceptance was hampered by entrenched cultural traditions and the social conditions of the times (e.g., limited transportation, limited communication technology), the process of Islamization of the diverse groups was paramount for maintenance of social order and providing a means for the social control of dissent. For the believers of Islam, the *Shari'a* provides "the path to follow" for a morally proper life and establishes the appropriate boundaries of conduct and the procedural rules to determine when they are violated and what should be done to the offender. It is the totality of the reach of Islam in all aspects of life that provides its power as a mechanism of social control and as a source of unity for disparate groups.

The substantive content of the *Shari'a* are the legal norms that existed in the *Qur'an,* the *Sunnah,* traditions of the earliest Muslims, and customary practices. These principles and ideas were developed into a systematic and coherent legal system in the mid-eighth century. Variation in schools of Islamic jurisprudence evolved from the work of early jurists working in different regions of the expanding Muslim empire.[20] This variation is important because it illustrates the variety of Islamic practices across different regions. However, the basic principles underlying the *Shari'a* have remained relatively unchanged since its inception.

As a forum for dispute resolution and enforcing administrative regulations, the rules of evidence and procedural safeguards associated with *Shari'a* justice have been viewed at various times as being too cumbersome, rigid, or inflexible for meeting the challenges of a changing world. In fact, the growth of criminal and commercial matters and "public interests" in the modernizing and industrial world of the nineteenth century and beyond required greater legal flexibility than traditional Islamic jurisprudence could provide.[21]

The response to this threat to the pervasiveness of Islamic law involved the application of doctrines that allowed secular rulers and judges to administer law in the public interest in *non-Shari'a* courts, as long as they do not contradict the principles of the *Shari'a*. Secular law in the areas of criminal misconduct, commercial regulations, and constitutional protections was initially derived from the practices of pre-Islamic predecessors (e.g., laws of the Byzantine Empire). The civil codes of Western Europe (especially France and Germany) were also widely used as the basis for the development of a more comprehensive and responsive legal system in the Muslim world.

THE RESURGENCE OF ISLAMIC FUNDAMENTALISM IN THE TWENTIETH CENTURY

Throughout the history of Islam, there has been an uneasy marriage between theory and practice of the *Shari'a* law. As early as the eighth century, it was apparent to legal scholars that "*Shari'a* law had come into being a doctrinal system independent of and essentially opposed to current legal practice."[22]

The schism between the state authorities (e.g., amirs, military commanders, civil governor, other political officials) and the religious authorities has grown through time, but the ties between them have never been completely severed. This is the case because of the mutual dependence of the respective parties. Specifically, jurists are obligated by the *Qur'an* to acknowledge the unity of the Islamic state (and by implication the necessity of an effective head-of-state), whereas rulers always have to make some outward deference to *Shari'a* to mobilize and motivate public support for them.[23] For much of the history of Islam, as long as the sacred law (*Shari'a*) received formal recognition as the religious ideal, the law did not have to be fully applied in practice.[24]

The gap between the universal application of *Shari'a* in theory and its actual use in practice varies across time, place, and substantive area. For example, the strongest union of theory and practice of Islamic law appeared to be in Medina during and shortly after Muhammad's life. *Shari'a* courts were also central among the early 'Abbasid rulers, but they never attained the position of a supreme judicial authority independent of political control.[25] Given the relative attention to these topics in the *Qur'an*, it is unsurprising that the theory and practice of *Shari'a* are most consistent in the areas of family law and inheritance. Since the late nineteenth century and as a result of encroachment of European legal traditions, many of the areas of criminal law and commerce in Muslim countries that relate to the relationship between individuals and the state have increasingly fallen within the domain of secular codes, secular authority, and adjudication in non-*Shari'a* courts.

Over the last half of the twentieth century, however, there has been a precipitous rise in Islamic identity and the resurgence of *Shari'a* justice within many Muslim countries. The rise in different forms of Islamic fundamentalism and reformism is directly tied to the growth of Western social problems in Muslim countries (e.g, rising crime rates, growing economic inequality), primarily Western multinational penetration in the economic domain and daily social lives of Muslims, and the ethnocentric views of diverse and competing cultures.

The most dramatic examples of modern Islamic resurgence include the overthrow of the existing secular or semisecular governments and the subsequent establishment of Islamic states in Pakistan and Iran. The rise in power of the Taliban in Afghanistan is another contemporary example of the rejection of Western ideas in the Muslim world and a return to the basic beliefs and practices of Islam. Recent episodes of national and international terrorism (e.g., the "9/11" attacks on America by members of Al-Qaeda) and the calls for *jihad* (a holy war) are the latest manifestations of cultural conflicts between various Muslim factions and the Western world.

SOCIAL CONTROL IN ISLAMIC SOCIETIES

As a "path to follow," the *Shari'a* provides a clear and comprehensive "road map" for living a pure spiritual life as a Muslim. It is both prescriptive and proscriptive, covering all of the most basic elements of human existence. For its most ardent believers, Islam serves as an absolutely ubiquitous mechanism of social control. It offers its righteous followers on the Day of Judgment an eternal life of heavenly bliss and unwavering physical pleasure (e.g., soft cushions, rich food, soothing drinks, voluptuous virgins), a world in sharp contrast to the meager and dismal living conditions of the nomads of the Arabian desert. For violators of its sacred rules of conduct, the traditional Islamic law provides a clear message of swift and severe punishment (e.g., amputation, death by stoning, beheading) and the lingering fear of eternal damnation through Allah's almighty power.

Islam is similar to other religions in its offering of a code of conduct or path of righteousness for its followers. For example, comparable living creeds are found within Christianity, Judaism, Buddhism, and Confucianism. There is also variation in theory and practices within each of these alternative religious or belief systems, similar to the sects and schools of Islam. Ultimately, the effectiveness of Islam or any other religion as a mechanism of social control depends on the extent to which it is internalized by its followers and implemented in practice.

Of the areas covered within the Islamic system, the most attention in the Western world has focused on the criminal law and punishments under the *Shari'a*. The general characteristics of Islamic criminal law, criminal procedures, and legal punishments are described below.

PUNISHMENTS UNDER ISLAMIC LAW: THEIR PURPOSE AND NATURE

Punishment in pre-Islamic Arabia was based primarily on the principle of retaliation (*lex talionis*). Lacking a state or central authority in nomadic and tribal life to regulate conflict and disputes, punishment for wrongdoing was privately dispensed by the victim and affiliates such as extended family or patron tribes. However, because of the nature of communal life and strong kinship solidarity, there was also collective responsibility for any serious misconduct committed by a clan member.

Under these conditions of private wrongs and collective responsibility, the normative mechanism of exacting revenge involved retaliatory attacks against both the offender and his extended kinship group and tribe. Such retaliatory acts and blood vengeance evolved largely into a sacred duty and became a fundamental aspect of pre-Islamic culture.[26] The pursuit of full and complete retaliation was also responsible for the continuation of the perpetual interclan and intertribal feuds within the region.

Through Allah's divine revelations to Muhammad and the teachings of the Prophet, Islam provided an alternative to the punishment of blood vengeance. This alternative was the acceptance of "blood money" (*diyya*). The principles of how each clan or subdivision of the community was responsible for the collection of its members' blood money were laid out in "the Constitution of Medina," whereas Muhammad's doctrines about bodily resurrection and life after death provided the spiritual basis for the acceptance of blood money over blood vengeance.[27] Because God will severely punish the wrong-doer on Judgment Day, exact revenge will ultimately be achieved through eternal Hell. With revenge satisfied through eternal damnation, the value of blood money as punishment for wrongdoing is that it provides some financial restitution to meet the immediate worldly needs of victims and their families.

Given its basis in a religion that covers all aspects of human existence, it should come as no surprise that Islamic law has evolved into a comprehensive legal tradition. Within the domain of criminal law, the *Shari'a* covers issues of public safety (e.g., the protection of individuals from physical attacks and public insults), the family (e.g., the protection of the stability of the family structure by punishing sexual activity outside of marriage), property (e.g., its protection against theft, destruction, or unauthorized interference), and state and religion (e.g., the protection of both against subversive activity).[28] As forbidden acts against God and/or the society, offenses within this domain are treated with widespread condemnation and severe punishment. The overall severity of the Islamic penal code is the product of its historical roots in the extremely harsh, hostile, and violent tribal societies of seventh-century Arabia.[29]

> Islamic criminal law covers wrongdoing in the areas of public safety, family relations, property and its illegal acquisition, and subversive activities against the state and religion.

Similar to other legal traditions, various purposes and philosophies underlie punishment within Islamic law (*Shari'a*). These include retribution, restorative justice, rehabilitation or reformation, and deterrence (both specific and general deterrence). The multiple purposes of Islamic criminal law are reflected in the nature and magnitude of the different types of punishments for crimes and forbidden behavior under the *Qur'an*. The three major types of crimes and punishments in Islamic law are *Hudud* (i.e., offenses against God), *Qesas* (i.e., private wrongs involving personal injury), and *Ta'azir* (i.e., offenses whose punishment is not fixed by the *Qur'an* or the *Sunnah*).

Hudud Offenses

The obvious connection between Islamic faith and Islamic law is found in the nature and punishment of *Hudud* offenses. These offenses are acts against God and their prosecution is initiated by the state. *Hudud* penalties are decreed by God: They are absolute, universal, nonnegotiable, and unpardonable – even under the sentiments of mercy.[30] There are seven *Hudud* offenses: apostasy (i.e., the voluntary renunciation of Islam), extramarital sexual activity (e.g., adultery, fornication), defamation (i.e., false accusations), theft, highway robbery, rebellion (e.g., efforts to overthrow the leader of the Islamic state), and use of alcohol.

As summarized in Table 6.1 and described below, *Hudud* punishments are mandatory for these offenses when particular circumstances are present. There are also specific rules of evidence and proof requirements for convictions for these crimes. Much of the Western criticism and outrage concerning the severity and rigidity of Islamic law is often based on an incomplete understanding of the substantive and procedural law surrounding *Hudud* crimes.

APOSTASY. Muslims who voluntarily convert to another faith, worship idols, or reject the tenets of Islam are punishable by death under the offense of apostasy. This severe penalty is imposed for such offenses because the abandonment of Islam constitutes "high treason."[31] Under its classification as a *hadd*, males are beheaded for apostasy while females are imprisoned until they renounce their alternative views and return to Islam. These *Hudud* punishments for apostasy are mandatory for all violators.

Before a death sentence is imposed for apostasy, males convicted of this offense will usually be given a several-day "grace period" to reconsider their position. Religious officials will visit the apostate and attempt to persuade him to return to Islam. If these efforts fail, he is then executed by beheading. Apostates who voluntarily denounce Islam and escape to non-Muslim states are considered "legally dead," thereby forfeiting all of their property to their Muslim heirs.[32]

The spiritual authority for the *hadd* punishment for apostasy is clearly specified in the *Qur'an* and the *Sunnah*. The adverse and eternal consequences of apostasy (*ridda*) are revealed in the *Qur'an's* tenet "And if any of you turn back from their faith and die in unbelief, their works will bear no fruit in this life and in the Hereafter; they will be companions of the Fire and will abide therein" (2:217). A passage in the *Hadith* is more direct: "whoever changes his religion, kill him." As with most other *Hudud* offenses, two witnesses or confessions are required for a conviction of apostasy.[33]

ADULTERY AND FORNICATION. Extramarital sexual activity (*zina*) is severely punished under Islamic law. *Hudud* punishments are restricted to adultery

TABLE 6.1: *Hudud* crimes and punishments

Offense description	Mandatory punishment
Apostasy: The voluntary renunciation of Islam by a Muslim who converts to another faith, worships idols, or rejects any of the tenets of Islam by word, deed, or omission.	Death by beheading for males and imprisonment until repentance for females.
Adultery and fornication: Sexual intercourse outside of the right to it arising from marriage or the ownership of a female slave.	Married person: Stoning to death. Unmarried person: 100 lashes. *Maliki* school also imposes 1 year in prison or exile for unmarried males in these acts.
Defamation: Acts include false accusations of illicit fornication, impugning the legitimacy of a woman's child, or launching charges against a male spouse.	80 lashes for a free person and 40 lashes for a slave.
Theft: The taking away of the personal property of another without the owner's permission while it is located in a secure place. The property must have a minimum value. Some items (like perishable food, birds, musical instruments for idle amusement) are not subject to *hadd* punishments.	Amputation of hand at wrist by an authorized doctor (1st offense). Amputation of second hand (2nd offense). Foot amputation at ankle or imprisonment until repentance (3rd offense).
Highway robbery: The taking away of personal property of another by violence or intimidation.	Death by beheading when robbery results in homicide. Cross-limb amputations when no homicide occurs. Imprisonment until repentance if arrested before commission.
Rebellion: The intentional, forceful overthrow or attempted overthrow of the legitimate leader (*imam*) of the Islamic state.	Death if rebels fight and are captured. *Ta'azir* (discretionary punishments to be determined by the judge) if they surrendered or are arrested.
Use of alcohol: Drinking wine or other intoxicating beverages.	80 lashes if a free person, 40 lashes for such persons in the *Shafi'i* school. 40 lashes for slaves.

and fornication. However, analogical reasoning (*qiyas*) has been used by some Islamic jurists to justify giving sodomy the same penalty as dictated by the *Qur'an* for adultery.[34]

The nature of the mandatory penalties for sex offenses varies by the defendant's status and the Islamic school that it followed within the jurisdiction. Married persons who commit *zina* offenses must be stoned to death, whereas unmarried persons must receive 100 lashes for these offenses.[35] Under the *Maliki* school of Islam, married violators of these sex offenses must be flogged before lethal stoning and unmarried persons are exiled after being whipped.[36] The severe punishments for adultery and fornication derive from their direct threat to the principles of family life, marriage, and communalism under Islam.

> "The fornicator sought easy pleasure without regard for *Shari'a* so he is made to suffer pain in order to recover his senses. . . . By pulling the self to pain, when it succumbs to prohibited pleasure, he reestablishes a certain equilibrium and avoids recklessness and folly."
> Ustadh Mahmoud's justification for the *hadd* punishment of 100 lashes for fornication by an unmarried male.
>
> *Source:* An-Na'im (1990:114)

Accusations of extramarital sexual activities are not taken lightly under Islamic law. For *Hudud* punishments to be applicable to these offenses, the *Qur'an* requires four male eyewitnesses or four confessions on four separate occasions in court proceedings to sustain a conviction.[37] The individuals must have been witnesses to the actual act of intercourse. Individuals who make legal allegations of *zina* offenses but are unable to present the required number of witnesses are themselves subject to punishment for defamation. Thus, although the punishment for these types of sex offenses is indeed harsh, the strict evidentiary requirements for proof of *zina* offenses and the adverse consequences for accusers who are unable to substantiate their claims serve to diminish the frequency of such cases in the *Shari'a* courts.

DEFAMATION. *Hudud* punishments for defamation are restricted to false accusations about adultery, sexual abnormality, defamation of a married Muslim, or making unfounded claims about the "illegitimate" birth of a woman's child. Unsubstantiated claims of sexual promiscuity and births out of wedlock deserve severe punishment under Islamic law to protect the individual and the society from the harm caused by the public humiliation of the victims of these allegations. As God's agent, the state initiates the prosecutions for these types of false accusations.

For persons convicted of making false accusations, the penalty is flogging. Unsupported accusations of adultery are punished with eighty lashes if the false statements are made by a free person. Slaves receive only forty lashes for the same offense. Given Muslim customs about dress and the exposure of the body, persons convicted of defamation are lightly clothed when they are whipped. Special conditions also apply to how the whipping is done (e.g., it is inflicted by scholars well-versed in Islamic law; blows are spread over the body but not to the head or face; males are flogged while standing and women are seated; the whipping should not lacerate the skin).[38]

THEFT. A great deal of public commentary has focused on the *Hudud* punishment of limb amputation for theft. However, whether this punishment must be given for theft offenses depends on the nature of the offense itself. For those convicted under the *hadd* for theft, the punishment must be amputation of the hand at the wrist (for first-time offenders), amputation of the second hand (for second-time offenders), and either foot amputation or imprisonment until repentance for third offenses.

As a punishment for crimes of theft, hand amputation has historical, symbolic, and practical significance in a number of different respects. Specifically, hand amputation of thieves epitomizes the historical law of retaliation (*lex talionis*), serves as a visible deterrent to others of the costs of misconduct, and has strong religious connotations in the *Qur'an's* description of the Last Day of Judgment (i.e., "each individual is handed his or her record book in either the right or left hand...the right [associated with] goodness and purity, the left with evil and pollution").[39] Under an Islamic concept of deterrence, meting out severe punishment for the "minor" crime of theft provides a clear signal to potential offenders that the spiritual community will not tolerate even seemingly trivial crimes.[40]

The types of thefts punishable by the *Hudud* penalty of amputation are very restrictive in their scope. For example, the stolen goods must be of some specified value (e.g., greater than 10 dirhams [75 U.S. cents]) and the property must have been under the full protective custody of the owner in a secure place. The property must have also been taken in a secret manner. Discretionary punishments (*Ta'azir*), rather than mandatory penalties (*Hudud*), are assigned to various special thefts, including the stealing of immovables (e.g., land, buildings), items available in large quantities (like wood, hay, grains), objects not usually subject to ownership (e.g., wild birds and fish), perishables (e.g., meat, eggs), and property deemed of no value (e.g., pork, alcohol).[41] For these types of thefts, the punishment of hand amputation may or may not be assigned upon conviction.

HIGHWAY ROBBERY. Persons who take the property of others through force or intimidation are punished by amputation, exile, or execution.[42] The specific punishment depends on the nature of the offense (e.g., robbery with murder is a capital crime) and the offender's prior record. The severe punishment for robbery rests on its threat to public order by disrupting commerce and creating fear among travelers.

Beheading and the subsequent display of the body in a crucifixion-like form is the punishment for bandits who murder and plunder. Cross-limb amputation (i.e., right hand and left foot) is the punishment for the first offense of robbery. Subsequent offenses require amputation of the remaining limbs. A judge (*qadi*) has the authority to impose an additional penalty of banishment for robbery. Banishment in this context is interpreted to mean imprisonment, internal exile, or expulsion of noncitizens from the state.[43] A pardon for banditry (but not the offenses associated with it) is also possible when the offender voluntarily surrenders and repents.

REBELLION. Armed rebellion against the Muslim state is mentioned as a separate *hadd* offense in some treatises on Islamic jurisdictions.[44] This act of rebellion (*baghi*) is viewed as a "war against Allah and His Messenger."[45] The nature of the punishment for rebels depends on the particular circumstances. For example, insurgents who are killed during the course of the uprising are said to be punished by *Hudud*. A similar situation exists for those who fight against the Islamic state and are captured – they are executed under the *hadd* penalty. Discretionary punishments in the form of *Ta'azir* penalties, however, are applied to rebels who surrender. Rebels are absolved from guilt when their allegations possess merit and the *imam* (the legitimate spiritual leader) has deviated from Islamic principles.[46]

INTOXICATION. Drinking wine or other intoxicating beverages is considered a *hadd* offense punishable by flogging even though neither the *Qur'an* nor *Sunnah* prescribed a specific punishment for this offense.[47] Alcohol use is generally condemned in Islamic law because of its perceived association with indolence, impairment of judgment, and the subsequent inattention to religious duties.

Although all alcoholic beverages are prohibited in most Islamic schools of jurisprudence, the *Hanafis* school restricts this prohibition only to drinks made from grapes, allowing consumption of other alcoholic beverages "until they cause intoxication."[48] Similar to principles in Western law, Muslims are not punished for the condition of being an alcoholic or drug addict. However, such persons under Islam are denied a place in Heaven as idol worshipers.[49]

> The use of drugs like marijuana is also subject to flogging (whipping) in Islamic law. Based on analogical reasoning about their adverse impact on public harm, use of these drugs is said to require the same criminal sanctions as alcohol use.

Qesas Offenses

Another class of crimes in Islamic law involve lethal acts against the person (homicide) and nonlethal offenses against the body (e.g., assaults, maiming). Contrary to *Hudud* acts against God, these *Qesas* offenses are "private wrongs" against the person.[50] Criminal prosecution for these offenses is initiated by the victim or heirs. Similar to most *Hudud* penalties, conviction for *Qesas* offenses requires two witnesses or confessions in open court. However, they differ from mandatory *Hudud* penalties in that victims or their closest kin have the right to choose between inflicting the prescribed penalty, accepting compensation (*diyya*), or even pardoning the offender.

MURDER. The most serious crime against the person in Islam is murder. The penalty for the intentional killing of another is death unless compensation (*diyya*) is demanded by the victim's family or they pardon the offender. The eternal and worldly damnation of murder is vividly and clearly expressed in the *Qur'an*, and the granting of compensation or other remission for the offender's sins is considered a onetime concession of a merciful God.[51] Possible penalties for intentional murder are death through retaliation by the victim's family, compensation of money or property to the victim's heirs, forfeiture of inheritance, or a pardon. No fixed monetary amount is established for compensation in the primary religious texts for Islamic law. However, the *Qur'an* does make reference to granting "any reasonable demand," and Allah is said to reward individuals who pardon an offender.[52]

Islamic law recognizes degrees of murder and manslaughter based on criminal intent, derivable from the circumstances of the offense and the choice of weapon used in the crime. Accordingly, willful or deliberate killings are those involving weapons or instruments that are considered lethal (e.g., clubs, sharp stones, fire). Voluntary manslaughters, in contrast, are unintentional killings through instruments not recognized as a lethal weapon. Criminal penalties for manslaughter include religious expiation (i.e., atonement by acts such as fasting, giving alms to the poor, the freeing of slaves) and the payment of blood money (*diyya*).[53] *Qesas* offenses involving lethal injuries also include accidental killings through mistakes, misadventure, or causing a lethal chain of events (e.g., opening a dam that ultimately drowns people). Punishments for these lethal offenses include any or all of the following: fines, exclusion from inheritance, religious expiation, or pardons.

NONLETHAL BODILY HARM. The retributive philosophy of "an eye for an eye" forms the basis of punishment for many *Qesas* offenses involving bodily injury. The *Qur'an* and *Sunnah* provide clear religious justification for seeking retaliatory equivalence for acts involving serious, permanent injury or disfigurement to the victim. Sporadic accounts of limb amputations, the surgical removal of an eye, and the severing of other body parts (e.g., ears, teeth, tongues, sexual organs) have been reported across the Muslim world as retaliatory punishments for comparable bodily injuries.

> Islamic criminal law allows for the payment of compensation (*diyya*) for crimes against the person that result in death or bodily injuries. *Diyya* is paid in camels or the equivalent amount of sheep, cattle, gold, or silver.
>
> *Source:* Siddiqi (1979:156–7)

As true of lethal harm, victims may demand compensation for their nonlethal physical injuries. Islamic jurists (judges) generally agree on a schedule of compensation that specifies the value of a human life and of various bodily parts.[54] The Western notion of "pain and suffering" as grounds for further compensation is not generally used within the context of Islamic law.[55]

Ta'azir Offenses

The remaining class of criminal acts under Islamic criminal law is called *Ta'azir* offenses. These crimes include all offenses for which the *Shari'a* has not proscribed a specific penalty. Offenses within this category are considered criminal acts because they threaten at least one of the five essential guarantees of Islam – the practice of religion, the development of the mind, the right to procreation, the right to personal security, and the possession of property and wealth.[56] Whereas *Hudud* and *Qesas* punishments are guided by retributive principles, the primary rationale for *Ta'azir* punishments is to reform and rehabilitate the offender. However, this goal of rehabilitation must be accomplished within the context of preserving social tranquility and public order in the community.

For purposes of maintaining and protecting the public welfare, *Shari'a* judges (*qadis*) are given wide discretionary authority in the local prosecution and punishment of *Ta'azir* crimes. This discretion is exercised within the range of acceptable punishments allowable in the *Qur'an*. For example, the *Qur'an* may specify imprisonment as the penalty for repeated minor offenses, but the local *qadi* has the discretion to impose any prison sentence of a duration between one day and life as long as it does not exceed the *hadd* punishment. For convictions for embezzlement, the appropriate penalty may vary from public disclosure and stigmatization to fines. Wide judicial discretion is also permitted in the number of lashes given as *Ta'azir* punishments. Some, but not all, Islamic jurists contend that *Ta'azir* punishment is null and voided when an offender repents and clearly demonstrates an adherence to Islam.[57]

Although there are various types of conduct that fall under the general category of *Ta'azir* offenses, there are several contexts in which these offenses are most prevalent. In particular, *Ta'azir* punishments are usually imposed in the following four circumstances:

- Acts that do not meet the technical requirements of *Hudud* or *Qesas* (e.g., thefts of property of insufficient value to qualify as a *hadd* offense, attempted but incompleted acts of adultery or assault).

- Offenses normally punished by *Hudud* but that in practice are often punished by *Ta'azir* because of extenuating circumstances (e.g., theft among relatives) or weak evidentiary proof (e.g., insufficient number of witnesses at trial). In theory, the *Shari'a* judge must convict or acquit the offender on the original *Hudud* charge.

- Acts condemned in the *Qur'an* and *Sunnah* or contrary to the public welfare that are not subject to *Hudud* or *Qesas* punishments. These offenses include the consumption of pork; usury; breach of trust by a public official; false testimony; bribery; contempt of court; and misleading the public through sorcery, fortune-telling, astrology, and palmistry.

■ Acts that violate Islamic norms such as obscenity, provocative dress, or a wife's refusal to obey her husband.[58]

When inflicting *Ta'azir* punishments, the judge considers the gravity of the offense and the moral character of the criminal. Following Muhammad's *hadith* or saying "forgive the mistakes of people of good rank," judges in these offenses are clearly allowed to impose less severe penalties or even dismiss charges for respectable people of honorable backgrounds. It is not uncommon for judges to pardon the *Ta'azir* offenses of the virtuous person and provide a severe punishment for the same offense committed by those of lesser social or religious standing.

PROCEDURAL RULES AND EVIDENTIARY REQUIREMENTS

All legal systems have procedural rules and evidentiary requirements that guide the application of the substantive law. Within most legal traditions, a fundamental guiding principle is that law should be applied uniformly to individuals regardless of religious or economic status. There are, however, several notable exceptions to this principle in Islamic law. For example, slaves and women in Islamic societies are not granted full legal protection under this equality principle, and they have little or no legal standing as witnesses in most cases. Similarly, non-Muslims are subject to the same criminal law as Muslims (except for the *Hudud* penalties for drinking, fornication, apostasy, and defamation because they are nonbelievers), but they are often only allowed to testify against other non-Muslims.[59]

Several major procedural safeguards are designed to preserve the integrity of the Islamic criminal process. First, the *qadi* of *Shari'a* courts are held to the highest standards of personal and judicial conduct. Judges who wrongfully punish defendants are subject to the same punishments they impose. Second, admissible evidence at trial is limited to eyewitness testimony, confessions, and religious oaths. Under Islamic law, these types of testimonial evidence are assumed to have high reliability.

According to Islamic criminal procedure, the accuser (plaintiff) is responsible for initiating court action. The plaintiff is required to present a particular number of witnesses (usually two) to support the accusations. These witnesses must be Muslim males of good character whose righteousness and sense of honor are beyond doubt.[60] Their testimony is limited to directly observed events and all witnesses must concur in the description of the time, place, and circumstances.[61]

An unequivocal form of evidence in Islamic law involves the taking of a holy oath. Oath-taking under *Shari'a* is a customary practice when there is no confession and the accuser (plaintiff) is unable to provide the required number of eyewitnesses for testimony. Under this tradition, the *qadi* designates which party will first challenge the other to swear under oath about the truth of their claims. The order of challenge is important because cases are automatically resolved without repute in favor of whoever swears under this oath. If neither party swears an oath, the case is usually settled in favor of the defendant. Oath-taking is a serious matter for practicing Muslims because bearing false witness under God's oath will be severely punished on Judgment Day.

From the perspective of controlling misconduct through punishment, the rigid procedural rules (e.g., victim-initiated prosecutions, severe penalties for false accusations) and strict evidentiary requirements under Islamic law would seem to diminish the certainty of punishment. In fact, it is the lower certainty of conviction that has led some analysts to challenge the general deterrent value of the *hadd* penalty of amputation for theft.[62] However, the deterrent value of Islamic punishments for practicing Muslims lies in both the certainty and severity of the particular penalty in the living world and their eternal damnation by an omniscient God.

OTHER CONTROL MECHANISMS AND SANCTIONING BODIES

The *Shari'a* penal code is but one mechanism of social control in Islamic societies. Personal activities and state/international relations in post-Islam history have also been regulated through separate customs, local traditions, and alternative jurisdictions. For example, non-*Shari'a* control practices included the handling of petty commercial affairs by the inspector of the marketplace, petty criminal cases by the chief police officer, and a "master of complaints" who heard cases that the *qadi* failed to resolve.[63] These alternative jurisdictions have become known as complaint courts (*mazalim*).

As a response to changing social conditions, the *mazalim* courts provided a forum to settle criminal and civil cases without submitting to the rigid procedural and evidentiary requirements of the *Shari'a*. These new "secular" courts were accepted under Islamic law because the *Shari'a* gives the ruler power to enforce the law, to direct public security, and maintain social order.

By the end of the nineteenth century, certain aspects of traditional Islamic law had been largely abandoned in many Muslim countries and replaced by European-type codes as the basis for social control and order maintenance in the areas of commerce, civil administration, and criminal law.[64] Fueled by the Iranian revolution and growing support among Muslim traditionalists to return to orthodox practices, however, the secular movement within some Islamic countries has greatly eroded in the twenty-first century.

SAUDI ARABIA

The kingdom of Saudi Arabia provides a good example of the application of Islamic law in a semisecular legal system. This geographical area is the birthplace of Islam, containing the holy cities of Mecca and Medina. Saudi Arabia's current population is about 24 million and 90 percent of its permanent residents are of Arab ethnicity (10 percent Afro–Asian).[65] It is an oil-based economy, containing the largest reserves of oil in the world. Saudi Arabia's political monarchy is hereditary and its legal system is based on the *Shari'a*.

The legal system of Saudi Arabia is considered semisecular because of its dual judiciary, but it places supremacy on religious laws.[66] A hierarchy of *Shari'a* courts exercise general and universal jurisdiction, whereas a separate system of specialized, secular tribunals have jurisdiction over specific issues (e.g., commercial disputes). The substantive law, procedural rules, and evidentiary proof requirements in the *Shari'a* court of Saudi Arabia are similar to those practices described previously. These similarities include, but are not limited to, the following: Crimes are

"The legitimacy of the royal government in Saudi Arabia depends on its perceived adherence to the precepts of a puritanically conservative form of Islam."

Source: U.S. Department of State (1994)

classified as against God (*Hudud*) or private wrongs involving bodily injury (*Qesas*); reliable evidence is restricted to testimony, confessions, and oaths; and witnesses must be nonrelatives of good character.

As an indication of the inseparability of church and state in this country, the Saudi government prohibits its citizens from practicing any religion other than Islam and mandates the acceptable form of Islamic practice (i.e., the *Wahhabi* sect's interpretation of the *Hanabali* school of Islamic jurisprudence).[67] Various human rights organizations (e.g., Human Rights Watch, Amnesty International) have voiced strong outrage at the Saudi government's mandate of religious homogeneity and the subsequent persecution of the Shi'ite minority and non-Muslims (especially foreign nationals). Issues of human rights violations have focused on a variety of concerns, including prohibitions and severe restrictions on the freedoms of speech and press, peaceful assembly and association, unlawful arrest, discriminatory treatment, torture and conditions of confinement, unfair and secret trials, and the lack of adequate means of redress.

The major enforcement body used to control and regulate public conduct under Islamic law in Saudi Arabia is the *mutawa'een*, the religious police.[68] These moral enforcers are also called by the names of the committee of "public virtue" or "public decency" in other Muslim countries (e.g., Afghanistan, Iran, Iraq, Somalia). The *mutawa'een* are extremely vigilant in carrying out their responsibility of ensuring strict adherence to established Islamic codes of conduct. They are a visible presence in large public areas, making sure that all Islamic customs are followed. Common targets of swift reaction by the religious police include women (e.g., for not wearing headscarves in public, walking alone or in the company of a nonrelative male) and teenage boys (e.g., for being imprudent in their language or public behavior).[69]

Coupled with other police agencies within Saudi Arabia, the *mutawa'een* are a major source of social control and punishment in this country. Similar to police organizations in other countries, the *mutawa'een* are given enormous discretion in the means by which they carry out their strict mandate to enforce public virtue. Neither judicial warrants nor even strong probable cause are necessary for either the public security police or *mutawa'een* to search a suspect or make an arrest.[70]

> "The al-Mutawa'een take us forcibly from the market . . . they remove our turbans, remove our beard and the hair of our heads. Sometimes in anger they even shave our eyebrows. They insult us in the maximum possible manner . . . . This is an everyday affair in Saudi Arabia. . . ."
>
> Excerpts from a letter written to Excerpts International in 1994 by a member of the Sikh community in Saudi Arabia.

Human rights organizations have recorded numerous accounts of individuals being harassed and arrested by these authorities in a "heavy-handed" manner. Arbitrary arrests, extensive detention without communication with family members, torture, and various types of intimidation are widely reported in the *mutawa'een*'s performance of their duty as the moral police. Within the context of physical and psychological abuse of suspects, the religious police can be viewed as serving dual roles of formal law enforcers and informal agents of corporal punishment.

CRIME TRENDS IN SAUDI ARABIA AND OTHER ISLAMIC COUNTRIES

Comprehensive national data on the prevalence of crime and criminal sanctions in Saudi Arabia and other Islamic countries are not available. There are no national centers for collecting and disseminating police and judicial data in most of these countries. Even if national data archives existed, issues of press censorship and the general secrecy that shrouds criminal processing in many non-Western countries dramatically affect the quality and quantity of the available information.

The limited availability of national data has forced researchers and international agencies to rely on government reports of unknown validity, small case studies of particular local jurisdictions, and compilations of media accounts and insider reports of incidents of the most severe punishments (e.g., counts of executions, torture incidents). It is important to keep these caveats in mind in the following comparative analysis of crime trends and punishment practices in Saudi Arabia with other Islamic countries.[71]

Based on available official data from the 1970s, the level of serious crime in Saudi Arabia appears to be relatively low compared to neighboring Muslim countries in the Middle East.[72] Official counts of the incidence and crime rates for murder, sexual assaults (including rape), and property crimes for different Arab countries in this time period are presented in Table 6.2. Contrary to Saudi Arabia, these particular countries use state law, rather than the *Shari'a*, as their legal system.

TABLE 6.2: Crime in Arab countries in the 1970s (yearly averages and rates per 100,000 population)

Country	Murders		Sex offenses		Property crimes	
	Counts	Rate	Counts	Rate	Counts	Rate
Saudi Arabia	53	.5	352	3.2	818	7.4
Egypt	1,319	3.0	2,171	4.9	33,088	75.2
Kuwait	61	3.1	561	28.1	2,238	111.9
Syria	403	3.7	553	5.0	6,599	60.0
Sudan	979	4.5	1,524	6.9	56,242	255.6
Iraq	1,119	8.0	1,832	13.1	3,522	25.2
Lebanon	439	12.5	759	21.7	5,252	150.1

Data Source: Arab Crime Statistics (1981); Souryal (1987)

Across both incident counts and rates per 100,000 population, Saudi Arabia reports substantially lower levels of crime than any other Arab country within the region. This pattern holds for each type of crime. The official murder rate in Saudi Arabia was six times lower than the next closest country (Egypt) and about twenty-five times lower than the murder rate in Lebanon, the Arab country with the highest murder rate in the 1970s. Saudi Arabia's official rate of sexual offenses was at least four times lower than reported in Iraq, Lebanon, and Kuwait. Differences for property offenses were even greater, with Saudi Arabia's rate per 100,000 population at least eight times lower than most other Muslim countries in this study. Saudi Arabia's official crime rate is at least eight times lower than is found for comparable crimes in the United States in the same time period.[73]

Official crime data have been widely criticized in terms of both validity and reliability in the United States and other Western countries, and there is reason to believe that similar factors are operating to diminish the accuracy of these crime data in the Middle East. However, if social and political forces that decrease the frequency of crime reporting are similar across jurisdictions, Saudi Arabia's crime rates would still be relatively lower than other Muslim and non-Muslim countries.[74]

Although more recent crime data for various Muslim countries are not available, there are several reasons why Saudi Arabia's crime rate may remain comparatively low even at the beginning of the twenty-first century.

Factors that may contribute to the expected low crime rate in Saudi Arabia in this new century include the following: (1) It has been more politically stable and repressive than other countries within the Middle East, (2) its government mandates *Shari'a* law and its strict punishments, (3) the *mutawa'een* (religious police) exert wide and strict control over public behavior, (4) greater population homogeneity in ethnicity and religious belief, and (5) stricter following of Islamic practices (e.g., prohibitions on alcohol use, commingling of men and women, and inappropriate dress) that may reduce criminal opportunities and/or motivations.

CRIMINAL PUNISHMENTS IN SAUDI ARABIA AND OTHER ISLAMIC COUNTRIES

One of the major cornerstones of Islamic law is its harsh penal code. *Hudud* offenses are offenses against God, and punishment for them is absolute and severe (e.g., death, amputation, whipping). Death sentences for murder are permitted under the law of retaliation, and whipping is also discretionary punishment for other criminal offenses. Imprisonment and monetary fines are also used. Unfortunately, national data and estimates of punishment practices in the last ten years are of limited availability for Saudi Arabia and other Muslim countries.

Corporal Sanctions

Depending on their offense and prior record, convicted criminals in Saudi Arabia have been subjected to execution, amputations, and whippings. The *Qur'an* and *Sunnah* specify the number of lashes for particular offenses and the method of imposition. According to independent investigations and reports submitted to Amnesty International, public flogging is a regular and widespread practice throughout Saudi Arabia. The number of lashes ranges from dozens to thousands. For example, an Egyptian national convicted of robbery in 1990 was sentenced to 4,000 lashes in addition to imprisonment.[75]

Flogging is also an extrajudicial punishment used in various contexts, including the treatment of political dissenters and foreign nationals, traffic offenders, and anyone suspected of harassing women. Under the orders of the local emir to maintain public order, the *mutawa'een* have served as both the judge and executioner of these punishments. A local newspaper in Riyadh reported in September 2001 that 172 youths had been whipped since the beginning of a campaign to stop the harassment of girls.[76]

Although limb amputation is widely discussed within Islamic societies, available data suggest that this practice is relatively uncommon. There were only sixteen amputations reported during a twenty-five-year period in the reign of King Abdel Azis Al Saud, whereas a total of eighty-two cases of amputations were recorded by Amnesty International between 1981 and 1995.[77] Anecdotal evidence that limb amputation may be more common than these reports suggest is found within the context of war injuries in the Middle East. For example, the potential mislabeling of soldiers who have lost limbs in battle in Iraq as criminals has led to some discussion of modifying these practices (e.g., by also branding criminals' foreheads). Such a concern would only arise if limb amputation was not an uncommon punishment for criminals in this country.[78]

The most comprehensive data on corporal punishments involve incidents of executions that have been compiled and summarized by international human rights groups. The secrecy of criminal proceedings and the use of extrajudicial executions in many Muslim countries contribute to an underestimation of the prevalence of death sentences in these countries. However, media accounts of executions and direct reports by independent, nongovernment observers provide at least a minimum count of these practices.

Based on media accounts and confirmed reports by international agencies (e.g., Amnesty International, Human Rights Watch), Saudi Arabia ranks as one of the most prevalent countries in the use of capital punishment. This ranking holds for the number of executions and the execution rate per capita.[79] Among other Muslim countries, only Iran and Iraq appear to have comparable numbers of execution in the twenty-first century (see Table 6.3). At least sixty-nine executions have been reported in Saudi Arabia for every year since 1996, reaching a high point of at least 123 executions in the year 2000. Amnesty International estimates that at least 560 executions occurred in Saudi Arabia between 1990 and 1997.[80]

Contrary to most industrial societies that have private executions, legal executions in Saudi Arabia are public events, imposed after short and secretive trials with limited opportunities for appeal. The following vivid description of a public beheading in Saudi Arabia was provided by Associated Press correspondent Anwar Faruqi after witnessing these executions:

> Policemen clear a public square of traffic and lay out a thick blue plastic sheet about 16 feet by 16 feet on the asphalt. The condemned, who has

TABLE 6.3: Executions in select Muslim countries (minimum counts and rate per million capita)

Country	Year 2000		Year 2001	
	Counts	Rate	Counts	Rate
Saudi Arabia	123	5.1	79	3.3
Iran	75	1.1	139	2.0
Iraq	"scores"		"scores"	
Yemen	13	.7	56	2.9
Egypt	22	.3	4	.1
Sudan	0	0	3	.1
Uzbekistan	8	.3	4	.2
Pakistan	6	<.1	13	.1
Afghanistan	15	.5	51	1.8
Bangladesh	0	0	3	<.1
Indonesia	0	0	2	<.1
Malaysia	2	.1	5	.2

Data Source: Amnesty International (2002, 2001) *Annual Reports*

been given tranquilizers, is led from a police car dressed in his own clothing. His eyes are covered with cotton pads, bound in plaster and finally covered with a black cloth.

Barefoot, with feet shackled and hands cuffed behind his back, the prisoner is led by a police officer to the center of the sheet and made to kneel. An Interior Ministry official reads out the prisoner's name and crime before a crowd of witnesses.

A soldier hands a long, curved sword to the executioner. He approaches the prisoner from behind and jabs him with the tip of the sword in the back so that the prisoner instinctively raises his head.

It usually takes just one swing of the sword to sever the head, often sending it flying about three feet. Paramedics bring the head to a doctor, who uses a gloved hand to stop the fountain of blood spurting from the neck. The doctor sews the head back on, and the body is wrapped in the blue plastic sheet and taken away in an ambulance.[81]

Persons executed in Saudi Arabia have been convicted of a variety of offenses, including murder, apostasy, "magic and witchcraft," adultery, and "corruption of earth" (e.g., drug smuggling). Similar to other countries with disparities in social groups that received death sentences (e.g., blacks in the

United States), foreign nationals and members of the *Shi'a* minority seem to be especially vulnerable to death sentences in Saudi Arabia. For example, foreign nationals represent only a minority of the Saudi population (23 percent), but they account for over 60 percent of the persons executed in this country.[82] Extrajudicial executions of political dissenters, deaths in custody, and arbitrary killings of citizens by opposition group leaders have been common occurrences in other Muslim countries across the world.[83]

Incapacitative and Economic Sanctions

Although the most attention has focused on its widespread use of corporal punishment, Saudi Arabia also employs various types of incapacitative sanctions (e.g., imprisonment, temporary detention) and economic sanctions (e.g., threats on the restriction of trade, withdrawal of financial benefits, monetary fines for minor offenses, *diyya* or "blood money" for compensation for personal injuries). These sanctions are used for purposes of public security, order maintenance, the control of dissent, and restorative justice. Imprisonment is most often applied to *Ta'azir* crimes for incorrigible offenders (i.e., those in which previous flogging had been ineffective) and dangerous recidivists.[84]

Estimations of the imprisonment rate in the 1990s suggest that Saudi Arabia is less likely to use this incapacitative sanction than most other Muslim countries (see Figure 6.1). Saudi Arabia's estimated rate of forty-five per 100,000 is considerably lower than some Muslim countries (e.g., Tunisia, Lebanon, Iran, Qatar) and higher than others (e.g., Indonesia, Bangladesh).[85] Among twenty-five Muslim countries with estimates of national imprisonment rates, Saudi Arabia's prison rate is one of the lowest (ranked twenty-first of twenty-five). Its low incarceration rate is due, in part, to the low crime rate in Saudi Arabia reported earlier and its greater use of corporal punishment for the control of crime and deviance.

There are numerous instances in media accounts of the payment of compensation in lieu of corporal punishment in cases of personal injury. The payment of *diyya* to victims or their heirs for bodily injuries and death is permitted under Islamic law and somewhat encouraged as an alternative to death under *Qur'anic* verses of a compassionate and benevolent Allah who will reward the forgiver in heaven. Fines are levied as punishment for various minor offenses in Saudi society and are sometimes used in conjunction with other penal practices (e.g., flogging, pretrial custody).[86] Unfortunately, there

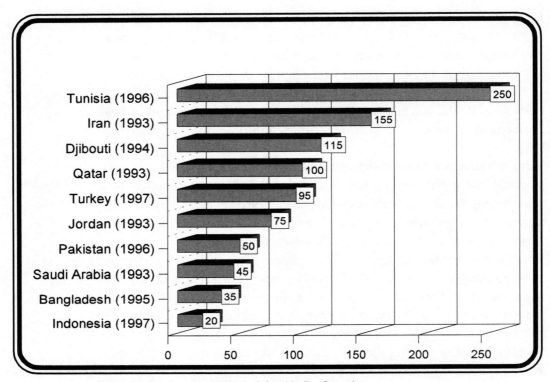

Figure 6.1. Imprisonment Rates in Select Muslim Countries.
Data Source: Walmsley (2000)

are no systematic data on the frequency of *diyya* payments and other economic sanctions for crime and deviance within Saudi Arabia or other Muslim countries.

A convicted Saudi Arabian murderer was spared execution after tribal sheikhs persuaded his victim's father to accept $1.33 million in return for his life. Thousands of men from the convicted murderer's tribe besieged the home of the victim's family to persuade them to spare the killer. After several hours, the victim's father agreed to the compensation.

Source: Reuters News (12/08/03)

The enormous wealth provided Saudi Arabia through its vast oil reserves has placed the Saudi government in a strategic bargaining position to either withhold or provide financial aid to various groups, organizations, and other countries. For example, the Saudi government has used its economic resources to help promulgate its particular Islamic beliefs to other countries across the world. Its wealth also provides financial sovereignty to make Saudi Arabia less vulnerable to threats and influence strategies by other countries and international bodies (e.g., UN sanctions, criticisms by international human rights organizations). Saudi Arabia's position of power in imposing economic sanctions is different than the impoverished conditions that characterize most other Muslim countries in the Middle East and across the world.

SUMMARY

When compared to other legal traditions and religions, Islamic law and faith are qualitatively different in origin, custom, and tradition. It emanates from the divine revelations of Allah and the teachings of the Prophet Muhammad in the fertile crescent of Arabia. Islam is an inclusive religion that covers all aspects of human existence and provides its followers a pathway for eternal bliss. The *Shari'a*, the Islamic law, contains a harsh penal code. This is especially true of *Hudud* crimes (e.g., theft, apostasy, adultery, defamation, alcohol use, rebellion) that are considered offenses against God. Punishment for these offenses is severe, absolute, and nonnegotiable (e.g., death by stoning or beheading, hand amputation, flogging). While the *Shari'a* courts were replaced in many countries by a secular legal system, traditional Islamic law has reemerged at the end of the twentieth century in response to a rise in Islamic orthodoxy or fundamentalism.

Saudi Arabia was considered a good example of the use of Islamic law within a semisecular legal system. Its government mandates the practice of Islam and *Shari'a* law. Compared to other Muslim countries, Saudi Arabia's official crime rate for murder, sexual assaults, and property offenses seems to be extremely low and its rates of corporal punishment (especially executions) relatively high. The religious police (*mutawa'een*) are major agents of social control in Saudi society that regulate and enforce Islamic standards of public virtue. Strict adherence to Islamic beliefs, opportunity-reduction practices, population homogeneity, widespread monitoring of public behavior by the religious police, and the threat of severe punishments are some of the factors that contribute to the low reported levels of crime and deviance in Saudi Arabia compared to other Muslim countries.

Notes

1. Erika Fairchild and Harry R. Dammer. 2001. *Comparative Criminal Justice Systems.* 2nd ed. Belmont, CA: Wadsworth. Page 60.

2. Israel Drapkin. 1986. *Crime and Punishment in the Ancient World*. New York: Lexington Books. Pages 254–5.

3. See Bryant W. Seaman. 1979. "Islamic Law and Modern Government: Saudi Arabia Supplements the Shari'a to Regulate Development." *Columbia Journal of Transnational Law*. Volume 18. Page 417. Cited in Matthew Lippman, Sean McConville, and Mordechai Yerushalmi. 1988. *Islamic Criminal Law and Procedure: An Introduction*. New York: Praeger. Page 25.

4. See Jethro Lieberman. 1983. *The Litigious Society*. New York: Basic Books; Marc Galanter. 1983. "Reading the Landscape of Disputes: What We Know and Don't Know (and Think We Know) About Our Allegedly Contentious and Litigious Society." *UCLA Law Review* 31(October): 4–71; Terance D. Miethe. 1995. "Predicting Future Litigiousness." *Justice Quarterly* 12 (3): 407–28.

5. Khisz Muazzam Khan. 1983. "Juristic Classification of Islamic Law." *Houston Journal of International Law* 6: 24–7. Cited in Matthew Lippman, Sean McConville, and Mordechai Yerushalmi. 1988. *Islamic Criminal Law and Procedure: An Introduction*. New York: Praeger. Page 29.

6. See Matthew Lippman, Sean McConville, and Mordechai Yerushalmi. 1988. *Islamic Criminal Law and Procedure: An Introduction*. New York: Praeger. Page 32.

7. Ibid.

8. Ibid. Page 33.

9. M. M. J. Nader. 1990. *Aspects of Saudi Arabia Law*. Riyadh, Saudi Arabia: Nader. Page 1.

10. Central Intelligence Agency. 2003. *The World Factbook*. Washington, D.C: U.S. Government.

11. Matthew Lippman, Sean McConville, and Mordechai Yerushalmi. 1988. *Islamic Criminal Law and Procedure: An Introduction*. New York: Praeger. Pages 7–8.

12. Abdullahi Ahmed An-na'im. 1990. *Toward an Islamic Reformation: Civil Liberties, Human Rights, and International Law*. Syracuse, NY: Syracuse University Press. Page 12.

13. For example, Muhammad's ideas about the unity of the universe and belief in one God were contrary to the religious beliefs of neighboring tribes that made pilgrimages to Mecca to worship in front of one or many of the 360 idols in the *Ka'aba*, the House of God. Similarly, his revelations about the need to change the social order by curtailing the extreme wealth and privileges of the rich were considered a direct threat to those with such resources. See Muhammad Z. Khan. 1962. *Islam: Its Meaning for Modern Man*. New York: Harper and Row. Page 16; Matthew Lippman, Sean McConville, and Mordechai Yerushalmi. 1988. *Islamic Criminal Law and Procedure: An Introduction*. New York: Praeger. Page 8.

14. Abdullahi Ahmed An-na'im. 1990. *Toward an Islamic Reformation: Civil Liberties, Human Rights, and International Law*. Syracuse, NY: Syracuse University Press. Page 12.

15. Matthew Lippman, Sean McConville, and Mordechai Yerushalmi. 1988. *Islamic Criminal Law and Procedure: An Introduction*. New York: Praeger. Pages 8–9.

16. Abdullahi Ahmed An-na'im. 1990. *Toward an Islamic Reformation: Civil Liberties, Human Rights, and International Law*. Syracuse, NY: Syracuse University Press. Pages 12–13.

17. Matthew Lippman, Sean McConville, and Mordechai Yerushalmi. 1988. *Islamic Criminal Law and Procedure: An Introduction*. New York: Praeger. Page 9.

18. Ibid. Pages 13–14.
19. See S. G. Vesey-Fitzgerald. 1955. "Nature and Sources of the *Shari'a*." In Majid Khadduri and Herbert Liebesny (eds.), *Law in the Middle East*. Washington, D.C.: Middle East Institute. Pages 91–2; Herbert J. Liebesny. 1972. "Comparative Legal History: Its Role in the Analysis of Islamic Law and Modern Near Eastern Legal Institutions." *American Journal of Comparative Law* 20: 38; Abdullahi Ahmed An-na'im. 1990. *Toward an Islamic Reformation: Civil Liberties, Human Rights, and International Law*. Syracuse, NY: Syracuse University Press. Pages 12–13.
20. Although nineteen separate schools of Islamic law were in existence from the seventh to nineteenth century, the four remaining *Sunni* legal schools are the *Hanafi* (followed mostly by Muslims in the Middle East), the *Maliki* (followed by many Muslims of North and Western Africa), the *Shafi'i* (followed by many Muslims of Indonesia and Malaysia), and the *Hanabali* (a minority sect in Saudi Arabia that became active after the *Wahhabi* reform movement in the nineteenth century). Another source of variation in Islam theology is the beliefs and practices of *Shi'a*, the only surviving significant minority of Muslims that disagree with the *Sunni* majority. They are distinct in the primary role of the *imam*, as the religious and political leader of the community, and differ in their beliefs about the infallibility of the transmission of the *Sunnah*. See Matthew Lippman, Sean McConville, and Mordechai Yerushalmi. 1988. *Islamic Criminal Law and Procedure: An Introduction*. New York: Praeger. Pages 26–8; Abdullahi Ahmed An-na'im. 1990. *Toward an Islamic Reformation: Civil Liberties, Human Rights, and International Law*. Syracuse, NY: Syracuse University Press. Pages 29–30.
21. See Matthew Lippman, Sean McConville, and Mordechai Yerushalmi. 1988. *Islamic Criminal Law and Procedure: An Introduction*. New York: Praeger. Page 33.
22. Noel J. Coulson. 1964. *A History of Islamic Law*. Edinburgh: Edinburgh University Press. Page 120.
23. S. G. Vesey-Fitzgerald. 1955. "Nature and Sources of the *Shari'a*." In Majid Khadduri and Herbert Liebesny (eds.), *Law in the Middle East*. Washington, D.C.: Middle East Institute. Page 91.
24. See Joseph Schacht. 1959. *The Origins of Muhammadan Jurisprudence*. Oxford: Oxford University Press. Page 84. It is important to note within this context that at least seventeen countries formally adhere to Islam by so declaring in their constitution. Other countries follow some components of Islamic law as a basis for their legal system. See M. Cherif Bassiouni. 1982. *The Islamic Criminal Justice System*. New York: Oceana. Page 3.
25. Noel J. Coulson. 1964. *A History of Islamic Law*. Edinburgh: Edinburgh University Press. Page 121. Cited in Abdullahi Ahmed An-na'im. 1990. *Toward an Islamic Reformation: Civil Liberties, Human Rights, and International Law*. Syracuse, NY: Syracuse University Press. Page 32.
26. See Bernard Lewis. 1961. *The Arabs in History*. New York: Harper and Row. Page 30; Robert Roberts. 1971. *The Social Law of the Qoran*. London: Curzon Press. Page 36.
27. Montgomery W. Watt. 1968. *Islamic Political Thought*. Edinburgh: Edinburgh University Press. Page 5.
28. Matthew Lippman, Sean McConville, and Mordechai Yerushalmi. 1988. *Islamic Criminal Law and Procedure: An Introduction*. New York: Praeger. Page 38.

29. Abdullahi Ahmed An-na'im. 1990. *Toward an Islamic Reformation: Civil Liberties, Human Rights, and International Law*. Syracuse, NY: Syracuse University Press. Page 142.

30. *Qur'an* 24:2. Cited in Sam S. Souryal, Abdullah I. Alobied, and Dennis W. Potts. 1994, "The Penalty of Hand Amputation for Theft in Islamic Justice." *Journal of Criminal Justice* 22(3): 249–65.

31. Muhammad Iqbal Siddiqi. 1979. *The Penal Law of Islam*. Lahore: Kazi. Page 106. Some modern Muslim writers contend that apostasy is not a *hadd* (the singular form of *Hudud*). This alternative view derives from the placement of higher authority on the *Qur'an* and its dictates about the freedom of consensus and the argument that the available *Sunnah* imposing the death penalty can be explained by the special circumstances of the cases in question. This minority view, however, does not preclude the imposition of severe punishment for apostasy under the discretionary power of *Ta'azir* punishments. See Abdullahi Ahmed An-na'im. 1990. *Toward an Islamic Reformation: Civil Liberties, Human Rights, and International Law*. Syracuse, NY: Syracuse University Press. Page 109; Shaikh Abdur Rahma. 1972. *Punishment of Apostasy in Islam*. Lahore: Institute of Islamic Culture. Chapter 2.

32. Matthew Lippman, Sean McConville, and Mordechai Yerushalmi. 1988. *Islamic Criminal Law and Procedure: An Introduction*. New York: Praeger. Page 48.

33. As will be discussed shortly, the exception is adultery, which requires four male eyewitnesses or four confessions on four separate occasions by the defendant in open court.

34. See Matthew Lippman, Sean McConville, and Mordechai Yerushalmi. 1988. *Islamic Criminal Law and Procedure: An Introduction*. New York: Praeger. Page 32. Although a death sentence is possible for sodomy, it is important to note that this crime is considered a *Ta'azir*, an offense in which the judge has discretionary power in the imposition of sanctions. Variability in lethal sentences for sodomy includes death by sword (followed by incineration of the body), live burial, stoning to death, or being thrown from a high building.

35. Technically, the *Qur'an* (24:2) specifies 100 lashes for *zina* (fornication), whereas the *Sunnah* makes the punishment stoning to death if the offender is a married person.

36. See M. Cherif Bassiouni. 1982. *The Islamic Criminal Justice System*. New York: Oceana. Pages 164–5. Cited in Matthew Lippman, Sean McConville, and Mordechai Yerushalmi. 1988. *Islamic Criminal Law and Procedure: An Introduction*. New York: Praeger. Page 46. The *Maliki* school of Islam is currently practiced in countries like Djibouti, Ethiopia, Kuwait, and Morocco.

37. Matthew Lippman, Sean McConville, and Mordechai Yerushalmi. 1988. *Islamic Criminal Law and Procedure: An Introduction*. New York: Praeger. Page 46. When the prerequisite of eyewitnesses is not satisfied, conviction is only possible if the adulterer confesses and requests the penalty. Aly Aly Mansour. 1982. "Hudud Crimes." In M. Cherif Bassiouni (ed.), *Islamic Criminal Justice System*. New York: Oceana. Page 199.

38. Matthew Lippman, Sean McConville, and Mordechai Yerushalmi. 1988. *Islamic Criminal Law and Procedure: An Introduction*. New York: Praeger. Page 43.

39. Frederick Mathewson Denny. 1985. *An Introduction to Islam*. New York: Macmillan. Page 96.

40. Sam S. Souryal, Abdullah I. Alobied, and Dennis W. Potts. 1994, "The Penalty of Hand Amputation for Theft in Islamic Justice." *Journal of Criminal Justice* 22(3): 249–65.

41. Matthew Lippman, Sean McConville, and Mordechai Yerushalmi. 1988. *Islamic Criminal Law and Procedure: An Introduction.* New York: Praeger. Page 46. Aly Aly Mansour. 1982. "Hudud Crimes." In M. Cherif Bassiouni (ed.), *Islamic Criminal Justice System.* New York: Oceana. Pages 197–8.

42. See *Qur'an* 24:2. Aly Aly Mansour. 1982. "Hudud Crimes." In M. Cherif Bassiouni (ed.), *Islamic Criminal Justice System.* New York: Oceana. Page 198.

43. Matthew Lippman, Sean McConville, and Mordechai Yerushalmi. 1988. *Islamic Criminal Law and Procedure: An Introduction.* New York: Praeger. Page 47.

44. See Safia M. Safwat. 1982. "Offenses and Penalties in Islamic Law." *Islamic Law Quarterly.* Volume 26. Pages 169–71. Cited in Abdullahi Ahmed An-na'im. 1990. *Toward an Islamic Reformation: Civil Liberties, Human Rights, and International Law.* Syracuse, NY: Syracuse University Press. Page 108. As noted by An-na'im (p. 108) and other texts, rebellion is often categorized as a form of highway robbery in Islamic law.

45. Muhammad Iqbal Siddiqi. 1979. *The Penal Law of Islam.* Lahore: Kazi. Page 140.

46. Aly Aly Mansour. 1982. "Hudud Crimes." In M. Cherif Bassiouni (ed.), *Islamic Criminal Justice System.* New York: Oceana. Pages 197–8.

47. It is reported that Muhammad said that one who drinks wine should be whipped without specifying the number of lashes. However, Muhammad himself had such an offender whipped forty lashes. This context provides the interpretative framework for the treatment of use of alcohol as a *hadd* offense. See Safai M. Safwat. 982. "Offenses and Penalties in Islamic Law." *Islamic Quarterly Review* 26: 169–71.

48. Matthew Lippman, Sean McConville, and Mordechai Yerushalmi. 1988. *Islamic Criminal Law and Procedure: An Introduction.* New York: Praeger. Page 47.

49. Ironically, addicts and alcoholics are permitted under Islam to use drugs or alcohol while overcoming their addiction. However, once they have been cured of their chemical dependency, the use of these illegal substances requires a *hadd* punishment of whipping. See Don Peretz, Richard U. Moench, and Safia K. Mohsen. 1984. *Islam: Legacy of the Past, Challenge of the Future.* New York: New Horizon Press. Page 109; Matthew Lippman, Sean McConville, and Mordechai Yerushalmi. 1988. *Islamic Criminal Law and Procedure: An Introduction.* New York: Praeger. Page 48.

50. The word *Qesas* means "equality" or "equivalence," implying that a person who commits a given offense will be punished in the same manner and by the same means used to harm the other person. See M. Cherif Bassioni. 1982. "Quesas Crimes." In M. Cherif Bassioni (ed.), *The Islamic Criminal Justice System.* New York: Oceana. Page 203.

51. *Qur'an* 2:178; 4:93; 25:68,69.

52. Matthew Lippman, Sean McConville, and Mordechai Yerushalmi. 1988. *Islamic Criminal Law and Procedure: An Introduction.* New York: Praeger. Page 52.

53. Ibid. Page 51.

54. Muhammad Iqbal Siddiqi. 1979. *The Penal Law of Islam.* Lahore: Zazi. Pages 156–7.

55. For example, Saudi Arabia does not recognize "moral injuries" (i.e., pain and suffering) under the principles of *diyya*. However, Article 76 of its Labor and Worker Regulations of 1969 does allow indemnity for moral injuries. See S. H. Amin. 1989. *Islamic Law and Its Implications for Modern Society.* Glasgow: Royston. Pages 369–70.

56. Osman abd-el-Malak al-Saleh. 1982. "The Rights of the Individual to Personal Security in Islam." In M. Cherif Bassiouni (ed.), *The Islamic Criminal Justice System*. New York: Oceana. Page 60.

57. Ghaouti Benmelha. 1982. "Ta'azir Crimes." In M. Cherif Bassiouni (ed.), *The Islamic Criminal Justice System*. New York: Oceana. Page 224. The nullification of punishment for repentance is clearly consistent with the meaning of *Ta'azir* (i.e., rehabilitative).

58. Ghaouti Benmelha. 1982. "Ta'azir Crimes." In M. Cherif Bassiouni (ed.), *The Islamic Criminal Justice System*. New York: Oceana. Pages 211–25. Cited in Matthew Lippman, Sean McConville, and Mordechai Yerushalmi. 1988. *Islamic Criminal Law and Procedure: An Introduction*. New York: Praeger. Pages 52–3.

59. Some jurists allow a non-Muslim to testify against a Muslim in a non-Muslim country and in noncriminal cases involving money or property. See Matthew Lippman, Sean McConville, and Mordechai Yerushalmi. 1988. *Islamic Criminal Law and Procedure: An Introduction*. New York: Praeger. Page 60.

60. There are other conditions required of witnesses, namely, that they be sane, of age of legal responsibility, free persons, non-family members, and refrained from sinful behavior. In some cases involving property or employment, some jurists will permit the testimony of female witnesses. Witnesses who make false testimony are guilty of a *Ta'azir* offense. See Muhammad Iqbal Siddiqi. 1979. *The Penal Law of Islam*. Lahore: Zazi. Page 117; Ma'amoun M. Salama. 1982. "General Principles of Criminal Evidence in Islamic Jurisprudence." In M. Cherif Bassiouni (ed.), *The Islamic Criminal Justice System*. New York: Oceana. Pages 116–18.

61. Matthew Lippman, Sean McConville, and Mordechai Yerushalmi. 1988. *Islamic Criminal Law and Procedure: An Introduction*. New York: Praeger. Page 70.

62. See Louis M. Holscher and Rizwana Mahmood. 2000. "Borrowing from the Shariah: The Potential Uses of Procedural Islamic Law in the West." In Delbert Rounds. *International Criminal Justice: Issues in a Global Perspective*. 2nd ed. Boston: Allyn and Bacon. Page 93; Sam S. Souryal, Abdullah I. Alobied, and Dennis W. Potts. 1994. "The Penalty of Hand Amputation for Theft in Islamic Justice." *Journal of Criminal Justice* 22 (3): 249–65.

63. Noel J. Coulson. 1969. *Conflicts and Tensions in Islamic Jurisprudence*. Chicago: University of Chicago Press. Pages 66–9.

64. Although the *Shari'a* was viewed as an idealistic and antiquated system of procedure and evidence, it remained responsible primarily for the administration and imposition of family law. For a general discussion of the changing role of the *Shari'a* over time, see Noel J. Coulson. 1969. *Conflicts and Tensions in Islamic Jurisprudence*. Chicago: University of Chicago Press.

65. This population estimate includes approximately 4 million foreign workers who play an important role in the oil and service sectors of the Saudi economy. See Central Intelligence Agency. 2003. *The World Factbook: Saudi Arabia*. Washington, D.C: U.S. Goverment. An estimated 85 percent of Saudis are Sunni Muslims and 15 percent are Shi'ite Muslims. Edward H. Lawson. 1991. *The Encyclopedia of Human Rights*. New York: Taylor and Francis. Page 1279.

66. Saudi Arabia in 1992 developed a codified system for law that derived from the adoption of the Basic Principles of Government, the Provisional System, and the System of the Majlis al-Shoura. Article 1 of Basic System makes explicit the religious context

of law and government: "The Kingdom of Saudi Arabia is an Arab and basic Islamic sovereign state. Its religion is Islam, and its constitution, the Holy *Qur'an* and the Prophet's *Sunnah*. . . . Saudi government holds that any law or decree that contradicts the *Shari'a*, as interpreted by the *Ulema*, must be overthrown." See Human Rights Watch. 1993. *The Events of 1992*. New York: Human Rights Watch, Inc. Page 331.

67. See U.S. Department of State. 1994. *Country Reports on Human Rights Practices for 1993*. Washington, D.C.: U.S. Government Printing Office. Page 1279. For a discussion of differences across Islamic schools and the Wahhabi movement that led to a strong association between Saudi royalty and *Hanabali*, see Madawi Al-Rasheed. 2002. *A History of Saudi Arabia*. Cambridge, UK: Cambridge University Press.

68. Other authorities with the power to arrest are the public security police (*al-Shurta*) and the general investigations (*al-Mabahith al-'Amma*). These enforcement units are under the Minister of the Interior. The *mutawa'een* are under the force of the Committee for the Propagation of Virtue and Prevention of Vice. See Amnesty International. 1997. *Saudi Arabia: Behind Closed Doors: Unfair Trials in Saudi Arabia*. [AI Index No.: MDE 230081997].

69. An extreme example of the seriousness with which the *mutawa'een* strictly adhere to their responsibility involved the death of fifteen girls during a fire in 2002 in a girls' school in Mecca. Presumably, the *mutawa'een* hampered rescue operations by preventing the girls from escaping the fire because they were not wearing headscarves and their male relatives were not there to receive them. Under Islamic law, women are not allowed in public without supervision of an immediate male relative. See Amnesty International. 2002. *Saudi Arabia Remains a Fertile Ground for Torture with Impunity*. [AI Index No.: MDE-230042002]. January 5, 2002.

70. See Amnesty International. 1997. *Saudi Arabia: Behind Closed Doors: Unfair Trials in Saudi Arabia*. [AI Index No.: MDE 230081997].

71. The more general problems of doing comparative historical analysis were previously discussed in chapter 3.

72. More recent comparative data on the nature of crime in Muslim countries in the Middle East and the rest of the world are not available. Saudi Arabia and other Muslim countries are rarely, if ever, included in international crime and victimization surveys. The crime data in the 1970s are the result of a crime survey conducted by the Arab Organization for Social Defense, an organization that operates in close association with the UN Social Defense Research Institute (UNSDRI) in Rome. The bibliographical reference for these data is: Arab Organization for Social Defense. 1981. *Arab Crime Statistics*. Baghdad, Iraq. Pages 55–68. For a discussion of these data and a summary of yearly counts of crime between 1970 and 1979 for each country, see Sam S. Souryal. 1987. "The Religionization of a Society: The Continuing Application of Shariah Law in Saudi Arabia." *Journal for the Scientific Study of Religion* 26(4): 429–49.

73. For example, the murder rate in the United States in 1975 was 9.6 per 100,000 population. The U.S. crime rate was 26.3 for sexual assault (rape) and 4,800 for property crimes (including the offenses of burglary, larceny, and auto theft). When compared to Saudi Arabia, the U.S. rates are 19.2 times higher for murder, 8.2 times higher for rape, and an incredible 648.6 times higher for property crimes. See Federal Bureau of Investigation. 1981. *Crime in the United States*. Washington, D.C.: U.S. Government Printing Office.

The far lower crime rate in Saudi Arabia than the United States was also replicated in 1981 based on official data on murder, rape, robbery, larceny/theft, motor vehicle theft, forgery, fraud, and drug abuse violations. The U.S. rate was at least six times higher for each offense than was found in Saudi Arabia for comparable offenses. See Badr-el-din Ali. 1985. "Islamic Law and Culture: The Case of Saudi Arabia." *International Journal of Comparative and Applied Criminal Justice* 9(2): 51–3.

74. See Sam S. Souryal. 1987. "The Religionization of a Society: The Continuing Application of Shariah Law in Saudi Arabia." *Journal for the Scientific Study of Religion* 26(4): 429–49. This author used various methods to attempt to validate the low rates of crime reported by government officials in Saudi Arabia. He conducted interviews with three sets of panels of individuals, comprised of members of the government, the clergy, and the general public. His personal interviews revealed several patterns about the reliability of government crime data (e.g., suggesting that rates should be increased by about fifteen percent), unreported offenses (e.g., minor juvenile offenses and "honor killings" of wives suspected of infidelity or daughters and sisters who were discovered to be pregnant out of wedlock), and unrecorded offenses (e.g., crimes of a political nature). We would expect these same factors, however, to be prevalent in other countries within this region as well. For a discussion of social and political factors influencing the reporting and recording of crime in the United States and other Western countries, see Clayton Mosher, Terance Miethe, and Dretha Phillips. 2002. *The Measure of Crime.* Beverly Hills, CA: Sage.

75. See Amnesty International. 1997. *Saudi Arabia: Behind Closed Doors: Unfair Trials in Saudi Arabia.* [AI Index No.: MDE 230081997].

76. Example cited in Amnesty International. 2002. *Saudi Arabia Remains a Fertile Ground for Torture with Impunity.* [AI Index No.: MDE-230042002]. January 5, 2002.

77. See Aly Aly Mansour. 1982. "Hudud Crimes". In M. Cherif Bassiouni (ed.), *Islamic Criminal Justice System.* New York: Oceana. Page 201. Amnesty International. 1997. *Saudi Arabia: Behind Closed Doors: Unfair Trials in Saudi Arabia.* [AI Index No.: MDE 230081997].

78. Under the government of Saddam Hussein, Iraq has imposed the punishment of ear and tongue amputation for political prisoners and other prisoners of conscience. It is unknown how many people have had body parts removed in judicial and extrajudicial sanctions.

79. In terms of numbers of executions, China is clearly the world leader in the imposition of state-sponsored executions. Amnesty International reports that at least 2,468 executions occurred in China in 2001. However, China's estimated execution rate of 1.9 per million residents in 2001 is about 1.7 times lower than the rate in Saudi Arabia. The number of executions in 2000 and 2001 in the United States (85 and 66, respectively) is somewhat comparable to estimates in Saudi Arabia, but the U.S. execution rate is at least ten times lower when adjusting for population size. See Bureau of Justice Statistics. 2002. *Capital Punishment, 2001.* U.S. Department of Justice. Washington, D.C.: U.S. Government Printing Office.

80. See Amnesty International. 1997. *Saudi Arabia: Behind Closed Doors: Unfair Trials in Saudi Arabia.* [AI Index No.: MDE 230081997].

81. Human Rights Watch Article. December 2001. "Human Rights in Saudi Arabia: A Deafening Silence." Associated Press. April 24, 2000.

82. These results are based on the 536 executions recorded by Amnesty International in which the nationality of the executed was known. A total of 332 persons executed were foreign nationals from Africa and Asian countries (including 143 Pakistani nationals) and 204 were Saudi Arabian nationals. See Amnesty International. 1997. *Saudi Arabia: Behind Closed Doors: Unfair Trials in Saudi Arabia.* [AI Index No.: MDE 230081997].

83. For example, investigations by the United Nations and international human rights groups have registered reports of extrajudicial executions and "disappearances" in the following countries in the late twentieth and early twenty-first century in which a large minority or the majority of the population is Muslim: Algeria, Egypt, Sudan, Guinea, Nigeria, Gambia, Senegal, Kazakstan, Kyrgyzstan, Uzbekistan, Tajikistan, Afghanistan, Bangladesh, Pakistan, Indonesia, Malaysia, and Turkey. See Amnesty International. 2002, 2001. *Regional Reports.* United Nations. 1996. "Human Rights Questions: Human Rights Questions, Including Alternative Approaches for Improving the Effective Enjoyment of Human Rights and Fundamental Freedom. Extrajudicial, Summary, or Arbitrary Executions." Report of the Special Rapporteur of the Commission on Human Rights on Extrajudicial, Summary, and Arbitrary Executions. United Nations General Assembly. Fifty-first Assembly. Agenda Item 110 (b). Political insurgence and extrajudicial killings have occurred within Saudi Arabia in 2003 in the context of indiscriminate bombings of civilians linked to the war in Iraq and the general instability of the Middle East.

84. See Ghaouti Benmelha. 1982. "Ta'azir Crimes." In M. Cherif Bassiouni (ed.), *The Islamic Criminal Justice System.* New York: Oceana. Page 217.

85. For the sources of these estimates of imprisonment rate, see Roy Walmsley. 2000. *World Prison Population List (2nd edition).* Home Office Research, Development and Statistics Directorate. Research Findings No. 116.

86. Fines were somewhat discouraged in early times because of fear that judges could employ it for personal gains, thereby plundering the community. See Ghaouti Benmelha. 1982. "Ta'azir Crimes." In M. Cherif Bassiouni (ed.), *The Islamic Criminal Justice System.* New York: Oceana. Page 218.

SUGGESTED READINGS

Abdullahi Ahmed An-na'im. 1990. *Toward an Islamic Reformation: Civil Liberties, Human Rights, and International Law.* Syracuse, NY: Syracuse University Press.

M. Cherif Bassiouni. 1982. *The Islamic Criminal Justice System.* New York: Oceana.

Noel J. Coulson. 1964. *A History of Islamic Law.* Edinburgh: Edinburgh University Press.

Matthew Lippman, Sean McConville, and Mordechai Yerushalmi. 1988. *Islamic Criminal Law and Procedure: An Introduction.* New York: Praeger.

Madawi Al-Rasheed. 2002. *A History of Saudi Arabia.* Cambridge, UK: Cambridge University.

CHAPTER SEVEN

Issues in the Sociology of Punishments

An examination of punishments within a comparative historical context brings up several basic questions about law, the structure of society, and the nature of social order. In this final chapter we explore and illustrate how a sociological analysis of punishment within a comparative historical framework can improve our understanding of these basic issues. We pay particular attention to the following concerns: (1) theories of law and society, (2) the effectiveness of state-sponsored punishments, (3) socioeconomic disparities in legal punishments, and (4) cultural values and the dramatization of "evil" societies.

THEORIES OF LAW AND SOCIETY

There are several well-established principles within the sociological study of law about the interrelationships between legal norms, criminal sanctions, and the nature of society. Both consensus and conflict models of social order have been used to describe the content of legal norms and changes in them over time in response to changing social conditions. As societies become more complex, it is widely assumed that legal norms and criminal sanctions also change in predictable ways. These views are reflected in the work of Phillipe Nonet and Philip Selznick on the movement from repressive to responsive law, Emile Durkheim's writings about the change from repressive to restitutive sanctions in modern societies, and Donald Black's arguments about how the quantity of law and its form are affected by the basic characteristics of societies. How the study of punishment within a comparative historical perspective informs these basic theoretical debates about law and society is addressed below.

CONSENSUS AND CONFLICT VIEWS OF SOCIAL ORDER

Consensus and conflict models represent the two extremes about the nature of social order. The consensus model focuses on the functional integration of society through shared norms and values, mutual cooperation, and compromise to maintain stability. Criminal offenses represent breaches of widely held community standards, and their punishment serves to reinforce the collective intolerance for particular acts. The conflict model, in contrast, views social order as precarious, based on conflict and dissension among individuals and competing interest groups. Social order is maintained through inducements, coercion, and using law and criminal sanctions as instruments of repression.

> Criminal punishments reflect shared public standards of morality under a consensus model of social order.

Across different time periods and in different countries, our examination of punishment reveals practices that are consistent with both consensus and conflict models. Support for both consensus and conflict perspectives can be found by looking at the offenses that are designated as capital crimes and the nature of public opinion in support of it.

Capital offenses in most time periods and places have included both acts that are considered *mala en se* and acts that are *mala prohibita. Mala en se* crimes are wrong in and of themselves and are said to violate widely held public standards of morality. Capital punishment for acts of murder and rape are often justified on the grounds that they violate clear community standards regarding the protection of human life and property. Robbery and burglary have also been justified as capital offenses in many countries because they violate consensual views about the protection of personal property.

> *Mala en se* crimes are wrong because of their intrinsic evil nature, whereas *mala prohibita* crimes are wrong because some political authority has defined them as illegal.

Mala prohibita crimes are considered wrong simply because some legal body deems them as illegal. For these offenses, there is not necessarily a shared consensus about the moral gravity or seriousness of the act, but they are defined as illegal for a variety of different reasons (e.g., personal values of legislators, special interests, responses to threat). Capital offenses within this category for particular historical periods include morality offenses (e.g., adultery, bestiality, witchcraft, and idol worship in Colonial America) and financial crimes (e.g., economic offenses in the post-economic reform era in China). With the possible exception of shared beliefs about these crimes as offenses against God in Islamic societies, none of these capital offenses necessarily represent violations of shared community standards. Instead, as proposed by a conflict perspective, these offenses are elevated to capital crimes to enhance and preserve the special interests of those who wield the power to get their desires protected by legal sanctions.

If the consensus model is correct in its contention that laws reflect public standards of morality, there should be a strong correlation between public attitudes toward the death penalty and actual execution practices. Support for this view is found in U.S. public opinion polls since the late 1980s, a time period in which the number of executions increased and over three-quarters of public survey respondents said they favored the death penalty for convicted murderers.[1] Widespread public support for capital punishment has also been noted in the context of China's "strike-hard" campaign in the late 1990s, when a plethora of executions were conducted for economic violations and to control social and political dissent. In Saudi Arabia, capital punishment is assumed to be universally upheld in public opinion because it is a nonnegotiable *Hudud* penalty for particular offenses under Islamic faith and law. Capital punishment could be justified in all three of these countries as a simple reflection of public consensus on the gravity of these acts.

Several additional facts about capital punishment and public opinion, however, question the general utility of the consensus model of law and society. First, no clear relationship exists between executions and public opinion when U.S. patterns are examined throughout the twentieth century (see Figure 7.1). The highest number of executions do not occur in time periods with the greatest public support for the death penalty. For example, public support for the death penalty in the United States was highest in the late 1980s and the 1990s, a period in which the actual number of executions was relatively small. Second, even in the period of highest public support, a large minority of U.S. citizens opposed it. In fact, the majority of African American respondents in most public surveys are opposed to the death penalty, providing direct evidence against the contention that these criminal sanctions reflect shared public opinions.[2] Third, public opinion remains strongly in favor of the death penalty in England, but executions in this country have been legally abolished since the mid-1990s.[3]

Collectively, the available evidence suggests that severe punishment practices are not simply a reflection of public standards of morality. The use of

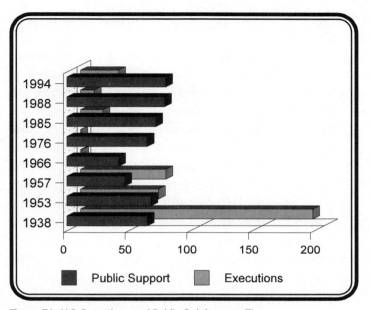

Figure 7.1. U.S. Executions and Public Opinion over Time
Data Source: Bohm (1991); Espy and Smykla (1991); BJS (2002)

the death penalty may serve numerous functions at different times and in different places, but it does not necessarily reflect public views about its appropriateness for particular offenses.

LEGAL EVOLUTION AND SOCIETAL COMPLEXITY

Most sociological perspectives in the study of law and society emphasize the dynamic nature of legal evolution and societal complexity. Both law and society are considered complex and dynamic social systems. Social, economic, and political changes in the structure of society influence the nature and scope of legal norms and criminal sanctions. Similarly, legal changes often invoke fundamental changes in social, economic, and political institutions in societies.

Different theoretical orientations explain how changes in society affect the nature and scope of laws. However, when applied to the extent and nature of criminal sanctions, most theorists (e.g., Durkheim, Nonet and Selznick, Braithwaite, Black) contend that restitutive sanctions would replace repressive sanctions in the transition from simple to more complex and advanced societies.[4] What does our comparative analysis of formal punishments tell us about the accuracy of these views?

Based on current practices worldwide, there is a strong inverse relationship between level of socioeconomic development and the use of corporal punishment. Countries with higher levels of industrial development are often more complex societies (e.g., they have a more extensive division of labor, generalized exchange networks, cultural diversity) and they are less likely to legally practice nonlethal and lethal forms of corporal punishments. In fact, the United States and Japan are the only large industrialized countries that have not abolished capital punishment, whereas nearly two-thirds of the developing countries of the world have retained it. Developed countries also typically have lower imprisonment rates than developing countries.[5] Overall, these results are consistent with theoretical expectations that less physically punitive sanctions are used in more economically developed and industrialized societies.

> As societies become more advanced over time, it is widely assumed that repressive sanctions are replaced by restitutive sanctions for purposes of maintaining social order.

When examined within the developmental histories of particular countries, however, this presumed relationship between societal complexity and types of sanctions is contradicted by various trends over time and location. For example, the United States has altered over time the nature of how it imposes capital punishment (from public hangings to gas chambers to private lethal injunctions) rather than abolishing this repressive sanction. Economic development in China, in contrast, has been associated with a rise in civil litigation and an increasing use of the death penalty for a growing list of financial crimes. Similarly, Saudi Arabia and other Muslim countries experiencing economic growth and development have also retained their use of various corporal punishments for crime and deviance. None of these trends are consistent with the presumed decline in corporal punishment and rise in restorative or restitutive sanctions that is widely thought to characterize a country's social, economic, and legal evolutions.

Under these conditions, general conclusions about the movement toward restorative justice and increases in "civilizing sensibilities" over time should be countered with statements about the context-specific nature of these trends in time and space.[6] Our comparative historical analysis of punishments suggests that the particular punitive response to changing environmental conditions is not uniform across social contexts. Contrary to conventional views about law and society, the transition from repressive to restitutive sanctions is neither a necessary nor a sufficient condition in the socioeconomic development of a country.

THE EFFECTIVENESS OF STATE-SPONSORED PUNISHMENTS

Formal punishments are widely used for various functions. Throughout history and across countries, various types of formal sanctions have been employed for purposes of social engineering (e.g., by reinforcing values or maintaining order), minimizing threats to prevailing practices, and deterring criminal and deviant behavior. The effectiveness of state-sponsored sanctions in these areas is examined below.

SOCIAL ENGINEERING

The historical records are filled with numerous examples of the use of formal punishments to either reinforce values or maintain order. The Puritans in Colonial America established capital statutes for various morality offenses (e.g., bestiality, sodomy, adultery) and alternative religious views (e.g., idolatry, blasphemy, witchcraft) to fortify collective values and community solidarity. The severe corporal punishments for *Hudud* offenses under Islamic law are rooted in the protection of the Islamic faith and the preservation of public order. The maintenance and reestablishment of particular religious values also formed the basis for capital punishment for heresy under the reign of "Bloody" Mary Tudor in England during the mid-1500s. Capital punishment and civil litigation in China in the twenty-first century have played an important role in regulating and controlling unlawful economic activities in the wake of its movement toward a new economic order.

Whether punishments and their threat have been effective in this context to reinforce and preserve order is subject to some debate. From the Puritans' perspective, for example, strict punishments and the ostracism of those with alternative religious beliefs were initially successful for purposes of boundary maintenance and social solidarity. However, these closed, overly regulated communities ultimately succumbed under their own weight or through the inevitable intrusion of external forces (e.g., migration, centralization of law and power).[7] Similarly, although a number of persons have been executed in

China for economic violations in the postreform period, it is unlikely that the death penalty, in and of itself, will be able to curtail the groundswell of capitalist values and greed that has emerged under this new market economy. Massive civil unrest and political volatility in many primarily Muslim countries (e.g., Afghanistan, Indonesia, Somalia) have severely eroded the ability of legal sanctions to maintain or enhance social order.

Sociologists have long recognized that punishment is most effective in maintaining social order and enhancing constructive social change when it is associated with both the institutionalization and internalization of patterns of behavior. In other words, laws and formal punishments help institutionalize patterns of behavior (i.e., they define the limits of acceptable behavior), but individuals ultimately conform to these standards because they have internalized the proscribed behaviors as personal preferences (i.e., they comply because they want to, not because they are legally compelled to).

> Effective laws and formal punishments are those that lead to both the institutionalization and internalization of patterns of appropriate behavior.

Viewed from this perspective, the general ineffectiveness of formal punishments in maintaining conformity and social order may be due to an overemphasis on the "iron hand" of law. In fact, history is filled with numerous examples of repressive regimes that achieved only short-term success in maintaining order. However, those countries that maintain order in the face of social change have often used educational campaigns to help internalize new values into the belief systems of its citizens.[8] Such educational programs are common within China's recent history (e.g., where educational reforms are focusing on the new conflict between individuals' economic "self-interests" and communal solidarity) and, to a lesser extent, within the context of the resurgence of Islamic fundamentalism (e.g., where strict and uniform religious values are being promoted). By combining strict punishments with concerted efforts to instill uniform values and beliefs, these countries have been more successful than others in maintaining social order and controlling deviance within a changing social world.

PUNISHMENT AND MINORITY GROUP THREAT

Civil and criminal laws have been widely used over time and across different countries to disrupt, harass, imprison, and/or eliminate particular individuals and social groups that represent a threat to the prevailing authorities. Federal agencies in the United States like the Federal Bureau of Investigation (FBI), the Central Intelligence Agency (CIA), the Internal Revenue Service (IRS), and Immigration and

> Civil and criminal laws are widely used to regulate and control threats by minority group members of a society.

Naturalization Services (INS) have long histories of efforts to control internal dissension and external threats through civil and regulatory actions (e.g., deportation, fines, injunctions, asset forfeiture), imprisonment, and even corporal punishments like torture and extrajudicial executions during clandestine operations. Student protestors, union organizers, rival companies, and political opponents have also been selective targets of social-control efforts through unlawful surveillance activities, civil litigation, the spreading of negative publicity against the opposition, and other types of administrative or regulatory practices.[9]

The most extreme form of social control against individuals and groups that represent a threat to prevailing conditions involves capital punishment and extrajudicial executions. The use of death sentences for these purposes is widely observed across historical contexts in different countries (e.g., England, the United States, China, Saudi Arabia).

English history contains numerous examples of the use of capital punishment for controlling minority group threats. Challenges to the English Crown were often met with swift and lethal reprisals at the gallows or chopping block. Henry VIII faced numerous threats to his reign by nobles, lords, and "pretenders" that were effectively countered through both public and private executions.[10] The threat to her revival of Catholicism served as the justification for capital punishment for acts of heresy under the rule of Mary Tudor. Parliament's passage of the "bloodiest criminal code in Europe" in the late eighteenth century was linked to preserving economic interests and enforcing the "rightful" division of property by terror.[11] During the first quarter of the nineteenth century, the death penalty was directed specifically at the threat to social order posed by the "dangerous criminal classes" that inhabited London and other large urban areas within England. The fear of collective action by this mobile horde of persons viewed as "morally bankrupt" struck universal fear among the property classes and sparked various efforts besides the death penalty to control them (e.g., increased imprisonment, transportation to other countries).

The use of the death penalty for controlling minority group threats had a different structure and content in American society, but had similar dire consequences for the targets of these social control efforts. The capital codes of the early settlements in Massachusetts were closely linked to the preservation of particular religious values. "Outsiders" and nonbelievers in many of these closed and isolated communities were subject to rigorous prosecution and persecution through various types of criminal sanctions (e.g., placement in stocks for public humiliation, hanging of alleged witches) as a means of reinforcing community solidarity against these threats. Minority group threat on the expanding western frontier in the 1800s involved the resolution of conflict between the Native Americans and white settlers; range wars between cattle and sheep herders; the post Civil-War exploits of criminal gangs and vigilante groups like Quantril's Raiders and the James–Dalton gang; and interpersonal disputes involving claim jumpers, horse thefts, and cattle rustlers. Union and labor disputes, political violence against opposition candidates and voters, and the civil rights movement became new contexts for minority group threat. However, the lynching of blacks during the Reconstruction period and throughout the first half of the twentieth century is probably the single best example of how executions served to control threats from a particular minority group.

Whatever the particular context of minority group threat, it is important to note that both legal and extralegal means of dispute resolution were available. Military courts, for example, were available, at least in theory, to mediate the Native American–white conflict. Territorial court magistrates were on a traveling circuit and may have been called upon to address criminal acts or resolve particular conflict situations. Similar judicial channels were present for dealing with issues of race, civil rights, and politics. However, extrajudicial executions were often more prevalent for resolving these issues in American history for several reasons. These include the greater speed and finality of extrajudicial executions (i.e., they could be conducted "on the spot"), their greater predictability of outcome compared to the uncertainty of verdicts by judges and juries, and the greater terror and subsequent acquiescence for those with similar personal characteristics who may be subjected to the same type of vigilante justice.

The use of punishment in China as a strategy for controlling minority group threat has encompassed a wide range of social, economic, and political groups. Death sentences and extensive "educational" retraining in labor camps have long been used to control individuals and groups that threaten prevailing political and ideological thought. Historically, both the Confucians and Taoists were targets of repressive social-control efforts at particular times by the ruling party in ancient China. More recently, Tibetan nationals and Falung Gong groups have been subjected to numerous control efforts. The activities of ethnic Muslims (e.g., Uighurs) have also been targeted in the "strike-hard" campaigns of the last two decades. Economically, a number of capital statutes have been developed in the wake of the economic reforms and the movement toward a market economy. Persons who engage in major economic violations are subject to lengthy imprisonment or death sentences under these new policies.

Minority group threat in Saudi Arabia has resulted in social control efforts directed at the Shi'ite minority and non-Muslims (especially foreign nationals). Social control efforts by the Saudi government and the *mutawa'een* (the religious police) against these groups involve prohibitions and severe restrictions on their basic human rights (e.g., freedoms of speech, peaceful assembly, and religious practices; right to a fair trial and appeal) and discriminatory treatment (e.g., unlawful arrests, torture, and cruelty while in custody). These minority groups (especially Pakistani nationals) are also drastically overrepresented in available reports of legal executions in Saudi Arabia.[12] The religious beliefs and lifestyles of foreign nationals and non-Sunni Muslims are a direct threat to the prevailing social order in this country.

> Members of the *Shi'ite* minority and non-Muslim, foreign nationals have been subjected to various types of coercive social control efforts in Saudi Arabia.

Because all countries highlighted here have used capital punishment and other sanctions for controlling minority group threat, it is important to ask whether such efforts are effective. The answer to this question is situationally specific. In particular, both legal and extrajudicial executions have been effective in eliminating certain individuals or groups of individuals that pose a specific threat. However, these sanctions have not eliminated the basic problems that motivated these control efforts and sometimes have been counterproductive to the prevailing authorities through the development of martyrs and the subsequent organization of disparate individuals and groups to form a collective response against this oppression. The civil rights struggle in the United States and the battles of ethnic and religious groups in China are a testament to how state and extrajudicial social-control efforts can ultimately result in constructive social changes that may be antithetical to their original intentions.

THE DETERRENT VALUE OF PUNISHMENT

Aside from its use for social engineering and reducing minority threat, a primary justification for formal punishments involves their deterrent effect on criminal offending. Deterrence asks this basic question: Does the threat or imposition of criminal sanctions lead to higher levels of law-abiding behavior? Criminal sanctions are widely thought to have the highest deterrent value when the punishments are certain, severe, and swift. In general, deterrence is also considered most effective on instrumental crimes (i.e., crimes done for some explicit, planned goal rather than spontaneous or impulsive acts) and when potential offenders have low commitment to crime as a livelihood.[13]

> Threat of legal sanction has the greatest deterrent value when punishments are swift, certain, and severe.

Two types of deterrence are often discussed within this context of criminal sanctions.[14] First, specific deterrence involves using criminal sanctions or their threat to deter an individual from committing a further criminal act. Second, general deterrence refers to whether the threat or imposition of criminal sanctions given to one person deters others from engaging in criminal behavior. Low recidivism rates and low crime rates, respectively, are often viewed as the basic indicators of the effectiveness of these two types of deterrence. Available data suggest there are wide differences across countries in the potential deterrent value of criminal sanctions.

Of the countries highlighted in our comparative analysis, basic patterns of crime and recidivism are the least consistent with the principles of deterrence in the United States. National data on convicted offenders released from prison indicate that about two-thirds of U.S. offenders are rearrested within three years.[15] U.S. crime rates and imprisonment rates also exhibited a positive correlation over most of the last half of the twentieth century, when deterrence would predict a negative correlation between crime rates and severe punishments.[16] In contrast, available data on crime rates and recidivism in China and Saudi Arabia are far more consistent with the deterrence doctrine. Both countries appear to have relatively low crime rates and their punishments are relatively severe and certain. Recidivism rates also seem to be extremely low in these countries.[17]

Although low crime rates and low recidivism rates in China and Saudi Arabia are often attributed to the deterrent effect of severe and certain punishments, there are several other factors besides punishments that may explain these patterns. For example, potential crime-inhibiting factors in Saudi Arabia compared to other countries include all of the following: (1) it has been more diligent in its repression of deviance than other countries, (2) its government mandates *Shari'a* law and its strict and nonnegotiable punishments for *Hudud* offenses, (3) the *mutawa'een* (religious police) are authorized to exert wide and strict control over public behavior, (4) greater population homogeneity in ethnicity and religious belief than is found in other countries, and (5) stricter following of Islamic practices (e.g., prohibitions on alcohol use, commingling of men and women, and dress) that may reduce criminal opportunities and/or motivations. China's low crime rate is also explained by deterrence factors (i.e., swift, certain, and severe punishments) and strong mechanisms of informal and formal social control that link the individual to the wider community (e.g., the promotion of communitarian values, neighborhood surveillance, emphasis on filial piety).

This book has focused on the social control and deterrent effects of state-sponsored sanctions. However, it is important to emphasize that compliance to societal norms is most commonly achieved through a wide range of social control mechanisms outside the area of criminal sanctions. These include the deviance inhibiting effects of various institutions (e.g., family, education, religion, economic), cultural values and traditions, and general ethical and moral beliefs. The low levels of reported crime and deviance in China and Saudi Arabia are directly tied to these alternative mechanisms of control and the subsequent use of severe criminal punishments when the threat and implementation of formal sanctions fail to achieve conformity. If these patterns are applied to other countries in the modern world, they suggest that criminal punishments are best viewed as a necessary but not a sufficient condition for deterring crime and deviance.

> The low crime rates in China and Saudi Arabia are attributed to both their system of formal punishments and various informal mechanisms of social control.

Although the joint influences of severe formal punishments and strong informal mechanisms of social control in China and Saudi Arabia may result in lower levels of crime and repeated deviance, it is also the case that these gains in crime reduction are often at the expense of personal liberty and individual freedom. Compared to the United States, both China and Saudi Arabia are widely viewed as repressive countries with extreme limits on personal freedoms and human rights. Thus, state-sponsored punishments may be highly effective in deterring crime and deviance, but the enforcement and implementation of these punishments may seriously erode the basic freedoms that underlie fundamental aspects of human rights.[18]

SOCIOECONOMIC DISPARITIES AND PUNISHMENT

An area of basic concern within the sociological study of law involves the issue of disparities in the application of criminal sanctions. The notion of equal treatment under the law is firmly entrenched in modern democratic societies. However, much research has focused on whether this legal tenet is actually followed in practice. The issue of differential treatment across socioeconomic groups has been widely explored in previous research. This research literature has examined whether sex, race, age, and income differences exist in criminal processing outcomes and, if so, what accounts for this differential treatment (e.g., is it *de jure* or *de facto* discrimination?).[19]

Previous research in the United States consistently reveals major differences by sex, race, age, and income in the risks of receiving severe formal sanctions like capital punishment. These differences are enormous in many cases when execution rates per million population are computed across particular decades of the last 100 years (see Table 7.1). For example, execution rates were about 500 times higher for males than females in the period around 1900 and 1920, and remained about 200 times higher in the mid-twentieth century before dropping to a rate of nearly fifty times higher at the turn of the new century. Execution rates for blacks were about ten times higher than the rate for whites during the first half of the twentieth century, decreasing to about twice as high by the end of the century.[20] The execution rates were roughly twice as high for persons under thirty than their older counterparts up until the 1980s, after which time persons over thirty had the higher execution risks.

Although these differences between social groups are substantial in many cases, it is important to note that they may be explained by a variety of factors other than systematic discrimination against particular groups. For example, the change in execution rates for different age groups, especially in

TABLE 7.1: U.S. execution rates per million population over time

Comparison	1898–1902*	1918–22	1938–42	1958–62	1978–82	1998–2002
U.S. rate	7.49	5.07	5.63	1.38	.02	1.37
Males	14.54	10.04	11.26	2.79	.05	2.73
Females	.03	.02	.06	.01	–	.06
Ratio:	484.7 : 1	502.0 : 1	187.7 : 1	279.0 : 1	–	45.5 : 1
Black	36.34	22.22	29.59	7.48	.04	3.46
White	2.90	2.75	2.73	.61	.02	1.22
Ratio:	12.5 : 1	8.1 : 1	10.8 : 1	12.3 : 1	2.0 : 1	2.8 : 1
Ages 15–29	4.03**	5.83	10.17	3.32	.02	na
30 or older	2.16	2.89	4.32	1.46	.04	na
Ratio:	1.9 : 1	2.0 : 1	2.4 : 1	2.3 : 1	.5 : 1	na

Notes:
*Execution rates are based on the number of executions in the five year period for each decade.
**used 1910 census data for computing rate.
"–" represents decades in which there were no executions for this group.
"na" means data are not available.
Source: Espy and Smykla (1991); BJS (2002); U.S. Census Reports (1900–2000)

the 1980 period and beyond, can be attributed to the following factors: (1) the amount of time on death row pending execution has increased over time, contributing to the older age of those executed in more recent years; (2) fewer juveniles who are adjudicated as adults for serious violent crimes are given the death penalty because of increasing modifications of state laws that exclude juveniles from capital punishments; and/or (3) the higher commission of capital-murder killings by older offenders now than was true in the past.[21] By taking into account these other factors, we would be in a better position to isolate the particular basis for differential treatment.[22]

Differential treatment within China has focused on the legal processing and punishment of various religious groups, political dissenters, and internal migrants. International human rights organizations (like Human Rights Watch and Amnesty International) have voiced strong concerns about the torture, imprisonment, execution, and general oppression of the Falun Gong, Uighur Muslims, Tibetans, and other groups that may threaten the prevailing political authority. Studies of criminal processing have shown that migrants or transitory residents are given more severe sentences than other offenders for theft-related crimes even after controlling for other factors that influence sentencing decisions.[23] However, differential treatment in China is not exclusively directed at socially or economically disadvantaged groups. Media reports of executions in China over the last decade often include descriptions of these punishments being given to managers, business executives, and political leaders for economic crimes, violations of national security, and political corruption.[24]

Differential treatment is unique in Saudi Arabia in that it is institutionalized in law. For example, women and non-Muslims have less legal standing within this country in various criminal and civil matters, and men of "high virtue" are considered less deserving of punishment than those of lesser personal character. Although socioeconomic status plays a fundamental role in criminal processing in other countries (e.g., defendants in the United States who cannot make financial bail or are represented by public defenders have higher risks of conviction), discriminatory treatment in Saudi Arabia is more overt and firmly entrenched in its Islamic legal tradition.

The diversity of the scope and nature of differential treatment across countries and over time provide evidence of the value of a comparative historical approach to the study of punishments. Differential treatment is found within each country, but its particular form and structure are context-specific. It is institutionalized in Saudi Arabia against women and non-Muslims, discriminatory in actual practice rather than law per se in the United States (i.e., *de facto* rather than *de jure*), and has operated to the detriment of both rich and poor in China. This variation across context would not have been observed by focusing exclusively on socioeconomic disparities in one country at a particular point in time. Regardless of whether these disparities in punishment are *de facto* or *de jure*, their presence seriously threatens the presumption of equal treatment that is the foundation for criminal justice in many countries.

CULTURAL VALUES AND PERCEPTIONS OF "EVIL" SOCIETIES

Statements about the civility of particular countries are often based on the nature and type of their formal punishments. Western Europe is often considered more compassionate and civilized than other world regions because its countries have abolished capital punishment for ordinary crimes. In contrast, countries such as Iran, Iraq, Saudi Arabia, and China are often viewed as barbaric by Western society because they use the death penalty, impose it in many cases in public locations, and use methods like beheading and a single bullet to the head that physically brutalize the body. The desire to appear more humane, civilized, and/or "therapeutic" is one reason why the United States has moved to lethal injection as the primary method of execution in the states that still retain capital punishment.

From a social constructionist's perspective, definitions and designations of countries as "evil" or "uncivilized" based on their punishment practices are problematic in a variety of respects.[25] In fact, this perspective assumes that definitions of all behavior are socially constructed by those who have the power, wealth, and means of imposing and disseminating their beliefs as the legitimate social reality. When applied to the question of capital punishment across countries, constructionists would ask how these classifications of "evil" versus "civilized" countries are developed and what types of behaviors are included under the definition of "executions." What seems especially pertinent in these classifications is how extrajudicial executions are counted.

There is little doubt that the number of state-sponsored executions worldwide represents only a small fraction of the number of acts of lethal violence. This pattern holds true throughout the twentieth century and across different world regions.

Compared to the relatively small number of persons legally executed for criminal acts, millions were killed in the Holocaust of Nazi Germany and the genocide involving the Turks and Armenians in the first quarter of the twentieth century. More recently, European countries have been involved in other types of lethal oppression of ethnic and religious groups, including prolonged clashes between Protestants and Catholics in Northern Ireland and the extrajudicial killings of various ethnic groups in the former Yugoslavia. Civil strife and mass genocide have a long history in various African countries.[26] Similar human carnage is found in the extrajudicial executions by paramilitary groups, state police, and "death squads" in South American countries and Asia. Extrajudicial lynchings of blacks by vigilante groups up through the first half of the twentieth century in the United States were less widespread than the genocides in other countries, but no less harrowing to its victims and those threatened by these attacks.

When placed within this context of mass deaths and killings, the ranking of countries as "evil" or "uncivilized" on the sole basis of "legal" executions and other types of corporal punishment seems extremely dubious. As discussed in chapter 3, most countries that have death squads and other extrajudicial means of lethal violence against their citizens also have retained capital punishment. However, some countries have abolished capital punishment for ordinary crimes like murder (e.g., Cambodia, Chile, Colombia, Israel, Haiti), but have long and continuing histories of civil violence, death squads, and "disappearances" that are linked to acts of commission or omission by state authorities. Other countries (e.g., China, Iran, Iraq) have both retained capital punishment and appear to widely use extrajudicial means of eliminating dissents and other threats. In contrast, Great Britain and other Western European countries have limited the use of both state-sponsored and extrajudicial violence against their citizens.

These patterns involving capital punishment and other forms of lethal violence should reinforce the idea that there is wide variability in practices across comparative historical contexts. Without a wider understanding of the sociopolitical context in which punishments are given, our judgments and public proclamations about the relative civility of different countries will continue to be highly subjective, impressionistic, and ethnocentric.

UNIVERSAL AND CONTEXT-SPECIFIC PATTERNS

One of the primary strengths of a comparative historical analysis is its ability to provide an empirical foundation for assessing the generality of observed findings across contexts. Our comparative analysis across countries and world regions allows us to evaluate statements about the nature of universal and context-specific punishment responses across time and place.

Punishment is a ubiquitous feature of all societies and countries examined in this book. Its function and form vary across social, political, economic, and historical contexts, but punishment practices and rituals associated with them appear to be common elements of all human societies.

Aside from the universality of punishment, however, other aspects of its structure and nature are context-specific. Through our comparative historical analysis, we have identified the following major exceptions to each of the "facts" that derive from the current literature in the sociology of punishments:

- The shift from repressive to restitutive sanctions is neither a necessary nor a sufficient condition for the historical transition to an advanced or modern society. The United States is one of the most advanced industrial societies of the world and still uses various types of repressive measures against its own citizens and other countries (e.g., the death penalty, economic embargoes, military action). Both China and Saudi Arabia also continue to impose death sentences and other repressive measures (e.g., torture, extrajudicial punishments) even in their recent history of economic development and growth.

- Punishment has not necessarily shifted from public to private settings through the evolution and development of societies. Although some support can be found for the claims of Foucault and others that punishments in modern society have become privatized regimes rather than public ceremonies, this assertion is overstated and clearly contradicted by numerous exceptions.[27] For example, China, Guatemala, Pakistan, and several countries in the Middle East (e.g., Iran, Lebanon, Saudi Arabia, Yemen) have in the last few decades either broadcasted executions on national television stations or conducted public executions in front of mass crowds.

- Contrary to Donald Black's theory about the behavior of law, there are numerous instances across different settings where the style of law is penal rather than compensatory when applied to persons of relatively equal rank.[28] China has executed numerous political officials and business executives for corruption and economic crimes in the past decade, whereas Henry VIII in England gained notoriety by using imprisonment and executions as a way to eliminate threats from particular nobles and "pretenders" to his throne. However, Donald Black's hypothesis received some empirical support in that those who are often given the most severe penal sanctions (e.g. death sentences) are typically persons of social disadvantage (e.g., non-Sunni Muslims in Saudi Arabia, blacks in the United States, religious minorities and internal migrants in China).

- State-sponsored punishment is used in all modern societies to maintain order and eliminate minority group threats, but the characteristics of the particular threatening group are a reflection of the particular time and place. Within China's evolving social and economic order, overly greedy capitalists and religious minorities (e.g., Falun Gong, Uighur Muslims) have become the new "villains" for state control. In contrast, racial profiling and biases against African Americans remain a central issue in current U.S. crime-control practices, whereas the issues of homeland security and terrorist threats have become the primary focus of numerous repressive measures. The current minority group threat in countries experiencing a rise in Islamic fundamentalism involves the intrusion of Western culture, lifestyles, and beliefs. Rather than being uniform or constant over time and place, the nature of the minority threat and the punitive response to it are both context-specific and similar across contexts.

As these examples illustrate, there are both elements of common universal trends and context-specific patterns in punishment practices over time and place. However, it was only through a comparative historical analysis that we were able to evaluate the generality of these basic factors that underlie the sociological study of punishments.

SUMMARY AND CONCLUSIONS

The examination of punishment responses from a comparative historical perspective has allowed us to explore basic questions within the sociological study of law. State-sponsored sanctions across different contexts have been used to reinforce values, to eliminate or reduce minority group threat, and to deter criminal behavior. The supreme corporal punishment – the death penalty – has been successful in achieving some of these goals (e.g., reinforcing Puritan values in Colonial America, reducing threats to the Crown in Tudor England), but it has not been shown to have a positive effect on deterring criminal behavior. The low crime rates reported in China and Saudi Arabia are best explained by factors related to both deterrence (i.e., certain and severe punishment) and strong informal mechanisms of social control that minimize the occurrence of crime and deviance.

Socioeconomic disparities in the application of punishments are found across contexts and time periods. Minority group members and disadvantaged groups are often the targets of disparate treatment. Our examination of practices in the United States, China, and Saudi Arabia illustrates that differential treatment takes a different form and nature within each context.

Finally, attention to formal punishments challenges our strongly held value judgments about the relative civility of different countries. Accordingly, we have tried to demonstrate that these judgments are socially constructed and, therefore, are highly subjective and ethnocentric representations of our own cultural values. By considering the nature and magnitude of extrajudicial executions within countries, our labels of countries as "civilized" or "barbarian" would change dramatically.

We hope that this focus on punishment has shown the reader the value of a sociological approach to the study of this crucial aspect of human behavior. The use of punishment is often context-specific, and its purposes and functions can only be fully understood by its systematic examination through a comparative historical approach.

Notes

1. For a review of U.S. public opinion polls on the death penalty, see Roger Hood. 1996. *The Death Penalty: A World-Wide Perspective.* 2nd ed. Oxford, England: Clarendon Press. Pages 150–5; Phoebe C. Ellsworth and Lee Ross. 1983. "Public Opinion and Capital Punishment: A Closer Examination of the Views of Abolitionists and Retentionists." *Crime and Delinquency* 29: 116–69; Robert M. Bohm. 1991. "American Death Penalty Opinion, 1936–1986: A Critical Examination of the Gallup Polls." In Robert M. Bohm (ed.), *The Death Penalty in America: Current Research.* Cincinnati, OH: Anderson Publishing; Death Penalty Information Center. 2004. *Summaries of Recent Poll Findings.* See Death Penalty Information Center Web site: http://www.deathpenaltyinfo.org.

2. For example, analysis of data from the national Gallup polls in the United States indicates a wide gap in support for capital punishment by race that has continued over time. During the mid-1930s, over 60 percent of white respondents favored the death penalty for murder compared to about 40 percent of black respondents. By the mid-1980s, the corresponding proportions in favor of capital punishment by race were about 75 percent and 46 percent, respectively. See Robert M. Bohm. 1991. "American Death Penalty Opinion, 1936–1986: A Critical Examination of the Gallup Polls." In Robert M. Bohm (ed.), *The Death Penalty in America: Current Research.* Cincinnati, OH: Anderson Publishing. Page 120.

3. See Lord Windlesham. 1987. *Responses to Crime: Penal Policy in the Making.* Volume 1. Oxford, UK: Clarendon Press. Page 163. An article in *The Guardian* on August 21, 2002 noted that 76 percent of British respondents to a poll in 1995 supported the death penalty, but that support had dropped to only 56 percent in 2002.

4. See Emile Durkheim. 1933 [1893]. *The Division of Labor in Society.* Translated by George Simpson. New York: Free Press; Phillipe Nonet and Philip Selznick. 1978. *Law and Society*

in Transition: Toward Responsive Law. New York: Octagon Books; Donald Black. 1978. *The Behavior of Law.* New York: Academic Press; John Braithwaite. 1989. *Crime, Shame, and Reintegration.* New York: Cambridge University Press.

5. See Roy Walmsley. 2000. *World Prison Population List.* 2nd ed. Research Findings No. 116. England: Home Office Research, Development, and Statistics Directorate. Pages 1–6. The United States is a clear exception to this general pattern.

6. See Norbert Elias. 1978 [1939]. *The Civilizing Process I: The History of Manners.* New York: Urizen Books. Norbert Elias. 1982. *The Civilizing Process II: Power and Civility.* New York: Pantheon.

7. In English history, Mary Tudor's efforts to reestablish Catholicism through strict legal sanctions and the revival of heresy laws were also relatively short-lived and largely ineffective.

8. Within the United States, these educational programs designed to change values and beliefs include ongoing efforts at drug prevention education (e.g., DARE [Drug and Alcohol Resistance Education]) and various public service announcements and programs designed to decrease drunk driving ("friends don't let friends drive drunk"), domestic violence, and hate crimes. Unfortunately, although possibly changing values in some individuals, there is no convincing evidence that these educational programs have been effective in reducing the incidence of these harmful behaviors.

9. See Steven Vago. 1994. *Law and Society.* Upper Saddle River, NJ: Prentice-Hall.

10. See Graeme Newman. 1978. *The Punishment Response.* Philadelphia: J. P. Lippincott.

11. Douglas Hay. 1975. "Property, Authority, and the Criminal Law." In Douglas Hay et al., *Albion's Fatal Tree: Crime and Society in Eighteenth-Century England.* New York: Pantheon Books. Pages 19–20.

12. See Amnesty International. 1997. *Saudi Arabia: Behind Closed Doors: Unfair Trials in Saudi Arabia.* [AI Index No.: MDE230081997].

13. William J. Chambliss. 1967. "Types of Deviance and the Effectiveness of Legal Sanctions." *Wisconsin Law Review* Summer: 703–19.

14. Aside from specific and general deterrence, the literature also discusses marginal deterrence and partial deterrence. Each type of deterrence was defined and discussed in chapter 2.

15. See Bureau of Justice Statistics. 2002. *Recidivism of Prisoners Released in 1994.* Washington, D.C.: United States Department of Justice. 06/02 NCJ 193427.

16. The deterrent effect of punishments in the United States is also thought to be relatively weak because of the low certainty of criminal punishment in this context. National police data indicate that less than 20 percent of serious crimes are known to the police, and the certainty of punishment becomes even less likely when rates of case dismissal by prosecutors and judges and trial acquittals are also considered. For data on clearance rates for different index crimes in the United States, see Federal Bureau of Investigation. 2002. *Crime in the United States.* Washington, D.C.: U.S. Government Printing Office.

17. For example, estimated recidivism rates in China are in the range of 5 to 10 percent, whereas no direct estimates of repeat offending are available for Saudi Arabia. However, studies of crime and criminal justice in both of these countries rarely mention recidivism as a serious problem. This anecdotal evidence provides some

indication of the relative rarity of repeat offending in these countries, especially when compared to patterns in the United States. See Xinhuan News Agency. 1991. *Chinese State Council White Paper on Human Rights.* Xinghua News Agency, Beijing. http://www.tibetjustice.org/materials/china/china8.html.

18. The United States is currently experiencing a similar situation in its response to national and international acts of terrorism. In particular, individual rights considering unlawful searches, seizures, and interrogations have been weakened as government officials try to increase the potential deterrent value of certain and severe punishment for acts of terrorism (including the expansion of capital statutes in these cases). Unfortunately, the deterrent value of these efforts is likely to be minimal because of particular aspects of terrorists and their actions (i.e., they are often unlikely to be deterred because they may have high commitment to crime as a "mission" against real or perceived oppression).

19. *De jure* discriminatory involves actions that have a discriminatory purpose, whereas *De facto* discrimination occurs when some action or policy has a disparate impact regardless of its purpose.

20. When race and gender are considered simultaneously, black males have execution rates that far exceed those for any other combination of race and gender. For example, execution rates around 1900 for black males were a staggering 2,400 times higher than the rates for white females. This execution ratio between black males and white females for the 1940 and 1960 periods was 854:1 and 1,548:1, respectively. Even at the beginning of the twenty-first century, execution rates for black males were still about 100 times higher than for white females.

21. For an examination of changes in homicides by age and motive over time in the United States, see Terance D. Miethe and Wendy Regoeczi. 2004. *Rethinking Homicide: Exploring the Structure and Process Underlying Deadly Situations.* Cambridge, UK: Cambridge University Press.

22. Whether or not racial and gender differences in execution rates are representative of discriminatory treatment also cannot be determined from these simple comparisons for several obvious reasons. First, each of these groups with comparatively higher execution rates than their counterparts (e.g., males vs. females) may simply reflect differential involvement in executable types of offenses (e.g., males are far more likely than females to commit homicide and homicide is the most common capital offense in the twentieth century). Second, groups may differ in their likelihood of committing different types of homicide (e.g., instrumental murders during other felonies versus "heat of passion" killings or manslaughter). The higher execution rate for black offenders, for example, may reflect their greater involvement than whites in felony-homicides rather than voluntary manslaughter, with felony-murders being more widely designated as capital offenses. Third, other offender, offense, and case attributes (e.g., more extensive prior criminal records, multiple victims, greater public endangerment, weaker legal representativeness) may also account for these group differences in execution rates. Under these conditions, group differences in U.S. execution rates across the twentieth century are substantial, but these differences do not necessarily represent systematic and overt discriminatory treatment against particular social groups.

23. See Hong Lu and Kriss A. Drass. 2002. "Transience and the Disposition of Theft Cases in China." *Justice Quarterly* 19: 69–96. Transients are treated more severely in China because they pose a threat to informal social control that derives from neighborhood and residential stability. Internal migrants in China are viewed in a manner similar to the "dangerous classes" in urban England in the nineteenth century.

24. Our preliminary analysis of over 1,000 capital and noncapital cases in China also supports this observation about differential treatment to the detriment of higher-status offenders. Specifically, persons with high-status jobs in China (e.g., managers and public officials) are over 1.6 times more likely to receive a death sentence than lower-status workers. However, these differences by employment are eliminated once we adjust for the fact that high-status employees are more apt to commit major economic and corruption offenses, types of crimes that are more often treated as capital offenses in contemporary China.

25. For a discussion of the social constructionist perspective, see Joel Best. 1990. *Threatened Children: Rhetoric and Concern about Child Victims*. Chicago: University of Chicago Press; Philip Jenkins. 1994. *Using Murder: The Social Construction of Serial Homicide*. New York: Aldine de Gruyter; Richard C. McCorkle and Terance D. Miethe. 2001. *Panic: The Social Construction of the Street Gang Problem*. Upper Saddle River, NJ: Prentice-Hall.

26. For example, the mass killings in Burundi involving both Hutus and Tutsis have resulted in an estimated 600,000 deaths from the 1970s to the early 1990s. An estimated 1.1 million people in Sudan, 600,000 Ugandans, and 400,000 Nigerians have also been killed by acts of democide and genocide. See Irving Horowitz. 2002. *Taking Lives: Genocide and State Power*. 5th ed. New Brunswick, NJ: Transaction Publishers.

27. See Michel Foucault. 1977. *Discipline and Punish: The Birth of the Prison*. New York: Pantheon. David Garland. 1990. *Punishment and Modern Society: A Study in Social Theory*. Chicago: University of Chicago Press. Page 70.

28. Donald Black. 1978. *The Behavior of Law*. New York: Academic Press.

REFERENCES

Albanese, Jay S. 1995. *White Collar Crime in America.* Upper Saddle River, NJ: Prentice-Hall.

Ali, Badr-el-din. 1985. "Islamic Law and Culture: The Case of Saudi Arabia." *International Journal of Comparative and Applied Criminal Justice 9*(2): 51–3.

Amin, S. H. 1989. *Islamic Law and Its Implications for Modern Society.* Glasgow: Royston. United Kingdom.

Amnesty International. 1996. "Iraq, State Cruelty: Branding, Amputation, and the Death Penalty." [AI Index: MDE 14/03/96].

Amnesty International. 1996–2003. *Annual Reports. Regional and Country Reports.* Available through Amnesty International's Web site www.Amnesty.org.

Amnesty International. 1997a. *Female Genital Mutilation: A Human Rights Information Pack.* [AI Index: ACT 77/05/97].

Amnesty International. 1997b. *Saudi Arabia: Behind Closed Doors: Unfair Trials in Saudi Arabia.* [AI Index: MDE230081997].

Amnesty International Report. 2000a. "Dominican Republic: Killings by Security Forces." [AI Index: AMR 27/001/2000].

Amnesty International. 2000b. "Guatemala: Further Executions Loom." [AI Index: AMR 34/022/2000].

Amnesty International Report. 2000c. "Socialist Republic of Vietnam: The Death Penalty – Current Developments." [AI Index: ASA 41/001/2000].

Amnesty International Report. 2001. "Jamaica: Killings and Violence by Police – How Many More Victims." [AI Index: AMR 38/003/2001].

Amnesty International Report. 2002a. "Dominican Republic." [AI Index: POL 10/001/2002].

Amnesty International Report. 2002b. "Jamaica." [AI Index: POL 10/001/2002].

Amnesty International. 2002c. *Saudi Arabia Remains a Fertile Ground for Torture with Impunity.* [AI Index: MDE-230042002].

Amnesty International. 2003. *The Death Penalty: Death Penalty Statistics.* See Amnesty International's Web site www.Amnesty.org.

Andrews, D. A., I. Zinger, J. Bonta, R. D. Hoge, P. Gendreau, and F. T. Cullen. 1990. "Does Correctional Treatment Work? A Psychologically Informed Meta-Analysis." *Criminology* 28: 369–404.

An-na'im, Abdullahi Ahmed. 1990. *Toward an Islamic Reformation: Civil Liberties, Human Rights, and International Law*. Syracuse, NY: Syracuse University Press.

Arab Crime Statistics. 1981. *Arab Organization for Social Defense*. Baghdad, Iraq. Cited in Sam S. Souryal, "The Religionization of a Society: The Continuing Application of Shariah Law in Saudi Arabia." *Journal for the Scientific Study of Religion* 26(4): 429–49.

Bassiouni, M. Cherif. 1982a. *The Islamic Criminal Justice System*. New York: Oceana.

Bassiouni, M. Cherif. 1982b. "Quesas Crimes." In M. Cherif Bassiouni (ed.), *The Islamic Criminal Justice System*. New York: Oceana, 203–9.

Benmelha, Ghaouti. 1982. "Ta'azir Crimes." In M. Cherif Bassiouni (ed.), *The Islamic Criminal Justice System*. New York: Oceana, 211–25.

Benn, Charles. 2002. *Daily Life in Traditional China – The Tang Dynasty*. Westport, CT: Greenwood Press.

Bentham, Jeremy. 1789. *An Introduction to the Principles of Morals and Legislation*. London: T. Payne.

Best, Joel. 1990. *Threatened Children: Rhetoric and Concern about Child Victims*. Chicago: University of Chicago Press.

Biles, David. 1995. "Prisoners in Asia and the Pacific." *Overcrowded Times* 6(6): 5–6.

Black, Donald. 1978. *The Behavior of Law*. New York: Academic Press.

Bodde, Derek, and Clarence Morris. 1973. *Law in Imperial China*. Philadelphia: University of Pennsylvania Press.

Bohm, Robert M. 1991. "American Death Penalty Opinion, 1936–1986: A Critical Examination of the Gallup Polls." In Robert M. Bohm (ed.), *The Death Penalty in America: Current Research*. Cincinnati, OH: Anderson Publishing, 113–45.

Bonger, Willem. 1916. *Criminality and Economic Conditions*. Boston: Little, Brown.

Bowers, William J. 1984. *Legal Homicide: Death as Punishment in America, 1864–1982*. Boston: Northeastern University Press.

Bozan, Jan, Xunzheng Shao, and Hua Hu. 1981. *A Concise History of China*. Beijing: Foreign Language Press.

Braithwaite, John. 1989. *Crime, Shame, and Reintegration*. New York: Cambridge University Press.

Brockeman, Rosser H. 1980. "Commercial Contract Law in Late Nineteenth-Century Taiwan." In Jerome Alan Cohen, R. Randle Edwards, and Fu-mei Chang Chen (eds.), *Essays on China's Legal Tradition*. Princeton, NJ: Princeton University Press, 76–136.

Brundage, W. Fitzhugh. 1997. *Under Sentence of Death: Lynchings in the South*. Chapel Hill: University of North Carolina Press.

Bun, Kwan Man. 2001. *The Salt Merchants of Tianjin – State-Making and Civil Society in Late Imperial China*. Honolulu: University of Hawaii Press, 71–2.

Bureau of Justice Statistics. 2002a. *Capital Punishment 2001*. Washington, D.C.: U.S. Department of Justice. December 2002. NCJ 197020.

Bureau of Justice Statistics. 2002b. *Recidivism of Prisoners Released in 1994*. Washington, D.C.: United States Department of Justice. 06/02. NCJ 193427.

Cai, Dingjian. 1997. "China's Major Reform in Criminal Law." *Columbia Journal of Asian Law* 11: 213–18.

Case Collections. 1999. Beijing: The Chinese People's University Publishing House.

Central Intelligence Agency. 2003a. *The World Factbook. China*. Washington, D.C. Web site location: www.odci.gov/cia/publications/factbook/geos/us.html.

Central Intelligence Agency. 2003b. *The World Factbook. Saudi Arabia*. Washington, D.C. Web site location: www.odci.gov/cia/publications/factbook/geos/us.html.

Central Intelligence Agency. 2003c. *The World Factbook. The United States*. Washington, D.C. Web site location: www.odci.gov/cia/publications/factbook/geos/s.html.

Chalk, Frank, and Kurt Jonassohn. 1990. *A History and Sociology of Genocide*. New Haven, CT: Yale University Press.

Chambliss, William J. 1967. "Types of Deviance and the Effectiveness of Legal Sanctions." *Wisconsin Law Review*, Summer: 703–19.

Chambliss, William, and Robert Seidman. 1982. *Law, Order, and Power*. 2nd ed. Reading, MA: Addison-Wesley.

Chen, Albert H. Y. 1996. "The Developing Theory of Law and Market Economy in Contemporary China." In Wang Guiguo and Wei Zhenying (eds.), *Legal Developments in China: Market Economy and Law*. Hong Kong: Sweet & Maxwell, 3–21.

Chen, Paul H. 1979. *Chinese Legal Tradition under the Mongol – The Code of 1291 as Reconstructed*. Princeton, NJ: Princeton University Press.

Chen, Xingliang. 1997. *The New Horizon of Contemporary Criminal Law in China*. Beijing: Chinese University of Politics and Law.

Christie, N. LS. 2000. *Crime Control as Industry: Toward Gulags, Western Style*. 3rd ed. New York: Routledge.

Clear, Todd R., and George F. Cole. 2000. *American Corrections*. 5th ed. Belmont, CA: West/Wadsworth.

Clinard, Marshall B., and Robert F. Meier. 1985. *Sociology of Deviant Behavior*. 6th ed. New York: Holt, Rinehart and Winston.

Cohen, Jerome A., R. Randle Edwards, and Fu-mei Chang Chen (eds.). *Essays on China's Legal Tradition*. Princeton, NJ: Princeton University Press.

Coulson, Noel J. 1964. *A History of Islamic Law*. Edinburgh: Edinburgh University Press.

Coulson, Noel J. 1969. *Conflicts and Tensions in Islamic Jurisprudence*. Chicago: University of Chicago Press.

Creel, Herrlee Glessner. 1980. "Legal Institutions and Procedures during the Chou Dynasty." In Jerome Alan Cohen, R. Randle Edwards, and Fu-mei Chang Chen (eds.), *Essays on China's Legal Tradition*. Princeton, NJ: Princeton University Press, 26–55.

Crockett, George W., and Morris Gleicher. 1978. "Inside China's Prison." *Judicature* 61: 409–15.

Cullen, Francis, Bruce Link, and Craig Polanzi. 1982. "The Seriousness of Crime Revisited: Have Attitudes toward White-Collar Crime Changed?" *Criminology* 20: 83–102.

Curran, Barbara, 1977. *The Legal Needs of the Public: The Final Report of a National Survey.* Chicago: American Bar Foundation.

Davis, Stephen B. 1987. "The Death Penalty and Legal Reform in the PRC." *Journal of Chinese Law* 1: 303–34.

Death Penalty Information Center. 2004. *Summaries of Recent Poll Findings.* See Death Penalty Information Center Web site: www.deathpenaltyinfo.org.

Denham, James M. 1997. *A Roque's Paradise: Crime and Punishment in Antebellum Florida, 1821–1861.* Tuscaloosa: University of Alabama Press.

Denny, Frederick Mathewson. 1985. *An Introduction to Islam.* New York: Macmillan.

Dijk, Jan J. M. van, Pat Mayhew, and Martin Killias. 1991. *Experiences of Crime Across the World: Key Findings from the 1989 International Crime Survey.* 2nd ed. Boston: Kluwer Law and Taxation Publishers.

Dikotter, Frank. 1997. "Crime and Punishment in Post-Liberation China: The Prisoners of a Beijing Gaol in the 1950s." *China Quarterly* 149: 147–59.

Dikotter, Frank. 2000. "Crime and Punishment in Early Republican China: Beijing's First Model Prison, 1912–1922." *Late Imperial China* 21: 140–62.

Dikotter, Frank. 2002a. "The Promise of Repentance – Prison Reform in Modern China." *British Journal of Criminology* 42: 240–9.

Dikotter, Frank. 2002b. *Crime, Punishment and the Prison in Modern China.* NY: Columbia University Press.

Drapkin, Israel. 1986. *Crime and Punishment in the Ancient World.* New York: Lexington Books.

Durkheim, Emile. 1933 [1893]. *The Division of Labor in Society.* Translated by George Simpson. New York: Free Press.

Durkheim, Emile. 1938. *The Rules of Sociological Method.* New York: Free Press.

Dutton, Michael. 1992. *Policing and Punishment in China – From Patriarchy to "the People."* Cambridge, UK: Cambridge University Press.

Edwards, R. Randle, 1980. "Ching Legal Jurisdiction over Foreigners," In Jerome A. Cohen, R. Randle Edwards, and Fu-mei Chang Chen (eds.), *Essays on China's Legal Tradition.* Princeton, NJ: Princeton University Press, 222–69.

Elias, Norbert. 1978 [1939]. *The Civilizing Process I: The History of Manners.* New York: Urizen Books.

Elias, Norbert. 1982. *The Civilizing Process II: Power and Civility.* New York: Pantheon.

Ellsworth, Phoebe C., and Lee Ross. 1983. "Public Opinion and Capital Punishment: A Closer Examination of the Views of Abolitionists and Retentionists." *Crime and Delinquency* 29: 116–69.

Emsley, Clive. 1987. *Crime and Society in England, 1750–1900.* London: Longman.

Erickson, Kai. 1966. *Wayward Puritans.* New Haven, CT: Yale University Press.

Espy, M. Watt, and John Ortiz Smykla. 1991. *Executions in the United States, 1608–1991: The Espy File.* [Data File]. Inter-University Consortium for Social and Political Research. Ann Arbor: University of Michigan.

Fairchild, Erika, and Harry R. Dammer. 2001. *Comparative Criminal Justice Systems.* 2nd ed. Belmont, CA: Wadsworth/Thomson Learning.

Federal Bureau of Investigation. 1981. *Crime in the United States.* Washington, D.C.: U.S. Government Printing Office.

Federal Bureau of Investigation. 2002. *Crime in the United States.* Washington, D.C.: U.S. Government Printing Office.

Foucault, Michel. 1977. *Discipline and Punish.* New York: Pantheon.

Friedrichs, David O. 2004. *Trusted Criminals: White Collar Crime in Contemporary Society.* 2nd ed. Belmont, CA: Wadsworth.

Fu, Zhengyuan. 1996. *China's Legalists.* Armonk, NY: M. E. Sharpe.

Galanter, Marc. 1983. "Reading the Landscape of Disputes: What We Know and Don't Know (and Think We Know) About Our Allegedly Contentious and Litigious Society." *UCLA Law Review* 31(October): 4–71.

Garland, David. 1990. *Punishment and Modern Society: A Study in Social Theory.* Chicago: University of Chicago Press.

Gibbs, Jack P. 1975. *Crime, Punishment, and Deterrence.* New York: Elsevier.

Goitein, Solomon D., and A. Ben Shemesh. 1961. *Muslim Law in Israel: An Introduction to Muslim Law.* Jerusalem: Mifal Hashichpul and Gvilim.

Gottfredson, Stephen D., and Don M. Gottfredson. 1992. *Incapacitation Strategies and the Criminal Career.* Sacramento, CA: Information Center, California Division of Law Enforcement.

Greenwood, Peter. 1982. *Selective Incapacition.* Santa Monica, CA: Rand Corp.

Griffin, Larry J., Paula Clark, and Joanne C. Sandburg. 1997. "Narrative and Event: Lynching and Historical Sociology." In W. Fitzhugh Brundage (ed.), *Under Sentence of Death: Lynchings in the South.* Chapel Hill: University of North Carolina Press, 24–47.

Grossman, Mark. 1998. *Encyclopedia of Capital Punishment.* Santa Barbara, CA: ABC-CLIO Publishers.

Hall, David D. 1999. *Witch-Hunting in Seventeenth-Century New England: A Documentary History, 1638–1693.* 2nd ed. Boston: Northeastern University Press.

Hay, Douglas. 1975. "Property, Authority, and the Criminal Law." In Douglas Hay et al., *Albion's Fatal Tree: Crime and Society in Eighteenth-Century England.* New York: Pantheon Books.

Hobbs, A. B. 1991. "Criminality in Philadelphia: 1790–1810 Compared with 1937." In Eric H. Monkkonen, *Crime and Justice in American History: Historical Articles on the Origins and Evolution of American Criminal Justice. The Colonies and Early Republic.* Vol. 1. London: Meckler, 339–43.

Holscher, Louis M., and Rizwana Mahmood. 2000. "Borrowing from the Shariah: The Potential Uses of Procedural Islamic Law in the West." In Delbert Rounds, *International Criminal Justice: Issues in a Global Perspective.* 2nd ed. Boston: Allyn and Bacon, 82–96.

Hood, Roger. 1996. *The Death Penalty: A World-Wide Perspective.* 2nd ed. Oxford, UK: Clarendon Press.

Horowitz, Irving. 2002. *Taking Lives: Genocide and State Power.* 5th ed. New Brunswick, NJ: Transaction Publishers.

Human Rights Watch. 1993. *The Events of 1992*. New York: Human Rights Watch, Inc.

Human Rights Watch. 1996a. "The Small Hands of Slavery – Bonded Child Labor in India." New York: Human Rights Watch. [HRW Index No.: ISBN 1-56432-172-x.]. September 1, 1996.

Human Rights Watch. 1996b. "Thirst for Justice: A Decade of Impunity in Haiti." New York: Human Rights Watch. September 1, 1996.

Human Rights Watch. 1997. "The Human Rights Record of the Haitian National Police." New York: Human Rights Watch. January 1, 1997.

Human Rights Watch. 2001a. "Defending Human Rights – The Role of the International Community, Saudi Arabia." New York: Human Rights Watch.

Human Rights Watch. 2001b. "China/APEC Summit: Crackdown in Xinjiang." New York: Human Rights Watch. October 18, 2001.

Human Rights Watch. 2001c. "Human Rights in Saudi Arabia: A Deafening Silence." New York: Human Rights Watch Article, December 2001. Associated Press (AP) April 24, 2000.

Human Rights Watch. 2002a. "Singapore: Asia's gilded cage." Human Rights Features. New York: Human Rights Watch. April 17, 2002.

Human Rights Watch. 2002b. "China: Repression Against Falun Gong Unabated." Press Release Report. New York: Human Rights Watch. [HRW Index No.: 270x]. February 7, 2002.

Human Rights in China. 2002. *Institutionalized Exclusion: The Tenuous Legal Status of Internal Migrants in China's Major Cities*. Human Rights in China. November 6, 2002.

Inverarity, James, Pat Lauderdale, and Barry Feld. 1983. *Law and Society: Sociological Perspectives on Criminal Law*. Boston: Little, Brown.

Ivashko, Sergei. 2001. "Duma Discusses Abolishment of Death Penalty." Cited in Johnson's Russia List Web site: Johnson@erols.com.

Izzo, R., and R. R. Ross. 1990. "Meta-Analysis of Rehabilitation Programs for Juveniles: A Brief Report." *Criminal Justice and Behavior* 17: 134–42.

Jenkins, Philip. 1994. *Using Murder: The Social Construction of Serial Homicide*. New York: Aldine de Gruyter.

Johnson, Wallace. 1979. *The Tang Code*. Princeton, NJ: Princeton University Press.

Judicial Document Selections of the People's Court. Beijing, 2000. Law Publishing House.

Judicial Document Selections of the People's Court. Sichuan, 2000. Law Publishing House.

Judicial Document Selections of the People's Court. Zhejiang, 2000. Law Publishing House.

Kealey, Linda. 1991. "Patterns of Punishment: Massachusetts in the Eighteenth Century." In Eric H. Monkkonen (ed.), *Crime and Justice in American History: Historical Articles on the Origins and Evolution of American Criminal Justice. The Colonies and Early Republic*. Vol. 1. London: Meckler, 344–67.

Khan, Khisz Muazzam. 1983. "Juristic Classification of Islamic Law." *Houston Journal of International Law* 6: 24–7.

Knight, John, and Lina Song. 2002. "Rural-Urban Divide: Economic Disparities in China." In Thomas Buoye et al. (eds.), *China: Adapting the Past, Confronting the Future*. Ann Arbor: University of Michigan Press, 377–81.

Kronenwetter, Michael. 2001. *Capital Punishment: A Reference Handbook*. 2nd ed. Santa Barbara, CA: ABC-CLIO.

Lamb, David M. 2003. "Regulations of The Peoples Republic of China on Protecting the Safety of Computer Information." Cited in *Cyber Crime: The Cyber Criminal Epidemic*. November 24, 2003 at www.geocities.com/chopshoptuning/paper.html.

Lane, Roger. 1997. *Murder in America: A History*. Columbus: Ohio State University Press.

Latessa, Edward J., and Harry E. Allen. 1999. *Corrections in the Community*. 2nd ed. Cincinnati, OH: Anderson Publishing.

Lawson, Edward H. 1991. *The Encyclopedia of Human Rights*. New York: Taylor and Francis.

Lawson, Stephen. 2001. "China cracks down on internet cafes." CNN.com/sci-tech. April 19, 2001.

Law Yearbook of China (1987–2003). Beijing: Law Yearbook of China Publishing House.

Lewis, Bernard. 1961. *The Arabs in History*. New York: Harper and Row.

Lieberman, Jethro. 1983. *The Litigious Society*. New York: Basic Books.

Liebesny, Herbert J. 1972. "Comparative Legal History: Its Role in the Analysis of Islamic Law and Modern Near Eastern Legal Institutions." *American Journal of Comparative Law* 20: 38–52.

Lippman, Matthew, Sean McConville, and Mordechai Yerushalmi. 1988. *Islamic Criminal Law and Procedure: An Introduction*. New York: Praeger.

Liu, Yongping. 1998. *Origins of Chinese Law – Penal and Administrative Law in Its Early Development*. Oxford, NY: Oxford University Press.

Lo, C. W. 1995. *China's Legal Awakening*. Hong Kong: Hong Kong University Press.

Lu, Hong, and Kriss A. Drass. 2002. "Transience and the Disposition of Theft Cases in China." *Justice Quarterly* 19: 69–96.

Lu, Hong, and Terance D. Miethe. 2003. "Confessions and Criminal Case Disposition in China." *Law and Society Review* 37: 549–78.

Luo, Wei. 1998. *The 1997 Criminal Code of the People's Republic of China: With English Translation and Introduction*. Buffalo, NY: William S. Hein.

Luo, Wei. 2000. *The Amended Criminal Procedure Law and the Criminal Court Rules of the PRC*. Buffalo, NY: William S. Hein.

MacCormack, Geoffrey. 1990. *Traditional Chinese Penal Law*. Edinburgh, England: Edinburgh University Press.

Mansour, Aly Aly. 1982. "Hudud Crimes." In M. Cherif Bassiouni (ed.), *Islamic Criminal Justice System*. New York: Oceana, 196–201.

Mao, Gengsheng. 1999. *Interpretation of the Chinese Criminal Law*. Beijing: Tong Xin Publishing House.

Martinson, Robert. 1974. "What Works? Questions and Answers About Prison Reform." *The Public Interest* 35(Spring): 22–54.

Massey, James L., and Martha A. Myers. 1989. "Patterns of Repressive Social Control in Post-Reconstruction Georgia, 1882–1935." *Social Forces* 68(2): 458–88.

Mauer, Marc. 1991. *Americans Behind Bars: A Comparison of International Rates of Incarceration.* Washington, D.C.: The Sentencing Project.

Mauer, Marc. 1992. *Americans Behind Bars; One Year Later.* Washington, D.C.: The Sentencing Project.

Mayhew, Pat, and Jan J. M. van Dijk. 1997. *Criminal Victimization in Eleven Industrialized Countries: Key Findings from the 1996 International Crime Victimization Survey.* The Hague: Ministry of Justice.

McCorkle, Richard C., and Terance D. Miethe. 2001. *Panic: The Social Construction of the Street Gang Problem.* Upper Saddle River, NJ: Prentice-Hall.

McKnight, Brian E. 1992. *Law and Order in Sung China.* Cambridge, UK: Cambridge University Press.

Meier, Robert F. 1989. *Crime and Society.* Boston: Allyn and Bacon.

Meijer, Marinus J. 1980. "Slavery at the End of the Ching Dynasty." In Jerome Alan Cohen, R. Randle Edwards, and Fu-mei Chang Chen (eds.), *Essays on China's Legal Tradition.* Priceton, NJ: Princeton University Press, 327–58.

Melossi, Dario, and Mark Lettiere. 1998. "Punishment in the American Democracy: The Paradoxes of Good Intentions." In Robert P. Weiss and Nigel South (eds.), *Comparing Prison Systems: Toward a Comparative and International Penology.* Amsterdam: Overseas Publishers Association.

Miethe, Terance D. 1984. "Types of Consensus in Public Evaluations of Crime: An Illustration of Strategies for Measuring 'Consensus.'" *Journal of Criminal Law and Criminology* 75(2): 459–73.

Miethe, Terance D. 1995. "Predicting Future Litigiousness." *Justice Quarterly* 12(3): 407–28.

Miethe, Terance D. 1999. *Whistleblowing At Work: Tough Choices in Exposing Fraud, Waste, and Abuse on the Job.* Boulder, CO: Westview.

Miethe, Terance D., and Wendy C. Regoeczi. 2004. *Rethinking Homicide: Exploring the Structure and Process Underlying Deadly Situations.* Cambridge, UK: Cambridge University Press.

Miyagawa, Maxio. 1992. *Do Economic Sanctions Work?* New York: St. Martin's Press.

Miyazaki, Ichisada. 1980. "The Administration of Justice During the Sung Dynasty." In Jerome Alan Cohen, R. Randle Edwards, and Fu-mei Chang Chen (eds.), *Essays on China's Legal Tradition.* Princeton, NJ: Princeton University Press, 56–75.

Monkkonen, Eric H. 1991. *Crime and Justice in American History: Historical Articles on the Origins and Evolution of American Criminal Justice. The Colonies and Early Republic.* Vol. 1 and 2. London: Meckler.

Moore, Charles A. 1987. "Taming the Giant Corporation: Some Cautionary Remarks on the Deterrability of Corporate Crime." *Crime and Delinquency* 33: 379–402.

Morris, Norval, and David J. Rothman. 1995. *The Oxford History of the Prison*. New York: Oxford University Press.

Morris, Norval, and Michael Tonry. 1990. *Between Prison and Probation: Intermediate Punishments in a Rational Sentencing System*. New York: Oxford University Press.

Mosher, Clayton, Terance Miethe, and Dretha Phillips. 2002. *The Mismeasure of Crime*. Beverly Hills, CA: Sage.

Nader, M. M. J. 1990. *Aspects of Saudi Arabia Law*. Riyadh, Saudi Arabia: Nader.

Nagin, Daniel S. 1998. "Criminal Deterrence Research at the Outset of the Twenty-First Century." In Michael Tonry (ed.), *Crime and Justice: A Review of Research*. Vol. 23. Chicago: University of Chicago Press, 1–42.

Nelson, William E. 1991. "Emerging Notions of Modern Criminal Law in the Revolutionary Era: An Historical Perspective." In Eric H. Monkkonen (ed.), *Crime and Justice in American History: The Colonies and Early Republic*. Vol. 2. London: Meckler, 429–61.

Newbold, Greg, and Chris W. Eskridge. 1996. "History and Development of Modern Correctional Practices in New Zealand." In Charles B. Fields and Richter H. Moore, Jr. (eds.), *Comparative Criminal Justice – Traditional and Nontraditional Systems of Law and Control*. Prospect Heights, IL: Waveland, 453–78.

Newman, Graeme. 1978. *The Punishment Response*. Philadelphia: J. P. Lippincott.

Newman, Graeme. 1999. *Global Report on Crime and Justice: Published for the United Nations*. New York: Oxford University Press.

New Zealand Ministry of Justice Report. 2000. *Report of Monetary Penalties in New Zealand*. Available through the following Web site: www.justice.govt.nz/pubs/reports/2000.

Ning, Pu. 1994. *Red in Tooth and Claw: Twenty-Six Years in Communist Chinese Prisons*. New York: Grove Press.

Nonet, Phillipe, and Philip Selznick. 1978. *Law and Society in Transition: Toward Responsive Law*. New York: Octagon Books.

Palmer, Michael. 1996. "The People's Republic of China." In Peter Hodgkinson and Andrew Rutherford (eds.), *Capital Punishment – Global Issues and Prospects*. Winchester, UK: Waterside Press, 105–41.

Pasqualini, Jean. 1993. "Glimpses inside China's Gulag." *The China Quarterly* 134: 352–7.

Paternoster, Raymond. 1987. "The Deterrent Effect of the Perceived Certainty and Severity of Punishment: A Review of the Evidence and Issues." *Justice Quarterly* 4(2): 173–217.

Paternoster, Raymond. 1991. *Capital Punishment in America*. New York: Lexington Books.

Petersilia, Joan, Peter W. Greenwood, and Marvin Lavin. 1978. *Criminal Careers of Habitual Felons*. Santa Monica, CA: Rand Corp.

Peretz, Don, Richard U. Moench, and Safia K. Mohsen. 1984. *Islam: Legacy of the Past, Challenge of the Future*. New York: New Horizon Press.

Preyer, Kathryn. 1991. "Penal Measures in American Colonies: An Overview." In Eric H. Monkkonen (ed.), *Crime and Justice in American History: The Colonies and Early Republic.* Vol. 2. London: Meckler, 476–503.

Quinney, Richard. 1973. *Critique of Legal Order.* Boston: Little, Brown.

Quinney, Richard. 1977. *Class, State, and Crime.* New York: McKay.

Radzinowitcz, Sir Leon. 1948. *A History of English Criminal Law and its Administration from 1750.* London: Stevens and Sons Limited.

Rahma, Shaikh Abdur. 1972. *Punishment of Apostasy in Islam.* Lahore: Institute of Islamic Culture, chapter 2.

Rasheed, Madawi Al. 2002. *A History of Saudi Arabia.* Cambridge, UK: Cambridge University Press.

Reichel, Philip L. 1999. *Comparative Criminal Justice Systems.* 2nd ed. Upper Saddle River, NJ: Prentice-Hall.

Roberts, Robert. 1971. *The Social Law of the Qoran.* London: Curzon Press.

Roetz, Heiner. 1993. *Confucian Ethics of the Axial Age.* Albany: State University of New York Press.

Rojek, Dean G. 2001. "Chinese Social Control: From Shaming and Reintegration to 'Getting Rich is Glorious.'" In J. Liu, L. Zhang, and S. Messner (eds.), *Crime and Social Control in a Changing China.* Westport, CT: Greenwood Press, 89–104.

Rose, Lionel. 1988. *Rogues and Vagabonds: Vagrant Underworld in Britain 1815–1985.* London: Routledge Press.

Rossi, Peter, Emily Waite, Christine Bose, and Richard Berk. 1974. "The Seriousness of Crime: Normative Structure and Individual Differences." *American Sociological Review* 39: 224–37.

Rusche, Georg, and Otto Kirchheimer. 1939 [1968]. *Punishment and Social Structure.* New York: Russell and Russell.

Safwat, Safia M. 1982. "Offenses and Penalties in Islamic Law." *Islamic Law Quarterly* 26: 169–71.

Salama, Ma'amoun M. 1982. "General Principles of Criminal Evidence in Islamic Jurisprudence." In M. Cherif Bassiouni (ed.), *The Islamic Criminal Justice System.* New York: Oceana, 116–18.

Saleh, Osman abd-el-Malak al. 1982. "The Rights of the Individual to Personal Security in Islam." In M. Cherif Bassiouni (ed.), *The Islamic Criminal Justice System.* New York: Oceana, 55–90.

Schacht, Joseph. 1959. *The Origins of Muhammadan Jurisprudence.* Oxford, UK: Oxford University Press.

Schacht, Joseph. 1964. *Introduction to Islamic Law.* Oxford, UK: Oxford University Press.

Scheff, Thomas J. 1990. *Microsociology: Discourse, Emotion, and Social Structure.* Chicago: University of Chicago Press.

Schmalleger, Frank, and John Ortiz Smyka. 2001. *Corrections in the 21st Century.* New York: Glencoe McGraw Hill.

Schwed, Roger E. 1983. *Abolition and Capital Punishment.* New York: AMS Press.

Scobell, Andrew. 1990. "The Death Penalty in Post-Mao China." *China Quarterly* 123: 503–20.

Scully, Gerald. 1997. *Murder by the State*. Washington, D.C.: National Center for Policy Analysis.

Seaman, Bryant W. 1979. "Islamic Law and Modern Government: Saudi Arabia Supplements the Shari'a to Regulate Development." *Columbia Journal of Transnational Law* 18: 417. Cited in Matthew Lippman, Sean McConville, and Mordechai Yerushalmi, *Islamic Criminal Law and Procedure: An Introduction*. New York: Praeger, 25.

Sebok, Anthony J. 2001. "How Germany views U.S. Tort Law: Duties, Damages, Dumb Luck and the Differences in the Two Countries' Systems." tsebok@findlaw.com. Monday, July 23, 2001.

Shaw, Victor. 1996. *Social Control in China*. Westport, CT.: Praeger.

Shaw, Victor N. 1998. "Productive Labor and Thought Reform in Chinese Corrections: A Historical and Comparative Analysis." *The Prison Journal* 78: 186–211.

Siddiqi, Muhammad Iqbal. 1979. *The Penal Law of Islam*. Lahore: Kazi.

Simon, Rita, and Dagny A. Blaskovich. 2002. *A Comparative Analysis of Capital Punishment: Statutes, Policies, Frequencies, and Public Attitudes the World Over*. New York: Lexington Books.

Simons, Geoff. 1999. *Imposing Economic Sanctions: Legal Remedy or Genocidal Tool?* London: Pluto Press.

Simpson, Sally S. 2002. *Corporate Crime, Law, and Social Control*. New York: Cambridge University Press.

Smith, Abbott Emerson. 1947. *Colonists in Bondage*. Chapel Hill: University of North Carolina Press.

Sourryal, Sam S. 1987a. "Saudi Arabia's Judicial System." *The Middle East Journal* 25: 403–7.

Souryal, Sam S. 1987b. "The Religionization of a Society: The Continuing Application of Shariah Law in Saudi Arabia." *Journal for the Scientific Study of Religion* 26(4): 429–49.

Souryal, Sam S., Abdullah I. Alobied, and Dennis W. Potts. 1994. "The Penalty of Hand Amputation for Theft in Islamic Justice." *Journal of Criminal Justice* 22(3): 249–65.

Spear, C. 1844. *Essays on the Punishment of Death*. Boston: John Green. Cited in William J. Bowers. 1984. *Legal Homicide: Death as Punishment in America, 1864–1982*. Boston: Northeastern University Press, 140.

Spierenburg, Pieter. 1995. "The Body and the State: Early Modern Europe." In Norval Morris and David J. Rothman (eds.), *The Oxford History of the Prison*. New York: Oxford University Press, 49–77.

Spohn, Cassia C. 2000. "Thirty Years of Sentencing Reform: The Quest for a Racially Neutral Sentencing Process." In Julie Horney (ed.), *Policies, Processes, and Decisions of the Criminal Justice System: Criminal Justice 2000*. Vol. 3. Washington, D.C.: U.S. Department of Justice, National Institute of Justice, 427–502.

Straits Times. 2003. *China News Weekly*. Laogai Research Foundation. 05/05/03.

Strick, Anne. 1977. *Injustice for All*. New York: Penguin.

Tannenbaum, Frank. 1938. *Crime and the Community*. Boston: Ginn.

Tanner, Harold M. 1999. *Strike Hard!* Ithaca, NY: Cornell University Press.

United Nations. 1996. "Human Rights Questions: Human Rights Questions, Including Alternative Approaches for Improving the Effective Enjoyment of Human Rights and Fundamental Freedom. Extrajudicial, Summary, or Arbitrary Executions." *Report of the Special Rapporteur of the Commission on Human Rights on Extrajudicial, Summary, and Arbitrary Executions*. United Nations General Assembly, 51st Assembly, Agenda Item 110 (b).

U.S. Department of Justice. 1982. *Prisoners 1925–81*. Bureau of Justice Statistics. Bulletin NCJ-85861. Washington, D.C.: U.S. Government Printing Office. December 1982.

U.S. Department of Justice. 2003. *Prison and Jail Inmates at Midyear 2002*. Bureau of Justice Statistics. Bulletin NCJ-198877. Washington, D.C.: U.S. Government Printing Office. April 2003.

U.S. Department of State. 1994. *Country Reports on Human Rights Practices for 1993*. Washington, D.C.: U.S. Government Printing Office.

U.S. Department of State. 1998. *China Country Report on Human Rights Practices for 1998: "Population Control"* at www.laogai.org/reports/stdept/sdpop.htm.

Vago, Steven. 1981. *Law and Society*. 1st ed. Upper Saddle River, NJ: Prentice-Hall.

Vago, Steven. 1994. *Law and Society*. 4th ed. Upper Saddle River, NJ: Prentice-Hall.

Vesey-Fitzgerald, S. G. 1955. "Nature and Sources of the *Shari'a*." In Majid Khadduri and Herbert Liebesny (eds.), *Law in the Middle East*. Washington, D.C.: Middle East Institute, 91–2.

Vila, Bryan, and Cynthia Morris. 1997. *Capital Punishment in the United States: A Documentary History*. Westport, CT: Greenwood Press.

Walker, Samuel, Cassia Spohn, and Miriam DeLone. 2003. *The Color of Justice: Race, Ethnicity, and Crime in America*. 3rd ed. Belmont, CA: Wadsworth.

Walmsley, Roy. 2000. *World Prison Population List (second edition)*. Home Office Research, Development and Statistics Directorate. Research Findings No. 116.

Wang, Wen. 1999. "Illegal Drug Abuse and the Community Camp Strategy in China." *Journal of Drug Education* 29: 97–114.

Watt, Montgomery W. 1968. *Islamic Political Thought*. Edinburgh: Edinburgh University Press.

Whitmore, William H. 1890. "The Body of Liberties, 1641." *A Bibliographical Sketch of the Laws of the Massachusetts Colony from 1630 to 1686*. Boston: Rockwell and Churchill.

Windlesham, Lord. 1987. *Responses to Crime: Penal Policy in the Making*. Vol. 1. Oxford, UK: Clarendon Press.

Woo, Margaret Y. K. 1994. "Chinese Women Workers: The Delicate Balance between Protection and Equality." In Christina K. Gilmartin et al. (eds.), *Engendering China: Women, Culture, and the State*. Cambridge, MA: Harvard University Press, 279–98.

Wright, David Curtis. 2001. *The History of China*. Westport, CT.: Greenwood Press.

Wright, George C. 1997. "By the Book: The Legal Execution of Kentucky Blacks." In W. Fitzhugh Brundage (ed.), *Under Sentence of Death: Lynchings in the South.* Chapel Hill: University of North Carolina Press, 250–70.

Wu, Harry. 1994. *Bitter Winds: A Memoir of My Years in China's Gulag.* New York: John Wiley.

Xinhuan News Agency. 1991. *Chinese State Council White Paper on Human Rights.* Xinghua News Agency, Beijing. www.tibetjustice.org/materials/china/ china8.html.

Yu, Zongquan, Shuan Wang, and Rong Ran. Nov. 25, 2003. "On the Current Situation and Development of Fines." www.chinacourt.org.

Zatz, Marjorie S. 1994. *Producing Legality – Law and Socialism in Cuba.* New York: Routledge.

Zatz, Marjorie S. 2000. "The Convergence of Race, Ethnicity, Gender, and Class on Court Decisionmaking: Looking Toward the 21st Century." In Julie Horney (ed.), *Policies, Processes, and Decisions of the Criminal Justice System: Criminal Justice 2000.* Vol. 3. Washington, D.C.: U.S. Department of Justice, National Institute of Justice, 503–52.

Zellere, Evelyn, and Joanna B. Cannon. 2000. "Restorative Justice, Reparation, and the Southside Project." In David R. Karp and Todd R. Clear, *What is Community Justice?* Thousand Oaks, CA: Sage, 89–107.

Zhong, Shuqin. 1995. *The Theory and Practice of Anti-Corruption in New China.* Beijing: China Procuratory Publishing House.

AUTHOR INDEX

SUBJECT INDEX